Happy Christmas
1988.
from Bill & Irene.

The Manual of Woodturning

By the same author

Toy Making in Wood
Jewelry Making
Beginner's Guide to Power Tools
Beginner's Guide to Woodturning

The Manual of Woodturning

Gordon Stokes

PELHAM BOOKS
LONDON

First published in Great Britain by
PELHAM BOOKS LTD
44 Bedford Square
London WC1B 3DP
1979
Reprinted 1982, 1983 and 1985

Photographs by Terry Magowan
Line illustrations by V. J. Taylor

ISBN 0 7207 0991 1

Printed in Great Britain by
Hollen Street Press Ltd at Slough, Berkshire
and bound by Hunter & Foulis Ltd, Edinburgh.

Contents

Metric Conversion Table

inches		millimetres
$\frac{1}{16}$	=	1·5
$\frac{1}{8}$	=	3
$\frac{1}{4}$	=	6
$\frac{1}{2}$	=	13
$\frac{3}{4}$	=	19
1	=	25
2	=	51
3	=	76
4	=	102
5	=	127
6	=	152
7	=	178
8	=	203
9	=	229
10	=	254
11	=	279

feet		centimetres
1	=	30·5
2	=	61·0
3	=	91·4
4	=	121·9
5	=	152·4

Introduction

Woodturning, like pottery, is undoubtedly an art form, requiring considerable manipulative skill and dexterity on the part of the turner. Such skill, while it can be acquired by interested persons of reasonable intelligence, cannot be perfected in a short period of time. It is possible for a complete beginner to reach the intermediate stage in a matter of months if he or she is prepared to make sufficient effort, obtain information from sound sources, and to devote a sufficient period of time each day to practice and study. The gap between the intermediate stage and the overall excellence of the master craftsman is, however, a wide one bridged by very few, and even those who succeed in achieving this status would freely admit that they still have much to learn. In this lies most of the attraction of any creative craft.

Very few radical changes have occurred in the craft over the centuries as regards the tools used and the manipulation of them. Machines, however, have become more sophisticated, and woodturning has altered considerably in that it is now practised more as a satisfying and remunerative hobby than as a trade.

Before me as I write this introduction is a copy of a book on woodturning published about seventy years ago, and it is perhaps fitting that a manual which sets out to describe contemporary woodturning machinery and methods should refer in its opening pages to the craft as it was, and to the men who followed it. Those whose interest lies in the historical aspects of woodturning will discover, by reference to their public libraries, a number of very old works which will provide considerable food for thought. One such book was written by a man named Bergeron about 160 years ago. In it are described machines which display considerable ingenuity and which, although primitive by modern standards, were functional and produced work of excellent quality. Some of these relied for their motive power upon a bow with several strings. A cord connected to a foot-operated treadle was passed several times around the work and connected to the bowstrings. When the treadle was pressed the cord pulled on the strings, bending the bow, and when the foot pressure was released, the bow would return to its original shape and pull the cord back to its starting position. This was an improvement upon the pole lathe in that the bow, being fixed to the lathe itself, made the machine easy to move or transport.

Much has been written about the 'bodgers', who are sometimes believed to have been woodturners of incredible skill. From the old bodger, however, comes the verb 'to bodge'. A job which has been bodged is a job done badly or in a makeshift manner, and while the bodgers were no doubt a great band of characters, their woodturning skill was relatively slight. Their main occupation was the reduction of green timber to cylinders, which were then stacked criss-cross fashion in the open so that they could dry out before being taken into the factory for their final shaping. This sort of work was carried out in the open, particularly in the beech woods of Buckinghamshire. Most of the turning was done with a wide chisel and carried out on a pole lathe.

The pole lathe was a primitive instrument, very much suited to working under conditions of this kind. It consisted of two heavy posts, driven into the ground, with metal points or centres between which the wood was mounted. A crude foot treadle was used to drive the lathe by a cord passed several times round a pulley, or in some cases around the work, and the other end attached to the bough of a tree above the machine. Pressure upon the treadle would rotate the material five times towards the woodturner, and when the treadle was released the pull of the branch above would cause it to rotate five times in the opposite direction. It is, of course, obvious that a machine which spends fifty per cent of its time returning to the point from which it started in order for another cut to be made is at best only fifty per cent efficient. Material could be removed from the workpiece only when it was rotating towards the turner, and shavings would therefore fly from the machine in short bursts.

Lathes in use when Bergeron's book was published were mostly composed of wood, with metal headstock, tailstock and toolrest holder. Some books on woodturning still in print today advise the use of the lathe with a wooden bed on the grounds that the springiness of this bed has advantages. This refers to the fact that early tailstock centres could not rotate with the timber, so that a considerable amount of friction wore and burned the timber away and necessitated frequent tightening of the tailstock to keep the work securely positioned in the machine. With the introduction of 'live' or rotating tailstock centres this advantage has disappeared, and lathes with wooden beds are no longer made.

Some points made in the old books are as true today as when they were first written down. An example of this is a statement to the effect that the correct position of the cutting edge of the tool is one at a tangent to the circle which is turned. The author has been careful to point out that this refers to the circle left *after* the edge has passed.

It is, of course, the surface of the bevel ground on the tool which is at a tangent to the cutting circle, and this is clarified later, but this simple fact was as vital to success in the art of woodturning centuries ago as it is today. Some of the items illustrated in Bergeron's book are, by modern standards, weird to say the least, though they were no doubt considered extremely handsome in their day. One project included is a complete spittoon, described as useful for the parlour or the smoking-room. I have left readers of this manual to decide for themselves whether an artefact of this kind would be useful in their parlours or smoking-rooms, if they have them, since some may decide to make one. But there can be very few people today in whose lounges a spittoon is prominent.

I have not included a section dealing with the construction of 'barley sugar' or other forms of twist turning, since these are not true turnings but all made by turning a cylinder of suitable length down to the required diameter, marking out the spiral in pencil, cutting along the marked lines to the required depth with a fine-toothed saw, and carving the shape of the twist itself by means of rasps and carving tools. While carving the twist, the lathe is stationary, but the wood is held between centres for convenience.

I have been connected with woodturning for more than thirty years and have been delighted to see the tremendous upsurge of interest which has occurred over the past decade. In order for the body of a man or woman to be healthy, it is necessary for the mind to be in a similar condition. If the mind is employed in the acquisition of skill and knowledge and their application to creative projects, it is considerably more likely to be healthy than if used merely to absorb the dubious creations of others through the constant viewing of television. The satisfaction which can be derived from sharpening tools correctly and manipulating them against timber rotating under power so as to produce objects which are functional, beautiful, or both is impossible to describe, but it is worth much effort and endeavour.

The beginner should not expect the road to be smoothly paved, clearly signposted and adequately illuminated. The road to a high standard of skill is long and hard, beset with difficulties, frustrations and disappointments. It does, however, inevitably contain extremely gratifying moments in which all goes well and problems are put into their true perspective. Those who are easily discouraged might be best advised to find some less demanding occupation, but those who are prepared to continue to struggle along when the going gets rough, and to seek sensible and intelligent advice, can be assured of success in the end.

Should technical queries arise, or advice be needed on woodturning problems, the author may be contacted, by letter or telephone only, at 202 The Hollow, Bath, Avon. He regrets that he is unable to deal with personal calls at this address other than by prior arrangement.

1 The Lathe

The purchase of a lathe, even without the tools and ancillary equipment required for comprehensive use, can represent a considerable capital outlay. In view of this, the importance of careful selection cannot be over emphasized. The makes and models shown and described in this book have all been thoroughly tried and tested by the author over the years, and other machines, for one reason or another found to be unsatisfactory, have been excluded. If a machine featured in this manual is purchased, it is unlikely to cause dissatisfaction – but it is vital that the lathe chosen should be suitable for the specific needs of the individual concerned.

The purchase of a heavy-duty machine by someone who intends to indulge in woodturning only on odd occasions would hardly be sensible, since the lathe has been designed to cater for the exceptionally devoted hobbyist or the commercial turner. Conversely, the purchase of one of the light models for production purposes, where turning goes on for several hours each day, frequently with heavy workpieces, would almost certainly lead to disappointment. When the intention is solely to turn out bowls, plates, trays or other products which take the form of a disc, there is no need to purchase a lathe as such. For this purpose the bowl-turning head, described in chapter 6, will be quite adequate and will require a much smaller cash outlay.

Secondhand lathes are very scarce indeed, and by virtue of this fact they command high prices. Few people give up woodturning once they have passed through the inevitable confusion of the early stages, and most of the used machines which do become available do so as the result of permanent illness, death or emigration. In such cases, of course, the lathe rarely arrives at the stage of being advertised for sale; it is much more likely to be snapped up by a friend or relative of the owner.

If an opportunity does arise to purchase a secondhand lathe, some consideration should be given to the matter. Precipitate action may well result in the acquisition of a number of problems. There are still numerous old lathes in use whose manufacturers have been out of business for many years and for which no spare parts can be obtained. These, even when offered at attractive prices, may be anything but a bargain. Should the bearings be badly worn or any parts of the tool missing or broken, the cost of having replacements specially made on a 'one off' basis could be entirely prohibitive. Lathes are sometimes sold by schools after considerable use by pupils and students at evening classes. If the purchaser is prepared to pay the cost of reconditioning these machines, they are worth looking at – but such costs may be quite high.

If a really big lathe is offered as a secondhand unit, the motor should be checked to ensure that it will be suitable for use in the home workshop. Many such machines have motors from 2 to 5 horsepower and are of the three-phase variety, which may be useless for the home user. Should this be the case, the possibility should be checked of removing the motor and replacing it by a single-phase one or by a 1.5 horsepower unit. The cost of a new motor must, of course, be considered, and it should first be established that a smaller motor will in fact be a viable proposition on such a heavy lathe. It is likely that the push-button starter unit will also have to be replaced, and these are expensive items.

The machine may seem cheap, but if it is one of the big old cast-iron monsters of days gone by it may well be necessary to strengthen the workshop floor, at no small cost in these times, in order to support it safely. It may also need to be moved by professionals with special equipment, which will be very expensive indeed.

Since the chances of finding a good used lathe at the right sort of price are so slim, most beginners purchase new machines. The important aspects of such a purchase must therefore be examined here.

It should be appreciated that heavy advertising of specific machines does not necessarily indicate merit. Some machines sell quite well with minimal advertising, while others need high-pressure promotion to keep up their sales. In other words, the make and type which springs most readily to mind may or may not be the one to buy. Impatience to get started should be curbed until a variety of

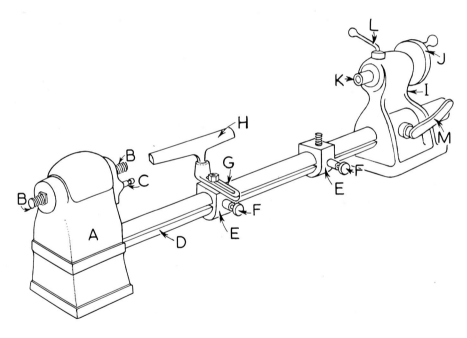

Figure 1. A typical lathe:

(A) headstock unit;	(B) spindle;	(C) indexing plunger;
(D) lathe bed;	(E) saddles;	(F) locating plungers;
(G) toolrest holder;	(H) toolrest;	(I) tailstock;
(J) tailstock handwheel;	(K) poppet barrel;	(L) poppet barrel clamping lever;
(M) tailstock clamping lever.		

machines has been examined. The main points for consideration are set out below as a guide, but as a final comment it should be noted that aesthetic charm or beauty of line should be considered last – if at all. Some of the most attractive lathes have bad points, and some which are far from beautiful are a delight to use. Money is often wasted by manufacturers on giving a product eye appeal which could have been put to far better use on the functional aspects.

Strength and Solidity

Is the lathe really sturdy – sturdy enough, that is, to absorb vibration and swing everything to be turned on it? If too light in construction, the machine may be satisfactory for most work, but useless for the odd heavy jobs where the wood itself is out of balance.

Bearings

The bearings which carry the lathe spindle must be of very high quality, since they are often subjected to considerable side pressure from heavy cuts and heavy end pressure from the tailstock. Top-quality needle roller bearings are quite satisfactory, though I have always preferred the robust phosphor bronze taper bearing, which stands up extremely well under the stresses of the job and is easily

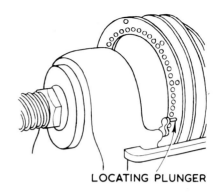

LOCATING PLUNGER

Figure 3. Some lathes are equipped with dividing heads which can be used to facilitate the accurate marking out of turned workpieces for fluting and reeding. They are also used for dividing wood into panels prior to carving.

adjusted by an unskilled operator when necessary due to wear. Roller bearings may be permanently sealed, requiring no lubrication by the operator, though provision may be made for the introduction of thin machine oil. In a phosphor bronze bearing, the oil used should be similar to that used in a car engine. Thin oil will run straight out at the bottom of the bearing housing. This type of bearing becomes quite warm in use – and is intended to

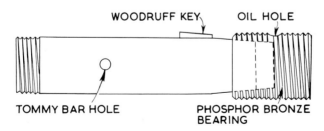

WOODRUFF KEY   OIL HOLE

TOMMY BAR HOLE

PHOSPHOR BRONZE BEARING

Figure 2. Assembly of phosphor bronze-type bearing and spindle. Woodruff key secures block. Tommy bar hole is provided so that spindle can be held when chucks, etc., are removed. Mating taper system of spindle and bearing makes attachment a very simple matter.

do so. Seepage of oil from the housing is also quite normal.

A few notes on maintenance of phosphor bronze bearings are in order at this point. The usual system is for adjustment to be carried out by means of two castellated rings, one at each end of the bearing. When adjustment is needed, the front ring – nearest the tailstock – is loosened, and the rear one is tightened until all play has been taken up. The effect of this adjustment is to draw the phosphor bronze bearing tighter onto the taper of the spindle. When the operation has been satisfactorily completed, the front ring is re-tightened. During the first few months of use this adjustment will be necessary quite frequently as the high spots wear down, but thereafter it will be needed less often.

If a faceplate is fitted to the machine while the bearing is warm, any wear can be detected by movement in the bearing as the faceplate is rocked from side to side. Bearings of this nature, which are allowed to run for long periods while in need of adjustment, may develop a 'step' in the inner surface and have to be replaced.

Headstock

The headstock of a lathe is a heavy metal yoke designed to support the spindle in a horizontal position so as to prevent any movement of the spindle (other than rotation about the horizontal axis) while under load. This unit should be a very heavy casting or it will fail to do its job. Lightweight headstocks are a perpetual nuisance.

Spindle

The lathe spindle should have flats ground on it to accept a spanner, or alternatively a hole may be drilled through it to permit the insertion of a tommy bar. The spindle can then be prevented from turning when faceplates or chucks are unscrewed from the mandrel, which is the threaded 'nose' of the spindle. Some items of this nature can become firmly fixed, and if the spindle cannot be locked their removal may present a real problem. The spindle also carries the stepped pulley block which permits it to be driven at various speeds.

Lathe Bed

The bed of a lathe is important since it carries the tailstock and the toolrest holders. If the bed is heavy and rigid there should be no trouble, but if it is of light construction the tailstock and toolrest holders may vibrate when the machine is under load.

One annoying feature with many lathes is the difficulty involved in sliding the tailstock and toolrest holders along the lathe bed. This the turner may need to do many times in a

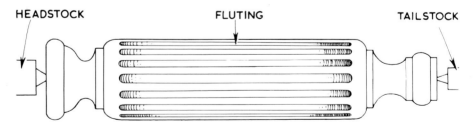

Figure 4. Fluted turning. Most workers perform this sort of operation with the aid of the dividing head and a portable router.

day, and if the movement is stiff or awkward there will be constant frustration. Lathe beds are made in many shapes, but one of the best consists of two rectangular bars set side by side on edge with a gap between them, through which pass the securing bolts of tailstock and toolrest holders. It is a simple system but, like most simple things, it is extremely effective.

Tailstock and toolrest holders on a good lathe will move freely along the bed under no more pressure than that of one finger. Lathe beds are made in a large number of different forms, but the more sophisticated patterns offer no advantage over the rectangular bars and usually cost more. A lathe bed normally has supports, or 'feet', at either end to lift the bed up above the bench on which it is mounted.

Tailstock

Strength, rigidity and accuracy of machining are the keynotes here. The absence of any one of these should be sufficient to dissuade the intending purchaser. As we shall see later, many woodturning problems that are blamed by inexperienced operators on the headstock and spindle, or even on their own lack of ability, are traceable to the tailstock.

The tailstock casting, then, should be very solid and capable of moving smoothly and easily along the lathe bed once the clamping lever has been released. Once positioned as required, it must be possible to clamp the tailstock with complete security. Bad tailstock clamps can lead to movement of the tailstock along the bed during operation, and serious injury could result if the workpiece were to fly

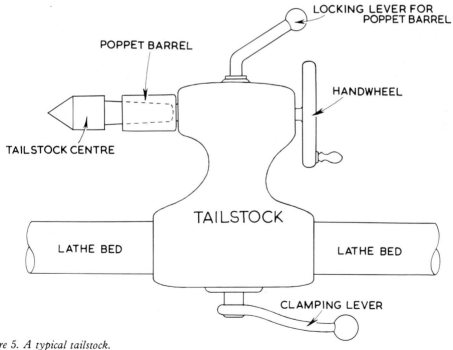

Figure 5. A typical tailstock.

from the lathe and strike the operator.

Turn the tailstock handwheel a few times when inspecting a new lathe, moving the poppet barrel back and forth through its full range of movement in and out of the casting. This whole movement will feel as smooth as silk on a good lathe, which has been engineered to fine tolerances and will be a pleasure to the operator. Handwheels which are stiff and sticky, and poppet barrels which move in a series of reluctant jerks, are signs of bad engineering. A lever is provided on the tailstock casting which enables the poppet barrel to be locked in any desired position through its range of travel. This lever does *not* require force in tightening, which may damage the mechanism, and a fairly short lever is desirable to prevent the application of undue leverage. This lever is of secondary importance, but it should be lightly tightened when stock is mounted in the machine. It is often useful to be able to remove the tailstock completely, and the clamping system should facilitate this.

On most lathes the poppet barrel is bored to accept centres, drill bits, etc. which have Morse tapered shanks – as is the headstock spindle. The Morse taper sizes generally used are number 1 (small), number 2 (medium), or number 3 (large). Cheaper lathes sometimes avoid this system, since from a production viewpoint it is expensive, and substitute a threaded section on the extreme end of headstock spindle and poppet barrel to which the lathe centres can be attached. This makeshift idea should be avoided if possible, since it severely reduces the versatility of the machine.

Centres, and other items supplied with a good lathe, are self-ejecting. Centres which are not self-ejecting can cause quite unnecessary problems when they need to be removed. They can become very tightly fixed indeed, and considerable force may be needed to move

them, which is obviously bad for the lathe over a period of time.

Self-ejection of centres is achieved by constructing the tailstock so that the end of the tapered shank strikes a projection inside the tailstock when the handwheel is wound fully back. It should be noted, however, that when centres or drills not supplied by the lathe manufacturer are used the shanks may be too short to reach the ejector.

Toolrest Holders

Commonly referred to in the woodturning trade as 'banjos', these items should again be very strong and incapable of flexing under heavy loads. They are supplied with a clamping system, for attachment direct to the lathe bed or to a 'saddle', and levers which allow the toolrest itself to be clamped *firmly* in a selected position. Check that the toolrest holders (there *must* be two) are not so badly designed as to prevent the toolrest from being dropped to at least $1\frac{1}{2}$ inches below the line of the centres.

Check too that two threaded holes, not one, are provided for the lever which clamps the toolrest in position. They should be at a 90-degrees angle to each other. This allows the lever to be moved if it is obstructing tool or hand during a cut.

Lathes which have only one toolrest holder should be avoided – or at least the cost of purchasing another should be considered – and where two banjos are supplied, a long toolrest which covers the whole run of the lathe can be used. This has two pins, rather than one as on short rests. Continuity of cut is essential in the production of flowing lines on long workpieces, and it is impossible to achieve with short toolrests, which have to be moved frequently. Finally, check that the system used to attach the banjo to lathe bed or saddle is an intelligent one. On some lathes this is very poorly designed, and a large projection of metal above the saddle or bed at this point severely reduces the size of workpiece which can be turned.

It is very important to note that the maximum thickness of a workpiece which can be turned on a given lathe is described as the 'swing over the bed'. A little thought will show that the true description must be 'swing over the highest obstruction', which is not the lathe bed but almost invariably the banjo or its securing nut. Some lathes are remarkably badly designed in this respect, having distances as small as $2\frac{1}{2}$ inches between the driving centre point and the first obstruction on the bed. As a result they are a source of constant and severe frustration. Types of centre used in head- and tailstocks are discussed on pages 22–4.

Saddles

Not all lathes are fitted with saddles, but if these are a feature, there *must* be two, not one. They are used mainly on lathes which have round beds, either of tubular or solid steel, to convert the undesirable round shape back to a flat one, so facilitating the attachment of the banjos.

Lathe beds which offer a flat surface in themselves, such as those with rectangular parallel bars, do not require saddles. A saddle is an attachment to the lathe bed; it has a flat upper surface and can be moved along the lathe bed to any desired point, where it is clamped firmly by a lever. Note that where saddles are used the swing over the highest projection is reduced by the thickness of the banjo *plus* the height of the saddle surface above the bed.

Drive

Modern lathes are powered, almost invariably, by electric motors – unlike the machine I used as a lad, which was powered by foot treadle. Make certain that the lathe chosen has a remote drive from an electric motor mounted either below or at the rear of the headstock, and that power is transmitted by a V-belt through stepped pulleys which provide a range of speeds. This is by far the best system, and it is used on all good-quality machines.

Assuming serious woodturning to be the aim, every effort must be made to avoid 'lathes' which use the spindle of the drive motor as a *direct* drive for the workpiece. This system means, of course, that the motor bearings are used as lathe bearings and so are subjected to pressures for which they were never intended.

In most cases 1 horsepower will be adequate, and many hobbyists manage quite well with three-quarters. I like $1\frac{1}{2}$ or 2 horsepower because I frequently get jobs that no one else wants, and many of these are large, heavy workpieces on which I use big tools. On such work, it is not difficult to use all the power from a 2 horsepower motor.

Motor Mounting

Particular attention should be paid to the system used for belt tensioning. This question of belt tension is important, and for many years I have emphasized it to my private students as a safety factor, as I will now explain.

The usual advice, if any, given by manufacturers is that the drive belt should be tensioned so that there is about half an inch of flex midway between the pulleys. This is not good advice, for two reasons. Firstly, unless the lathe has a simple and efficient system of motor mounting which permits quick release of the motor to relax the belt tension, speed changing will be carried out by forcing the belt from one set of pulleys to another. The resulting heavy tension causes strain on the motor bearing, so shortening its life. Secondly, and this is far more important, careful and precise belt tensioning can be used by beginners as a 'slipping clutch' system to protect them from themselves. When a belt is fully tensioned, a 'dig-in' with a tool, sudden twist of toolrest in holder or other incident will result in either an actual injury to the turner or, at least, a nerve-shattering experience. Power, speed and momentum of the workpiece may combine to break a toolrest, break the tool itself, split a large piece of wood from the job or tear the tool from the hand of the operator.

When the lathes in my workshop are in use for teaching, as they are most of the time, I have the belts tensioned with around 2 inches of flex at the central point so they drive the spindle under normal load but slip on the motor pulley the moment the load becomes abnormal. Should inept tool handling or other misfortune bring about an incident, the workpiece instantly ceases to rotate, while the motor pulley continues to do so. Use of this slack belt tension eases the mind of the beginner and removes much apprehension. Tension, in fact, is removed from both belt and operator.

One other feature should be checked. Many lathes are designed badly, so that when the motor is moved to alter belt tension it can twist on its mounting. If a lathe is run for long periods with the motor twisted in this manner, unnecessary strain will be placed on the motor bearing, and belt wear will be rapid. On a well-designed lathe the motor mount holds the motor square automatically when it is moved on the mounting.

Lathe motors should be of the induction type, which have no brushes and so do not cause any interference with radio or television. They should also be of the variety known as 'totally enclosed', of which the Brook Gryphon is a typical example. These motors are completely sealed against dust and are cooled by a plastic fan, which rotates at one end under a plastic cowl and directs cool air from the fan over the motor casing. Motors which draw cooling air through the casing should be avoided in view of the conditions under which they will be used.

Starter Unit

Cheap lathes tend to have cheap starter units or to be supplied without either motor or starter, the purchase of these being left to the new owner. The starter unit should in fact be a high-quality item which will operate efficiently over a period of years. Poor-quality starters will give trouble from the beginning and are a most unwise investment. All starters for woodworking purposes *must* be fully protected from dust, to which they are very sensitive.

Almost all units in use now are of the 'no volt overload' variety, which is important for safety reasons. These units will operate only when current is available because they are electro-magnetic. For example, if a machine stops running because of a local power cut or breakdown, the operator may forget to switch it off. In the case of the old type of manual switch, the machine will start up again when power is suddenly restored, possibly causing injury to anyone cleaning or adjusting it. This is impossible with the NVO switch, which switches itself off when the power is removed. Starter units also contain a thermal overload system, which is designed to protect the motor should it be subjected to prolonged and excessive loads. The principle is the same as that normally used in regulators on cookers, which use a small strip of metal formed from two laminated strips with widely differing coefficients of expansion. This causes the strip to bend when heated, and this bending movement breaks the electrical contact and switches off the motor. Never bypass a thermal overload. When the strip has cooled the motor can be started again. Some designs have a small 'reset' button which must be depressed first.

Some starter units have provision for running the motor in reverse, a very old idea used by woodturners to achieve fine surface finishes as described on page 140. When a lathe is fitted up in the workshop, a suitable site must be selected for the starter unit. This ideally should be one that will enable the motor to be switched off by the operator's knee or hip in an emergency. Switches on woodworking machines must always be within easy reach, *never* mounted on the wall behind the machine so that the operator is forced to reach across it to operate them.

Toolrests

All the hundreds of students who have taken my intensive two-day courses will be well aware of the importance I attach to the design of toolrests. The beginner needs all the help he can get, and many toolrests supplied with otherwise good lathes are no help at all – in fact quite the reverse. The sketches clarify the points I wish to make, and thorough study of them can be beneficial.

First, there is a danger in the misleading use of the expression 'hand rest' to replace 'toolrest', the latter being correct.

A new lathe owner, totally unfamiliar with

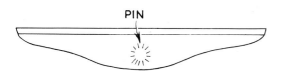

Figure 6. Plan view of a badly designed toolrest. This shape would be quite adequate for those who employ the scraper at all times. Woodturners use gouges and chisels, with their handles low, so that the tool contacts the toolrest along the back rather than the front edge, and the shape shown here renders the entire process extremely difficult.

the machine and relying upon the accuracy of a book or magazine article, may well take such a description to mean that the hand is upon the 'handrest' and the tool upon the hand, so that the fingers are between tool and rest. This quite obviously could result in a serious injury. Note, and note well, that the tool – any tool – must *always* be in firm contact with the toolrest during a cut (except when a scraper is used with the rotation of the lathe reversed). It is by no means necessary for the hand to contact the toolrest at all, though many people find it helpful to allow it to do so. This part of the lathe is therefore a toolrest and should be so regarded.

There is an unfortunate and distressing tendency, based on ignorance mixed with perversity, to produce bad toolrests. Some are bad because they have been made to look attractive, others because cheapness of production has been the object. The end result in every case is a toolrest which inhibits the ease and correct movement of the tools in one or more ways. Through the years I have quite literally thrown away toolrests from many makes of lathe order to replace them with more suitable items made for me at some expense. This is simply because I have needed to earn my living through woodturning and could not afford to be held back by perpetual struggles with strangely shaped toolrests designed (if that is the word) according to the whims of engineers who do not have to use them!

A good toolrest has three main points. First, it is straight. Second, it has a radius on its forward face. Third, the pin is long, allowing the rest to be raised near the top of large workpieces when required.

Many of these patterns would be fine if tools other than scrapers were not used at all. This manual, however, is concerned primarily with woodturning, and with scraping of wood only as a secondary and 'last resort' approach.

Woodturning, as practised by those who know what they are doing, is about cutting wood with chisels and gouges. These tools are almost invariably presented to the work with positive rake, or pointing upwards, as against scrapers which always enjoy negative rake – they point slightly down. It will be appreciated, therefore, that while a scraper is used off the forward edge of the toolrest where the maker has put a little flat strip along the length, chisels and gouges will be in contact with the back of the toolrest and so be forced into a wandering path as they move along. This is extremely frustrating and will hold students back. Reference to the sketches will help here. Cheap toolrests are often made from rectangular or other oddly shaped metal which is quite soft, and since chisels are made of tool steel, which is hard, the corners of the chisels dig into the toolrest, leaving small indentations. Subsequent attempts to produce flowing shapes with flawless surfaces will be doomed by these indentations, which will momentarily halt the progress of the tool along the rest, causing rings and ridges on the work.

Ideally, a lathe should have a minimum of three toolrests, one quite short for use on small items, another about 12 or 14 inches long for general work, and a third with two pins running the full length of the lathe.

Toolrests must be of fairly heavy section to give rigidity. Any tendency for the toolrest to flex when supporting a tool near its extremities is likely to provoke a dig-in and so is dangerous.

Lathe Centres

These are of great importance. They form the only support for the work in the lathe, and poorly designed centres can give rise to problems which the turner, expert or tyro, could well do without.

In bygone days when woodturners

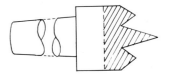

Figure 7. Two-pronged driving centre, now difficult to obtain, but useful if it can be found. Note that the central point should project beyond driving points. The shaded area should enter the wood.

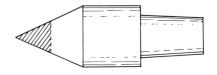

Figure 8. Tailstock centre is cone-shaped, whether or not it rotates with the timber, and should enter the wood by approximately the depth shown in the shaded portions.

abounded, lathe makers could not market weird devices which were inefficient. Men whose livings depended on the ability to produce work of high quality in a short time, often on a piece-work basis, would not accept equipment which by its poor design would reduce their earning capacity. In those days the manufacturer had little choice but to produce what his customer demanded.

Today, the main part of the market is with the hobbyist, the beginner, who has little means of knowing what he wants and is forced to conclude that the equipment offered is correct as a result of considerable knowledge on the part of the maker and his staff. This, with metal-turning lathes, is true, since the men who make them are fully trained in their use. Lathes for woodturning, however, are also made by engineers - not by woodturners - and the result is chaos. Woodturning lathes and their ancillary equipment should be designed by woodturners who fully understand the craft and made by engineers who understand engineering. Perhaps in time this utopian state will be reached.

Top-quality lathes offer as standard equipment a *two*-pronged driving centre (sometimes referred to as a fork centre) and an accurately machined cone-shaped tailstock centre upon which the wood rotates. Where machines are made to a price, the trend now is to supply a *four*-pronged driving centre, which I am reliably advised is much cheaper to manufacture.

It might seem reasonable to assume that the grip provided by four prongs must be superior to that offered by two, but this is not the case. Many workpieces consist of very hard timber, and for safety reasons the fangs or prongs of the driving centre need to be well buried in the wood. This burial is much easier with two prongs than with four, and nasty accidents have occurred through hard workpieces flying from the lathe due to insecure mounting. Two-pronged centres have always been for general purpose use for this reason, working in conjunction with a cone-shaped dead centre in the tailstock. The four-pronged centre was not designed for general use, but for the turning of thin workpieces which are likely to split during the turning if the wedge-shaped two-prong and cone tailstock centres are employed.

Such thin workpieces, driven by a four-pronged centre, should be supported at the tailstock end by a ring centre (sometimes called a cup centre). This has a central point, surrounded by a circular knife edge. Ring centres have little or no tendency to split the wood, but are unsuitable for use on large and heavy workpieces because, like the four-pronged drive centre, they cannot easily be buried to a satisfactory depth.

Note that a tailstock centre which rotates with the wood in a special ball or needle roller

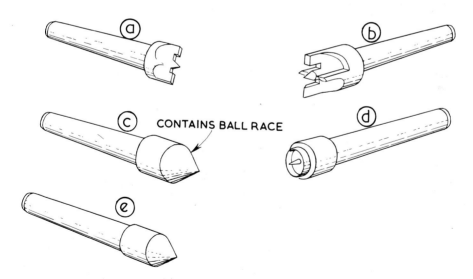

Figure 9. Lathe centres – shanks are Morse tapered: (a) two-pronged drive centre; (b) four-pronged drive centre; (c) 'live' tailstock centre; (d) cup or ring centre; (e) 'dead' or non-rotating tailstock centre.

head is a revolving or rotating centre. A centre which remains stationary, the wood rotating on it, is a dead centre. Descriptions used by some writers, such as 'a cup', or 'dead centre' are nonsense.

The wisdom of purchasing a rotating centre, which is an expensive item if it is well made, is perhaps debatable. Once the job has been correctly set up on a rotating centre, no further attention need be paid to the tailstock until the work has been completed. When a dead centre is used, grease, oil or wax must be applied to reduce friction and so prevent burning.

Such centres also have a tendency to enlarge the hole in which they run, necessitating the periodic tightening of the tailstock. This phenomenon is more marked in cases where the job is heavy and out of balance. Failure to keep the tailstock support tight can in extreme cases result in the wood flying from the lathe. Looking at the matter from another angle, once the correct use of a dead centre becomes habit the device is perfectly effective and has, of course, served countless woodturners well over the centuries.

The real drawback to a rotating centre is that sooner or later (sooner in the case of cheap versions) wear takes place, and the centre develops play. It is, of course, vital that the revolving point should have no movement other than that of rotation about its longitudinal axis, otherwise fine and accurate cutting becomes almost impossible. Just as movement of a dead centre within a hole which it has enlarged is detrimental to quality work, so movement of a rotating centre in its mounting produces inaccuracies.

MISCELLANEOUS EQUIPMENT

The items mentioned here will be needed as proficiency with the lathe and tools is acquired. They can be purchased as the need arises.

Dividers

A large pair of dividers is useful for marking out circles on timber prior to cutting to shape with a bandsaw. The use of dividers leaves the centre clearly marked, which facilitates mounting the workpiece on faceplate or chuck.

Calipers

Various types are used in woodturning. Calipers for outside measurement are necessary for the production of precise diameters. These should be of the spring type, having a threaded bar with knurled nut for adjustment. Outside calipers are frequently used on work which is revolving, and there is a chance with simple calipers that the adjustment will move under pressure from the wood. Use of sprung calipers greatly reduces this possibility.

Inside calipers are needed for jobs such as vases or goblets. The lathe should be stationary when they are used.

The Columbus pattern vernier caliper is relatively expensive but extremely useful for measurement where one part of a turning must fit inside another. A typical example is the fitting of a pin (or round tenon) on a table lamp stem into a hole in the base, as described on page 151. This type of caliper also has provision for measurement of depth, which has many applications for the woodturner.

Faceplates

At least one faceplate is supplied with the majority of lathes, but many turners purchase extra ones to facilitate production of repetition work. A faceplate is simply a metal disc, normally stiffened around its edge by an extra thickness of metal. It has an internal thread to its central hole, so that it can be screwed onto the lathe mandrel (end of the spindle), either

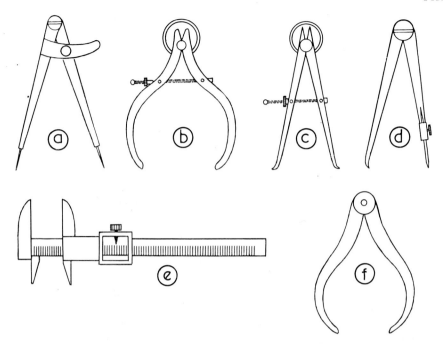

Figure 10. Dividers (a) to (d) and (f), very useful for marking out discs. All show various patterns of inside and outside caliper; (b) and (c) are spring-loaded, controlled by means of a small knurled nut; (f) will remain where set by virtue of the friction present at the hinges – checks must be made to ensure that this setting does not alter when the tool is subjected to pressure against the revolving timber; (d) is a hermaphrodite caliper, not commonly used by woodturners; (e) shows a Columbus pattern vernier caliper, which is a cheap copy of the very expensive tool used by metal-workers.

inboard or in some cases outboard as well.

Where both inboard and outboard faceplate mounting systems are employed, a minimum of two faceplates is needed. The threads cut on the inner and outer spindle ends are right and left hand respectively, which renders the faceplates self-tightening under load. Most faceplates have eight holes drilled right through and countersunk at the back for use in attaching the various workpieces.

Too little thought goes into the production of most faceplates, and too little importance seems to be attached to them. Most faceplates now are made from lightweight aluminium alloys, and it should be noted that this type can be permanently distorted by screwing it down tightly to an uneven surface. Work to be fixed on a plate of this nature should always be planed flat before mounting.

Woodscrew Chucks

A good lathe has two woodscrew chucks, the sizes generally being $1\frac{1}{2}$ inches by $2\frac{1}{2}$ inches in diameter. These are small metal units which screw onto the lathe mandrel, the smaller having a single central woodscrew and the larger a central screw plus a number of holes drilled round the edge to take additional screws.

These holes should be countersunk from the back.

For best effect, the screws used with woodscrew chucks should not be smaller than number 14, minimum 1-inch length. These are replaceable on good chucks – avoid any woodscrew chuck which has its central screw permanently fixed.

In some cases the screw projection from the plate can be adjusted by the turner, but few bother to make such adjustments since it is easier to reduce effective screw projection by interposing a disc of hardboard or plywood between chuck and work.

Long-Hole Boring Kit

These kits are available for most lathes. Their most common application is in the drilling of holes through blanks for table lamps to take the flex. The kit consists of (a) a shell auger $\frac{5}{16}$ inch; (b) a counterbore tool; (c) a centre finder; and (d) a drilling jig with ring centre. The use of this kit is explained on pages 189-92.

Jacobs Pattern
Three-Jawed Chuck

This has a Morse tapered shank to suit the lathe, the shank normally being detachable from the chuck. It is used principally for the drilling of holes with various types of boring bit or cutter, and on occasion for holding small drum sanders, rag mops for polishing, etc.

The chuck can be fitted into the tailstock and fed to work which is rotating on the headstock, or mounted in the headstock and fed into stationary material which is supported by the tailstock and fed to the cutter. This is not to be confused with the engineers chuck as used on metal-turning lathes, which should never be used in woodturning owing to the high risk of injury from the protruding jaws,

which are invisible when rotating at woodturning speeds.

Neither type of chuck should be used for holding wood unless the workpiece is very short, since the metal jaws compress the wood and loosen the grip, with the possibility of the workpiece flying from the lathe.

Dividing Head

Most good-quality lathes are equipped with some form of dividing head, though it is surprising just how many owners are unaware of the purpose of the device. Normally, it consists of a disc mounted on the headstock spindle, in which a number of holes has been drilled. Sometimes one of the drive pulleys is used to avoid the expense of fitting an extra disc.

Some form of positive locator is incorporated, so that the disc can be locked by engaging the locator in one of the holes. With a workpiece mounted in the lathe, one revolution of the disc will give one revolution of the work. Partial turning of the disc will, therefore, give equal movement to the work, and it becomes possible to divide a job into equal parts around its circumference for subsequent fluting, carving or drilling of holes.

The practice of locking the dividing head in order more easily to remove a jammed chuck or faceplate constitutes an abuse, since it can damage the locking mechanism.

Note Some lathes are fitted with expensive systems designed to permit an infinite variation of speed between about 100 rpm and the available maximum. The fact is that a novice will alter the speed far too frequently in the hope of effecting a magical improvement in the work (frequently with the reverse effect), while a more competent turner will rarely use the device. It is very doubtful whether such ingenious ideas are worth their high cost.

Other items of general use are described in the appropriate sections of the manual, as are the various jigs and chucks which the woodturner can make in his own workshop. All the lathe accessories mentioned in this chapter are dealt with more fully later in the book.

2 Tools

This section of the manual briefly describes the tools in general use by woodturners and explains their functions. Full instructional data is contained in succeeding chapters. Good woodturning is the result of considerable skill and manual dexterity, and a full understanding of each tool is necessary before practice can be expected to lead to progress.

There are two approaches to shaping wood in a lathe: scraping, and cutting with a paring action. These two methods are quite unrelated, and each should be studied carefully by any potential turner. Most comments by ill-informed writers and lecturers regarding the use of scraping tools and 'techniques' or processes which are said to involve scraping wood with cutting tools are a source of amusement to those who understand the craft thoroughly. The reasons for this will become apparent.

A recently published book on woodturning stated that only a few woodturners enjoy the satisfaction of mastering the cutting techniques. Perhaps this was true at one time, but today large numbers of people who have received good instruction use these techniques daily, and the number of competent woodturners is rising steeply year by year.

Woodturning is not a mystic art in which only the specially gifted may hope to succeed. It can be taught – by those who know not only how to turn wood but how to explain the basic principles to students in a simple and practical way. I have taught hundreds of men and women, many of whom now operate successful businesses, and a few of them are even teaching the craft. At one time I taught a great many people in different parts of the world by correspondence course. Unfortunately, although the success of this approach was spectacular, it had to be abandoned as uneconomic.

Cutting techniques are desirable wherever it is possible to use them, since they are very much faster than scraping methods yet produce vastly superior surface finishes which require little or no after treatment with abrasive materials. They are, however, difficult to

Plate 1. Shavings fly as a heavy gouge deals rapidly with the shaping of a yew disc.

master without a very good book or, better still, individual instruction of the *right kind*. Instruction of the wrong kind can produce very bad habits in a student and can prevent satisfactory progress. It must be clearly understood that the use of any scraping method will inevitably produce a greatly inferior finish to that of a cut with a paring action. A further point which seems to escape the notice of far too many people is that fine detail work is impossible on normal timbers when scrapers are used, particularly on the outsides of workpieces whose grain runs parallel to the lathe bed. Such an approach will destroy the finer parts of the job by dislodging small pieces of wood.

It is also an inescapable fact that wood which has been scraped will require a good deal of work with abrasive paper. This abrasion dulls the finer edges, and turnings which should have been fresh and crisp in appearance are ruined and bear the unmistakable mark of the novice. This is sad, because good instruction and personal effort could change a wood gnawer into a woodturner.

Certain situations in woodturning, particularly in the hollowing of end grain where the depth of an excavation exceeds its width,

demand the use of a scraper for safety reasons. Fortunately for the turner, a scraper is at its best when cutting end grain.

My advice to all my students on this subject is that they should scrape only when it has become awkward or dangerous to continue to use cutting methods. This is most important, and is explained fully on page 100. Dust as such is a certain sign of a poor finish – and a dust-filled workshop is as certain a sign of a poor woodturner.

There are certain common misunderstandings which seem to be perpetuated as one writer 'researches' from another. For around thirty-five years I have practised the craft of woodturning, and for the past fifteen or so I have had to analyze every move, every facet, in order to pass on its truths simply and accurately to my private students. The following descriptions of lathe tools are the result of this experience.

Gouges

For practical purposes these may be considered to run in a range of sizes from $\frac{1}{4}$ inch to 2 inches measured across the inside of the flute, or hollow part. At the time of writing, woodturning tools were not available in

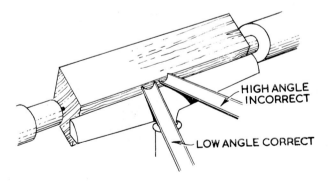

Figure 11. Use of the roughing gouge. Gouge must be held with handle very low in order to cut cleanly and maintain its cutting edge. If the handle is held too high the cut will be a partial scrape and the edge will rapidly deteriorate.

Britain or the United States in metric sizes, though they undoubtedly will be before very long.

This change will not benefit woodturners, though it may have some value to manufacturers or retailers. But speaking as a retailer of woodturning tools, I take leave to doubt it. Turners of my generation will undoubtedly continue to think in inches until too old to care, and it should be noted that where turning tools are concerned the sizes are purely nominal, one man's ½-inch gouge frequently being another's ⅝ inch. The three types of gouge are described below.

Roughing Gouge (Trade description 'half round'). This has been evolved as the safest and most efficient tool for the removal of the corners of square lengths of wood – in other words, work-pieces whose grain runs lengthwise.

Used and ground correctly these are delightful tools, easy to master and having no vices. Once the techniques of sharpening and controlling the roughing gouge are mastered, the tool will remove wood very quickly indeed and with a high degree of safety. It is much enjoyed by beginners, who with proper instruction can soon become quite proficient in its use. Roughing gouges should never be used on discs of any kind. It is possible for a highly skilled turner to control them in such situations, but even so great care must be taken.

The use of these tools should be reserved for timber whose grain runs in the same direction as the lathe bed. The smallest roughing gouge normally encountered is ¾ inch, the largest 2 inches.

Spindle Gouge As the name suggests, the spindle gouge with its curved outline is used for the turning of spindles, workpieces which are held in the lathe between driving and tailstock centres. It is also used for jobs which are held in a chuck, such as vases, candle holders, or similar items whose grain runs with the lathe bed rather than across it.

It should not be used in the turning of any form of disc except by a very experienced turner, since it was not evolved for such work and is extremely difficult to control in such cases.

Unlike the square-ended roughing gouge with its deep flute, the spindle gouge is shallow, and its profile is a fingernail shape. The corners are in fact ground away so that they do not impede the action of the gouge when it is used on curves and hollows.

The "nose' or central part of the edge of the spindle gouge, though frequently referred to in books and articles as significant, is almost never used. Normal sizes are from ¼ inch up to 2 inches, though the large sizes are of little use except on very big workpieces and so are not in much demand. The principal function of the spindle gouge is to shape curves.

Skew Chisel

This tool is certainly more feared by newcomers to the craft than any other because of the spine-chilling tales told by those who have failed to master it. This is unfortunate, since though very difficult to conquer without skilled instruction, the skew chisel is an easy tool to use once the fundamentals of its operation are understood. All the students who have passed through my workshop, from countries all around the world, have achieved within two days sufficient basic ability with this tool to ensure continuing improvement with practice and effort. The skew chisel takes its name from the fact that its cutting edge is ground at an oblique angle to the sides of the blade, unlike the wood chisel used by carpenters and joiners which is ground at 90 degrees. Some writers have tried to state exact angles of skew which should be imparted to these tools, but the reasons for the presence of the skewed

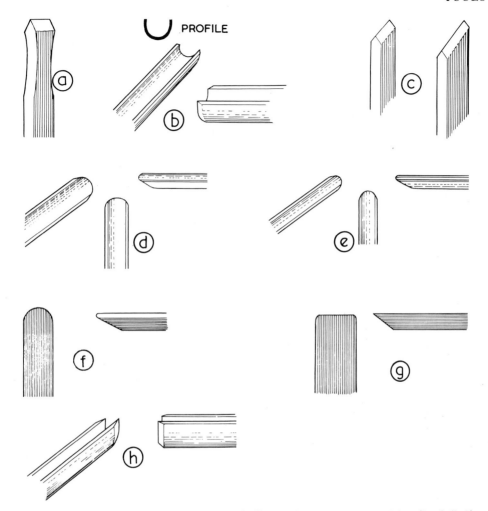

Figure 12. (a) parting tool (shape shown exaggerated); (b) roughing gouge, square end deep-fluted, 'half round' section; (c) $\frac{3}{4}$-inch and $1\frac{1}{4}$-inch skew chisels; (d) $\frac{1}{2}$-inch spindle gouge, curved end shallow-fluted; (e) $\frac{1}{4}$-inch spindle gouge as (d); (f) $\frac{3}{4}$-inch round-nosed scraper; (g) $1\frac{1}{4}$-inch square-ended scraper (note small radius on corners); (h) $\frac{3}{8}$-inch 'deep, long and strong' disc-turning gouge.

edge in the first instance, and for the angle chosen by the individual turner in the second, are discussed fully on pages 61–73 and should be considered carefully.

In brief, the degree of skew given to the edge of any skew chisel will be determined by certain quite definite factors. Chisels with either very small or greatly exaggerated angles of skew should be avoided by beginners until their purposes are understood, and compe-

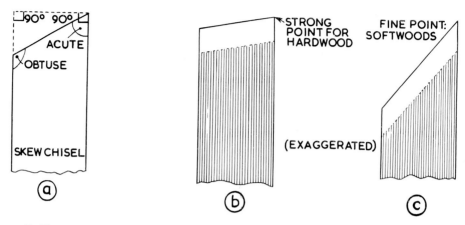

Figure 13. Skew chisel. (a) The reason for a skewed edge on a woodturning chisel is shown here. An angled edge produces acute and obtuse angles in opposite corners, these areas of the blade being used for differing purposes. The outline of a square-ended chisel is shown by a dotted line: this does not provide suitably shaped corners. (b) Small angle of skew produces strong corner for use on hard timbers. (c) Large angle of skew produces a fine point which will cut well on soft timbers without overheating.

tence has been achieved with standard specimens. Where suggested angles are shown in the illustrations it should be noted that they are merely suggestions, and that they can be varied as required.

The functions of the skew chisel, detailed in full in the section dealing with techniques, are the trimming of end grain; cutting of beads, shoulders and 'V' shapes; and the all-important smoothing cut which defeats so many keen novices unable to obtain good instruction.

The rapid removal of quantities of wood in the formation of shapes is the function of the gouge, not of the chisel, the latter being used where possible to follow the gouge, taking a very light cut and improving the surface finish.

Sizes of skew run from $\frac{1}{2}$ inch to 2 inches, with $\frac{3}{4}$ inch and $1\frac{1}{4}$ inches most useful for beginners. Some turners do use square-ended chisels, which have limited uses and are really only of practical value in the rapid removal of waste wood from between parting tool cuts, as described on page 163.

Parting Tool

The parting tool is of the chisel family and can best be described as a $\frac{1}{4}$-inch or $\frac{3}{8}$-inch square-ended chisel with a sectional shape designed to give rigidity when appreciable projection over the toolrest is necessary, and being 'ground in', or relieved, behind the cutting edge to prevent binding in the cut.

The rather strange shape to which new parting tools are formed by the makers is traditional but in no way functional. Newcomers to the craft are frequently confused by the fact that this tool appears to have two bevels. In fact, only the ground area immediately behind the cutting edge is the true bevel, and the long sloping surface behind it is quite unimportant.

Strange statements have been made about these tools. One writer even remarks that they are used horizontally with a scraping action

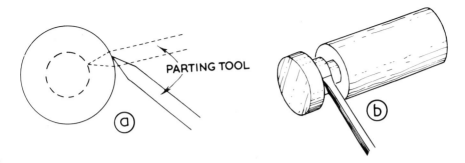

Figure 14. (a) The position of the handle of the parting tool should be kept low, so permitting the bevel to rub the wood. High handle position as indicated by dotted lines gives a scraping action and so blunts the tool. (b) Removal of waste between two sections of a turning can rapidly be achieved by means of a series of parting-tool cuts.

and so require frequent sharpening! The truth is that no woodturner with real knowledge of the craft would use a parting tool in this way if he could avoid it, and the tool is given *positive rake*, the handle held low so that the bevel rubs the wood and the edge is cutting.

Parting tool functions include the forming of recesses, cutting right through a workpiece, initial hollowing of small items in chuck work, setting out diameters along a spindle turning prior to shaping, and the cutting of 'pins' (small round tenons) on such items as furniture legs. All these processes are explained later in the book under the appropriate sections.

Disc-Turning Gouge

This tool is square ended and deep fluted, but it is narrower in relation to its depth than the 'half round' roughing gouge. Its shape gives it considerable strength, and it is usually of the classification 'long and strong'.

Many people refer to it as a 'bowl gouge', which is misleading to a beginner because, although it is certainly the type of tool used in bowl turning, it is used on discs of any kind and is not employed in turning work between centres or workpieces held on a chuck, where

the grain of the wood runs the same way as the lathe bed. This will be clear from the text and illustrations relating to work of this nature.

The disc-turning gouge is subject to exactly the same rules as govern the use of any of the other gouges, and it is unfortunate that it has come to be regarded as a special tool.

The 'long and strong' chisels and gouges are used very little nowadays, at least by experienced turners. They are still manufactured, but as in most cases they are neither necessary nor desirable it seems likely that they will ultimately disappear. Unfortunately, they are often purchased by beginners, who feel that extra length and strength are likely to justify the additional cost, which is considerable.

By and large this argument is fallacious. The 'long and strong' tools are difficult for a novice to sharpen and in use are devoid of sensitivity. They are relics of the past, essential tools in the days when huge pieces of wood had to be manually turned, for example in the construction of wooden columns or newel posts for big staircases. Considerable projection over the toolrest was required at times in work of this nature, so extra length was useful – and extra thickness gave strength to prevent the blade of the tool from flexing.

Standard strength gouges and chisels will be the most sensible buy for anyone taking up the craft, but the disc-turning gouge is often of the 'long and strong' type because it may need to be used with several inches projection over the toolrest when hollowing bowls.

Scrapers

These tools, like the gouges and chisels, will be dealt with as their use arises throughout the book, but in this preliminary examination of tools the humble scraper must be considered, although comment has been made earlier on the inadvisability of scraping wood except where no other approach is possible.

It is necessary to note that a scraper is sharpened in a special way (see pages 42–9) and that its action is quite different from that of a chisel or gouge. It does not have a sharp cutting edge, at least not in the accepted sense, but removes wood by a kind of cutting action. The 'burr' or wire edge on top of the blade is used to achieve this. It is quite unlike the chisel or the gouge in that its bevel *never* rubs the wood, and it can be used cutting 'uphill' and 'downhill' – from large diameter towards smaller, or vice versa. Sharpening of scrapers is discussed at the appropriate point in the book.

The conversion of an old file into a sort of scraping tool is an undesirable practice which can lead to very serious incidents.

Figure 15. Diagram of scraping tool, showing the 'wire edge' on top of the blade. Since the wire edge does the cutting, the tool obviously cannot cut if it is pointed upwards. The handle is therefore always held fractionally higher than the business end of the blade.

Plate 2. Some scraping is likely to be needed on many faceplate products. Note the downward-pointing attitude of the tool.

ANCILLARY EQUIPMENT

Faceplates

Faceplates are normally made from a light alloy, and care is needed in screwing them to workpieces. If the surface of the workpiece is not prepared flat and true, the soft metal plate may be distorted when the screws are tightened. Many lathes are supplied with only one faceplate about 7 inches in diameter, which is rather unfortunate.

These alloy plates are normally drilled with a pattern of eight holes countersunk at the rear to permit the fixing of workpieces by means of screws. A rim of thicker metal around the plate, plus some radial ridges on the back, combine to give strength. The faceplate is threaded internally at the centre to fit the lathe mandrel.

Most faceplates have a hole through the centre to permit the passage of a cutter when a hole has to be bored through the centre of the workpiece. For most of the thirty-odd years during which I have used lathes I have suffered annoyance due to the difficulty of locating faceplates accurately in relation to the centres of workpieces. In view of this I designed removable centring devices for my own faceplates which have small spikes projecting exactly from the centre. These can easily be located by feel in the small central depression made by the leg of a pair of dividers when marking out blanks prior to bandsawing for turning purposes. The centring devices can be removed in a few seconds when drilling operations through the wood are undertaken.

Woodscrew Chucks

These chucks are normally provided in two face diameters of $1\frac{1}{2}$ inches and 2 inches. They are simple pieces of equipment but are worth their weight in gold in any woodturner's shop.

The small chuck has a flat steel face with a woodscrew set in the exact centre. Woodscrew chucks which do not have provision for the easy removal of the centre screw, so that a fresh one can be fitted, are of little value, and

this is worth looking into when selecting a lathe.

In most designs the centre screw is retained by a grub screw or similar device. The $2\frac{1}{2}$-inch chuck is similar to the smaller one, but it has countersunk holes around its edge to permit the use of extra screws. There should be four holes at 90-degree intervals, and they are usually countersunk at the rear.

These chucks are fitted to the lathe in the same way as a faceplate, by screwing over the threaded mandrel. Some lathes do have a thread at each end of the spindle, some work being done 'outboard', or on the left-hand end of the spindle. It is worth noting in this connection that the outboard thread will be of the left-handed variety, and that faceplates, chucks, etc. which are fitted to the spindle threads are not interchangeable.

Faceplates and chucks will need to be duplicated so that both ends of the spindle can be used as work requirements dictate. Woodscrew chucks are used mainly for the turning of small discs and for holding relatively short workpieces, which have their grain running the same way as the lathe bed but need to be shaped or hollowed in a manner which precludes the use of the tailstock. A single-screw chuck with a $1\frac{1}{2}$-inch diameter face will cope

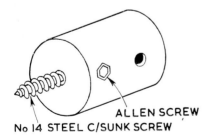

ALLEN SCREW
No 14 STEEL C/SUNK SCREW

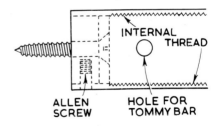

INTERNAL THREAD

ALLEN SCREW

HOLE FOR TOMMY BAR

Figure 16. Many modern production lathes are not supplied with a small woodscrew chuck. The type shown here can be made by any reasonably competent metal-turner and will be well worth the expenditure of a few pounds. The diameter of the cylinder is $1\frac{1}{2}$ inches; the length and thread pattern to suit the lathe in use.

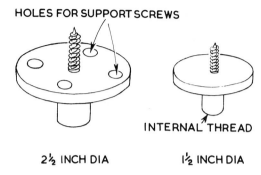

HOLES FOR SUPPORT SCREWS

INTERNAL THREAD

2½ INCH DIA   1½ INCH DIA

Figure 17. Woodscrew chucks: smaller version has central screw only; larger version is provided with holes for additional screws.

with blanks up to about 3 inches in length. Work of 8 or 9 inches can be held on the larger chuck if the extra screws are used in the holes provided.

The woodscrew chuck should have a hole somewhere in it which will enable a steel tommybar to be used to facilitate removal. Note that both faceplates and woodscrew chucks can become jammed on the mandrel of the lathe, and unless a bar can be used their removal may be a problem. This happens particularly with new lathes and is almost certain to occur if the lathe headstock bearing becomes warm in use and transmits heat to the faceplate or chuck mounting. Expansion allows the fitting to tighten, and if the plate or chuck is not removed before it cools fully it can be hard to shift. The problem can be overcome by the fitting of a leather or fibre washer between the rear of the faceplate collar and the shoulder of the spindle.

A jammed faceplate can usually be freed by screwing a length of wood across its face, with a foot or so projecting, and then holding the spindle with a wrench while the wood is given a sharp tap in the appropriate direction.

MOUNTING OF BLANKS FOR TURNING

It is important for any newcomer to woodturning to appreciate that serious injuries can result from improper mounting of workpieces between centres and on chucks or faceplates. Such accidents have happened – and will continue to occur while untrained operators use lathes – but if wood is fixed correctly to its mounting, and common sense is employed there is very little danger. Correct procedures in the fixing of workpieces are therefore vital to safety, and a lathe must never be started unless the work mounting has been checked – and checked again.

WORK BETWEEN CENTRES

It is most important for the driving and tailstock centres to be buried in the wood sufficiently (about $\frac{1}{4}$ inch deep) to ensure adequate support.

When soft pieces of timber are mounted they can be pushed onto the driving centre by pressure from the tailstock without creating undue strain on the headstock bearing, but the majority of blanks in use by woodturners are of hard timber, and a different procedure must be adopted.

Where there is a need for extreme accuracy in centring workpieces between centres, as for example in the making of legs for furniture or the turning of laminated blanks, the centre points at each end of the square workpiece can be located by either of the methods indicated in figure 57 (page 96), and a small depression made with a bradawl to help in locating the centres when the wood is offered up to the lathe.

The same systems are used by beginners when mounting blanks for general turning or for practice purposes, but an experienced turner can judge the centre accurately enough for most work.

In order to ensure safety when mounting workpieces which are hard, an old driving centre similar to the one in use should be driven firmly into the exact centre of the workpiece, with the aid of a hammer, to a depth of $\frac{1}{4}$ inch to $\frac{3}{8}$ inch, and then removed so that the wood can be placed on the driving centre in the lathe and tightened by reasonable tailstock pressure.

In the absence of an old driving centre, a piece of scrap steel ground to a similar shape will do as well. The centre of a workpiece which is to be cut to octagonal shape prior to turning should of course be marked before the corners are cut off.

The reduction of a square length of wood to octagonal section by the removal of the corners on a circular saw or planer is frequently advocated, but the process is quite unnecessary for a turner who has become proficient in the correct use of tools. If a large square workpiece has to be turned it may be found that it cannot be rotated in the lathe because the corners are fouling the toolrest holder. In such instances, of course, the wood will have to be reduced in overall size, and the removal of the corners will normally give the desired results.

When the workpiece has been fitted into the lathe under firm tailstock pressure and both centres have adequate grip, the tailstock pressure is eased by turning the handwheel back about a quarter of a turn. If the full pressure is left on, vibration and flexing will occur as the diameter of the job decreases.

Note that all clamping levers must be checked and double-checked for tightness and the workpiece rotated by hand to ensure that it will clear the toolrest before the lathe is started. Wood which has splits or loose knots should be rejected for turning purposes.

Mounting on Faceplates

Work turned on faceplates is normally in the form of a disc, with the grain running at right angles to the lathe bed rather than in the same direction, as is the case with spindle turnings. The fixing screws will, therefore, be entering the face of the wood, not the end grain, and will offer a secure hold of a suitable size and length.

Timber to be mounted on a faceplate should first be cut to a disc on a bandsaw, or by hand with bow or coping saw, and should be planed flat on at least one side. Screws used in faceplates should always be driven fully home. Examine the wood carefully for splits, and reject it if any are found.

Mounting on Woodscrew Chucks

The smaller woodscrew chuck, with its single screw, is used only for small workpieces. The screws of a woodscrew chuck are almost invariably in end grain, which offers less grip for a screw than face grain, so the mounting must be done carefully.

The ends of wood cut for turning on a screw chuck should be at exactly 90 degrees to the sides, and it is best to drill a pilot hole, say $\frac{1}{16}$-inch diameter, at the centre of the workpiece before fitting it to the chuck. It should be screwed on tightly, but just a little too much tightening will strip the thread in the wood and defeat the object. The exact amount of force needed to tighten the job will depend upon the density of the timber and can be judged accurately only after considerable experience. Setting up a workpiece on a $2\frac{1}{2}$-inch chuck is a similar procedure, but the extra screws used should be driven fully home. The gauge of the screw should be 14, though 12 will do if necessary.

Home-made Chucks

Various forms of chuck can be made by the

turner himself from oddments of wood, and some of these can be very useful. These chucks and their uses are dealt with in this book as they occur (see pages 83–101).

Timber for Woodturning

It should be appreciated that there is no specific wood which will meet all the general requirements of a turner, any more than for the carver or cabinet-maker. Inexperienced or unskilled lathe operators will find themselves badly restricted, in that only hardwoods of high density will respond to the scraping technique. Those who have mastered the gouges and chisels, however, will find that they can work successfully on all European timbers and on most of the tropical varieties. They will also have the extremely desirable ability to turn pine and other softwoods to a very high quality finish. This finish comes straight from the cutting edges if they are really sharp and correctly used, and little or no abrasive paper will be required.

It should be appreciated that properly executed cuts with sharp tools produce virtually no dust at all. Where tools are used with a scraping technique, however, a tremendous amount of dust is evident, and it is definitely advisable from a safety point of view to wear a face mask in such circumstances. This, of course, also applies where considerable sanding is done, which produces yet more dust.

Bear in mind that the dust produced by abrasive papers has small quantities of abrasive material mixed with it which could well cause damage to the lungs over an extended period. The answer, of course, is to *cut* cleanly at all times, and keep the use of sandpaper to a bare minimum. Very few trees produce timber which cannot be turned satisfactorily by a competent turner using cutting techniques, and there seem to be no European woods which are unsuitable. Certain tropical timbers, which the average woodturner is unlikely to encounter, are 'gritty' and have an abrasive quality which blunts any cutting edge after a few revolutions. Such timbers are sawn and machined with cutters tipped with tungsten carbide, an extremely hard metal which copes with them perfectly well.

Much confusion surrounds the subject of tungsten carbide; I am often asked to supply woodturning tools tipped with this material. Such tools are not at present available, and any manufacturer who considers the use of tungsten carbide for woodturning tools will need to investigate certain aspects of the matter rather carefully. Some years ago I had some made and tested them very thoroughly, and the main points which emerged were as follows:

1. Tungsten carbide is rather like glass, in that it is very hard indeed but extremely brittle. An accidental knock against the lathe, or another tool, is quite likely to chip out a piece of the cutting edge.
2. Sharpening of this type of cutting tool in the home workshop is not a practical proposition in view of its hardness; special machinery is required.
3. Tungsten carbide will not hold a fine cutting edge in the same sense as tool steel, from which chisels and gouges are normally made. A brand new tool tipped with this material cuts rather like an ordinary tool which has become blunt.
4. TCT (tungsten carbide-tipped) tools, if available, would be very expensive.
5. Woodturning scrapers cut with the 'burr' of metal left on *top* of the tool in the grinding process, or they are 'ticketed' – the extreme edge is bent upwards. TCT tools do not have the softness required for a good scraper.

In view of these points, it seems obvious that TCT tools are unlikely to become generally available. They might have limited value for those who wish to turn some of the really difficult timbers, but such wood usually has faults such as poor finishing and polishing qualities, objectionable colours, etc., and is therefore best avoided altogether.

Some of the timbers in general use among woodturners are listed here with brief comments on their turning qualities. Newcomers to the craft may find it interesting to keep a 'timber notebook' in the workshop, entering new types of timber as they are encountered with comments on their suitability or otherwise. The turner may well find, in browsing through this notebook after a few years, that he no longer agrees with some of his original views because he has gained experience and mastery of the techniques.

Beech

This wood is close grained and turns very well and is therefore popular with beginners. Grain pattern in the finished turning is uninteresting, but the wood stains well and is useful in furniture work.

Oak

Although this is an open grained wood it has interesting grain patterns and is a popular turning timber. Some turners work in oak exclusively. Like beech, it will take all normal polishes and finishing materials well.

Steel wool should not be used in finishing off oak turnings, since small particles of it will remain embedded in the wood, and the action of the timber on the steel will cause dark spots to appear. Oak is, of course, very hard, but hard timbers are fairly easy to turn. Most turners have far more difficulty with wood which is soft.

Japanese oak is very straight grained, has less knots than English oak, and so has advantages for furniture work, but knots which are sound - not cracked or loose in the wood - add character to a turned workpiece.

Elm

The decimation of elm trees by disease in recent years has resulted in large stocks of elm at the sawmills. At present it is relatively cheap, but in time as stocks are reduced it will become an expensive timber. Most of the available elm in England at the time of writing is unseasoned, some of it still very 'green' (see pages 146-7 for turning of wet elm).

When seasoned, elm has a wild and beautiful grain but is dusty stuff to turn. A face mask will be needed by many people, as this dust can attack the sinuses, causing severe discomfort. Elm, when dry, is often very abrasive, taking the cutting edges off tools quite rapidly. Small white specks can often be seen in the timber, and these will destroy a cutting edge very quickly; frequent tool sharpening is called for when turning elm.

Ash

This timber turns very well and has pleasing grain patterns. Being very light in colour, with a faint tint of pink, it is a popular wood for use in built-up turning (see pages 167–86) and is usually built up with a dark wood such as walnut, mahogany or elm.

Sycamore

In appearance very similar to lime, with a very light colour, this wood sometimes exhibits a very faint, greenish tint. This timber is soft and turns very well, but like most soft timbers it is difficult to finish on the quarter grain areas when turned in the form of a disc.

Lime

As stated, this is very much like sycamore, with good turning qualities. It is a favourite timber among woodcarvers, and some truly magnificent work was done in lime by the great Grinling Gibbons. It is another useful timber for laminated woodturning blanks, but it can be difficult to obtain.

Birch

Not available very often, this wood can be found at times in odd corners of country sawmills. It turns very easily and is almost white with dark markings. The production of birch plywood leaves lengths of wood about 4 inches in diameter by 4 feet or so long, which can be purchased cheaply. Unfortunately, this is always very wet and great care is needed to control its drying, as it is likely to split badly in the process.

Holly

This timber turns very well indeed. It is pale in colour and popular for laminated work, but it is difficult to obtain in large pieces.

Cherry

A very good timber for the woodturner, this is also pale in colour, often showing pronounced green streaks which can be most attractive. All the fruit woods turn well, though for some reason the wood from wild fruit trees, as opposed to the garden varieties, is superior. Apple and pear are excellent, the latter being another wood much favoured by woodcarvers.

Walnut

Both English walnut and American black walnut are much sought after for turning, but they are extremely expensive, almost prohibitively so. Turning qualities are good, and walnut takes polish very well.

Mahogany

Cuban mahogany, once freely available, is no longer so, but there are mahogany-type timbers such as utile (pronounced yewtilly) and sapele (sapeelee) which can be obtained easily enough and are commonly used for woodturning. They are soft, but not so soft as to be difficult to work. Care must be taken when turning such timbers in disc form, since their soft fibres will rough up badly in the

quarter grain areas at the slightest provocation. Timber of this type turns well between centres and is very pleasant to use in most forms of chuck work.

Afrormosia

An attractive, honey-coloured timber, this turns beautifully and is useful for most types of lathe work. It is quite freely available but not cheap.

Iroko

Similar in appearance to afrormosia, this timber does not turn quite so well and gives off a peppery odour which can irritate the nose and throat after a long turning session.

Plate 3. One reason for the high cost of items turned in yew can be seen here. The amount of waste in yew through cracks, holes and other faults can be very high indeed.

Yew

Without a doubt this is my personal favourite for woodturning. Now quite expensive, it is not easy to obtain in good quality. I now buy up good yew wherever I can find it and put it into store for future use. Some of it, with other timbers, is cut into discs and squares to be sold as woodturning blanks to customers in our shop in Bath, but I keep a fair percentage of each batch for my personal use.

The turning qualities of yew can only be described as excellent in every way. Shavings come away cleanly, the wood gives off a very pleasant aroma, and if cut cleanly with sharp edges the surface can be brought up to a good gloss merely by buffing with a handful of yew shavings. Branch wood from a yew tree should be kept for small turnings. The sapwood is milky white, and the colours run from pale fawn through to dark red - sometimes purple at the centre. A good spinning wheel properly turned in yew looks magnificent.

Care should be exercised when buying yew boards or blanks, since some will be virtually useless for turning purposes due to numbers of large and small shakes or cracks.

Softwoods

The classification of timbers as hardwoods or softwoods is confusing to beginners, who quite naturally expect a softwood to be soft and a hardwood hard. Bewilderment is inevitable when, for example, a piece of balsa wood, which is *very* soft indeed, is found to be a hardwood by classification, and yew, which is extremely hard, is classified as a softwood! The basis of this classification is that softwoods come from needle-leafed trees, which do not shed their leaves, whereas hardwoods come from broad-leafed trees, which do.

The successful turning of high quality workpieces from softwoods *which are soft* such as pine is impossible unless sharp tools are used with correct techniques, but a small percentage of lathe owners do master the art, which is a fascinating one. The difficulty of turning pine to a high standard means that such work can often command a higher price than a similar item turned from an expensive hardwood - which is food for thought for those who wish to augment their incomes through turning.

A turner who cannot turn pine and other soft timbers satisfactorily is obviously not fully competent, and the effort required to master such turning will be found worthwhile. Such items as salad or fruit bowls, clock cases, egg cups, pepper pots or mills and the like are very good selling lines today, since many people have pine or stripped pine kitchen furniture.

The turning of such materials is always demonstrated and explained to students on my intensive two-day courses. They are often amazed at the finish which can be produced on timbers they had considered impossible to turn. These softer woods cannot be scraped - they must be sliced cleanly with a paring action of gouge or chisel.

3 Tool Sharpening

The extreme importance of sharp edges on woodturning tools cannot be overemphasized. Having said that, it is necessary to point out that woodturning tools are not normally sharpened in the same way as carving or general woodworking tools.

In this section I will explain the methods which are used, but I must first point out that I use an oil-stone rarely, and that most of my cutting is done with tools which have been ground on a 60- or 80-grit carborundum wheel. The numbers refer to the number of holes in a square inch of the mesh through which the abrasive material is sifted before it is formed into a grinding wheel. An 80-grit wheel is composed of finer particles than a 60.

Woodworkers accustomed to sharpening tools for other forms of woodwork are apt to feel that an oil-stone must be used. In such cases there is little harm in oil-stoning a tool, but from many years of practical experience I am able to state quite categorically that in woodturning a tool taken straight from the grindstone will usually cut *better* than one which has been honed. The writer of an old book on the craft which I read many years ago explained this point very nicely by comparing the cutting actions of a bread knife (with a serrated edge) and a ham knife (with a smooth and finely honed edge). The fact is that the fibrous nature of wood responds best to the finely serrated edge of a tool which has been ground but not honed. These remarks, of course, refer only to turning and not to any other form of woodwork.

There is a motorized wet grinding wheel in my workshop, and students are often surprised to find that I do not use it for my turning tools. It is reserved for new carving tools which need shaping before they can be honed and stropped, and for such items as plane irons and wood chisels. Grinding on a water-lubricated stone of this nature certainly removes all possibility of the tools becoming overheated, but it is a long and rather messy business.

I have also found that turning tools ground on this wheel, which is very fine, do not cut as well as they do when ground on the 60- or 80-grit carborundum. Tool grinding is a vital part of woodturning, so it is dealt with here in some detail. Honing and stropping are also described, for the benefit of those who may wish to use oil-stones and strops.

The Grinding Process

Some lathes have provision for the fitting of a carborundum wheel at the inboard and outboard end of the lathe spindle. This can be rather a nuisance, since the stone will be used several times during most jobs, and the workpiece may have to be removed from the lathe, so that the stone can be fitted, and then be replaced.

Another objection often put forward is that the fine abrasive dust may get into the bearings of the lathe. This, of course, is quite possible, though I do know of several turners who have used grinding wheels in this way for many years without apparent ill effect. The decision is a matter for the individual, but I have used a Wolf double-ended grinder for some years now and have found it to be entirely satisfactory. The important fact in relation to grinding wheels is that, for woodturning purposes, they must be regarded as what they are - precision cutting tools - and not as rough pieces of rock rotating on a spindle.

A grindstone is rather like a large number of fine circular sawblades jammed together, the teeth being represented by the points of the abrasive grains and the gullets by the interstices between them. For a grindstone to be efficient it is vital that the points are sharp and the interstices empty. A grinding wheel, like a circular sawblade, becomes blunt in use, and the spaces between its grains become filled with metal particles, resin, dirt and grease. When this occurs a glaze can be seen on the wheel, and this must be removed without delay. Strange though it may seem, a grindstone must, in effect, be sharpened.

This is a very simple yet extremely important process, carried out by means of what is known in the trade as a 'devil stone'. In the past a devil stone could have been asked for in a shop by name, but today it would be easier to ask for a grinding wheel dressing stone. This is a very hard carborundum stick which is placed on the grinder rest and applied lightly but firmly to the wheel. It removes a thin layer from the surface of the wheel, thereby exposing new points and removing the foreign matter from between them.

I am frequently asked how often the devil stone should be used, which is a 'how long is a piece of string?' sort of question. The answer must depend upon how much use the grinder undergoes, but certainly the wheel should be dressed as soon as any sign of glaze appears. The dressing stone should also be used on a new grinding wheel, on which a smooth 'skin' forms during the manufacturing process.

A tool which should not be used is the grindstone dressing tool, an iron instrument which has a number of toothed metal discs mounted on a spindle in its head. The dressing tool is too coarse in action. Its main use is in shaping grinding wheels for special purposes, for example the shaping of a wheel to fit the gullets of a circular sawblade. A wheel which is badly out of shape can quickly be put right with a dressing tool, but the surface left on the wheel will be very rough, and a devil stone should be used after the dressing tool before any grinding is done.

A good-quality grinder is needed for woodturning. Cheap versions have poor bearings and are not worth buying except for occasional rough grinding work.

Assuming that the grinding wheel is clean and in good condition, overheating of the tools in the grinding process can be avoided by using little or no pressure of tool against wheel. If the tool is pressed hard against the revolving stone, or if the wheel is in poor condition, the temperature of the tool will be raised to a point where the temper of the metal is destroyed and the metal is rendered soft and incapable of holding a cutting edge for more than a brief period.

Because the question of pressure in grinding is so vital, I never use the adjustable grinding rests which are provided on most grinders other than to steady my hand. There are two reasons for this, one being that if the rest is used, it will need constant adjustment for various tools. The other, and more important reason, is that when a tool is placed on a grinding rest it becomes very difficult to tell how much pressure is being used. Little more than the weight of the tool itself is needed - just a very slight pressure is enough to keep the tool in contact with the wheel.

Water as a Coolant

The use of water as a coolant for tools during the grinding process is frequently advocated, the idea being to position a container of water near the grinder and dip the tools into this at intervals in order to remove the heat produced by friction against the wheel.

Theoretically the idea is sound, but it does not work as well in practice as might be expected. Anyone who has mastered the art of grinding woodturning tools, keeping his wheels clean, and using only the lightest pressure on the tools will not raise the temperature of the metal to a dangerous level. An operator of this calibre would experience no difficulty in removing a tool from the wheel part-way through the grinding, cooling it in water, and replacing it in the same position and attitude.

The turner most likely to need water as a coolant is the beginner who has not achieved complete mastery of the techniques and tends to overheat the tools. At this level of competence it will be very difficult indeed to replace a tool on the wheel correctly after cooling in water, and as a result a number of ground facets is likely to be found on the tool when the grinding is finished rather than the smooth continuous surface from heel to cutting edge which is needed, and which is the mark of the expert.

The technique of grinding woodturning tools on a dry wheel is not a difficult one, and is best achieved by practising with pieces of scrap steel begged or bought from the nearest light-engineering firm. Flat strips of steel can represent chisels, and pieces of steel tube or rod provide excellent gouge-grinding practice. Bevels can be ground on this scrap material, mistakes noted, and the bevels ground away again.

Practice of this nature will quickly produce the skill required to obtain sharp edges on the tools. Remember that it is virtually impossible to become a really good woodturner unless the art of using the grinder is mastered. Tools *must* be kept sharp by frequent light grinding. Honing can follow if desired, but it is by no means essential.

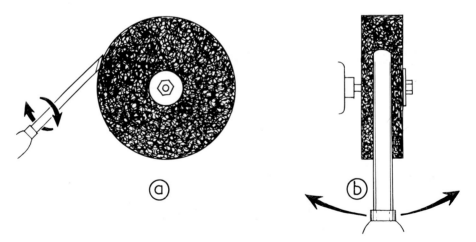

Figure 18. Tool sharpening. (a) Side view of gouge-grinding process. Gouge is placed on grinding wheel with heel only touching, the edge being fractionally clear of the stone. Rotation of the tool continues until sparks appear at the edge. (b) The beginner is advised not to adopt any side-to-side swing of the handle, which is unnecessary and which will make the correct grinding of the gouge much more difficult than it should be.

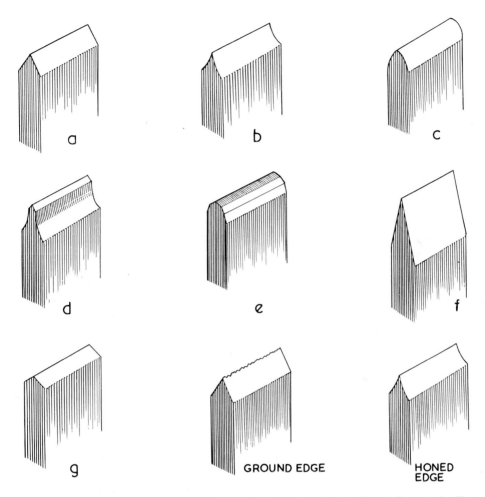

Figure 19. Exaggerated drawings of bevel shapes. (a) A tool ground on the side of a grinding wheel will have a perfectly flat bevel if the job is correctly executed. (b) If ground on the curved face of the grinding wheel, the tool will have a hollow-ground effect, the bevel surface being concave. (c) The convex bevel surface as shown here is undesirable as it renders the tool very difficult to control. (d) The concave bevel surface as at (b), which is an 'ideal' shape, will suffer, as shown here, if too much oilstoning is carried out. (e) Use of water as a cooling agent by a beginner may well result in a badly formed bevel surface consisting of a number of facets. (f) Extremely long bevel ground on tool, producing an edge which does not possess sufficient strength to stand up to repeated hard work. A high-quality edge could be produced on this, but it would not last many seconds. (g) A very short bevel has tremendous strength but will not give a sharp cutting edge. The ideal bevel angle lies somewhere between (f) and (g). A ground edge requires a 60 or 80 grit stone. A honed edge does not in fact cut as efficiently as a ground edge, except when used for very light final cuts. (This, of course, applies exclusively to woodturning tools.)

Grinding the Turning Tools

Grinding should always be performed on the curved face of the wheel, not on the flat side surfaces. It is important to appreciate that there is no magic angle to which gouges and chisels should be ground, in spite of common attempts to suggest the contrary. The sketches will clarify this point, and it will be noted that both chisels and gouges are ground with long bevels to suit soft timbers and much shorter bevels for harder ones. The ideal situation is one in which the tool is ground to give the correct combination of strength and sharpness for the timber in use. This explains to a large extent why professional turners, who understand the craft thoroughly, tend to have large numbers of tools. A recent rough check in my workshop produced seventy-two!

When working on oak, which is very hard, I select a gouge or chisel whose bevel is short enough to give the necessary strength – with sufficient metal at the extreme edge to dissipate the quite high degree of frictional heat produced in rubbing the bevel against a hard timber. For beech or ash I would choose a larger bevel and a longer one still for the softness of sycamore or lime.

There is no need, of course, for a raw beginner to involve himself or herself in this aspect; there will be time for it later. At first just one of each type of tool will do if the grinding angles are kept as in the original factory grinding. When real competence has been achieved and the turner feels fully confident, extra tools may be purchased and ground at various angles. What matters is the shape of cutting tools, both in profile and in the bevel surface. The bevel shape to aim for is shown in (b) of fig. 19. Here the tool has been ground on the curved face of the wheel. A hollow ground effect is produced, giving good bevel support qualities on convex surfaces and allowing easy oil-stoning for those who wish to stone their tools. If a tool is ground as in (a), on the flat side of a wheel, the support quality against a convex surface will be inferior, and it will be necessary to cut metal away from the whole area of the bevel surface when using an oil-stone slip to freshen an edge. If metal is not removed all over the surface, the angle of the grinding will be changed, spoiling the performance of the tool.

When the bevel surface is as shown in (b), however, the oil-stone slip lies across from heel to cutting edge, and the tool can be sharpened with a few rubs. Turning tools should never be rubbed on an oil-stone. Many workers who have come to woodturning from other forms of woodwork tend to apply the methods learned in earlier years, but the most effective method of honing turning tools is by means of an oil-stone slip. There must be two of these, one kept for gouges and the other for chisels. Gouges wear hollows in oil-stones, rendering them useless for the honing of chisels.

Honing

I do not advocate the honing of woodturning tools, but there is no harm in the process, and for the benefit of those who prefer to use an oil-stone slip after grinding, I will outline the procedure. It does sometimes give a slightly better cut, but this is mainly on very soft timber.

Most of the timbers used by woodturners are hard, for the very good reason that only a really skilled turner can produce good tool finishes on wood which is soft. Woodturning tools, however, have to endure two things which other woodwork tools do not, namely a high relative speed between tool and material and considerable frictional heat generated in rubbing the bevels on the wood. An edge honed to a fine pitch of perfection, as with carving tools, is excellent if pushed or tapped slowly along the work, but it will quickly be ruined if used on rapidly revolving wood.

It is not uncommon for turners who have never considered this aspect of the matter to hone their tool edges even in the early stages of the turning, which is a waste of time. In the heavy cutting which takes place in the early and intermediate stages of a turning project, a honed edge is much too fragile, and its unnecessary excellence quickly fades. On rare occasions I hone the edges of tools, but only for the final light cuts which finish the job.

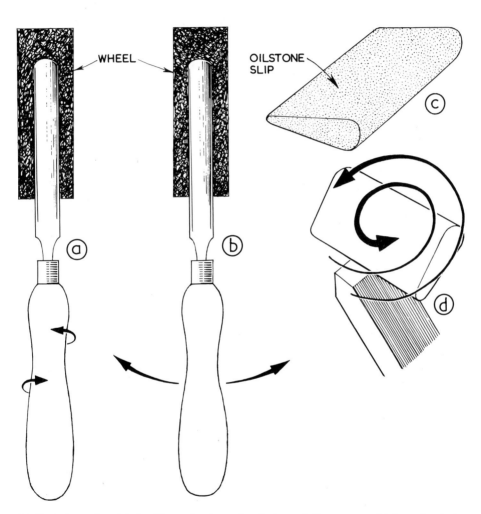

Figure 20. Tool sharpening. (a) A rolling action is employed when grinding a gouge. (b) Lateral swinging of the handle is unnecessary. (c) Oilstone slip. (d) Sharpening with slip. Commence with centre on heel of bevel only. Continue with rotary movement and tilt stone towards edge until oil creeps over it.

In the main my tools come straight from the 60- or 80-grit wheel to the wood, with no attempts made to remove the 'burr' or wire edge formed during the grinding. The removal of this 'burr' would be essential on normal woodworking tools, but in turning it is removed in seconds by the rapid passage of the hard timber over the cutting edge. When fitting a grinding wheel to a machine certain important points need to be noted. The 'skin' on the surface of a new wheel needs treatment with the dressing stone before any grinding is carried out.

New grinding wheels have thick paper washers on either side which must *not* be removed. Metal washers of quite large diameter are also used, and these spread the load of the retaining nut. The nut itself should be pulled up firmly but not overtightened.

The hole in the centre of the stone must be exactly the correct size for the spindle, or the stone will not run true. Some efficient form of protection for the face, and particularly for the eyes, must *always* be employed when the grinder is used.

A light touch is needed in grinding tools on a carborundum wheel, together with a steady hand. The tools are placed against the curved surface of the edge of the wheel, with the heel of the tool touching and the edge itself clear of the stone. The tool position is then adjusted by raising the handle until the edge is almost, but not quite, touching the wheel. If the tool is a chisel which is wider than the stone itself, it is moved slowly from side to side until sparks have been observed at the cutting edge throughout its length, then it is turned over so that the other side can be ground in exactly the same way. If the chisel is narrower than the wheel there is no need for the sideways movement. Parting tools are treated in the same way as chisels.

The successful grinding of a gouge requires a rolling movement from side to side, a knack which does not take very long to acquire. There is no necessity for the handle of the tool to be swung from side to side, though this method is taught in some quarters.

Gouges, like chisels, are presented to the stone so that initially only the heel touches, and the angle is then adjusted until the edge is nearly, but not quite, in contact, when the rolling movement can commence. This is done quite slowly and continues until sparks have been seen to appear along all parts of the cutting edge.

In the grinding of a gouge which is square across the end, as with roughing or deep-fluted disc-turning types, the sparks will normally appear first at the centre of the cutting edge. Beginners may find that in grinding such gouges there is a tendency for them to erode the central part of the edge; in fact, this is a common problem.

In order to avoid this and to end up with a square end equally ground all along the bevel, the correct action must be taken. It is necessary to raise the handle of the tool very slightly when rolling the tool back and forth once the sparks have appeared at the centre, so that this area receives no further grinding. When sparks have been observed at all parts of the edge, the job is done.

Gouges which have rounded or 'finger-nail' ends - i.e., spindle gouges - are quite different. With these tools the sparks appear at the corners first and at the centre last, so it is necessary gradually to reduce the rolling motion of the gouge until finally the sparks are seen at the centre. While the tool is rolled on the wheel the frictional heat will build up as the corners reach the stone, and they may become overheated. This can be avoided by easing the pressure as the corners are approached.

Note also that extremely delicate handling is necessary with very small tools if they are to survive the grinding with the temper of the steel undamaged.

In the early stages some beginners are inclined to worry because the grindstone rotates towards the cutting edges, and they feel that the tools may 'dig' into the stone. To this I can only say that after more than thirty years I have never known this to happen, nor have I heard of it occurring.

Oil-stones and Slips

For those who wish to use oil-stones or oil-stone slips on their tools, the main points are given here. It will be found that almost without exception those professional woodturners who really know their craft do not rub turning tools on oil-stones. Instead, they support the tools by propping them vertically, with the cutting edge uppermost, on some convenient part of the lathe, and rubbing the tools with an oil-stone slip. It is far easier with this method to avoid 'dubbing' or rounding over the edge. A medium-grade slip should be used, anointed with a thin machine oil. Some workers use a thin oil diluted with about fifty per cent paraffin, which they claim gives the stone a better 'bite'. A brand new slip will need to be thoroughly soaked in thin oil, as it is very absorbent. If this is not done the surface of the slip will be dry again in seconds.

The slip is placed on the heel of the bevel, a circular movement of the stone is begun, and with this movement continuing the slip is tilted towards the edge until oil can be seen creeping over the edge itself. This angle is maintained until the tool has been fully honed. Care must be taken not to tip the stone too far, or the edge will be 'dubbed' – in other words, a tiny second bevel will be formed at the edge.

In the case of a chisel or parting tool the honing process is relatively simple, since there is no need for the tool itself to be moved. When a slipstone is used on a gouge, however, the rotary motion of the stone must be maintained while the gouge is gently twisted back and forth so that all the edge receives treatment.

When the honing is complete the 'buff' or wire edge can, if desired, be removed from a gouge by placing the slipstone on edge, flat along the inside of the tool, and stroking towards the edge.

The purist may wish to go even further than the honing stage, finishing off the tools by stropping them on leather dressed with neatsfoot oil and flour-grade emery powder. The leather can be fixed to a board for use on chisels or rolled into tight wads for stropping the insides of gouges. The leather must be moved from the handle end of the tool towards the cutting edge, or it will be cut. Unless this is done purely for final cuts on a job it is a waste of time, since the edge so produced will be destroyed in a relatively few revolutions against hard timber.

4 Basic Lathe Work

As a matter of convenience I have divided basic lathe work into three parts - spindle turning, chuck work, and the turning of discs. To beginners this section, which deals with the fundamentals, is the most important of all, since unless they can cope relatively easily with all that it contains, they are not ready to pass on to the craft itself - the making of specific items.

Remember that all woodturning comes down to only three things - the cutting of convex curves, the cutting of concave curves, and the cutting of straight lines.

I have tried to explain, in words alone, exactly what I would teach by lecture and demonstration in the early stages of a woodturning course in my own workshop. It is by no means easy to put across the finer points of any manual skill in words, and I do not suggest that a book is a real substitute for practical tuition at the lathe, but I hope that a fair idea of what is involved can be gained by studying these pages.

In considering the basic woodturning techniques, it will be convenient to relate them to work held between centres. This is the simplest form of turning for a complete beginner. Initially, of course, the requirement is for a sound piece of timber. For practice purposes any sound piece of hard or soft wood can be utilized, but timber which is split or contains loose knots should be rejected. It must, of course, be noted that the really demanding operation for a woodturner is the achievement of a marble-smooth finish on *soft* timber. Many complete beginners imagine that hard timbers are more difficult to cope with, but this is not so. In hard timbers the fibres are densely packed and stand well to the cutting edge. When a wood is soft, however, great care and skill with sharp-edged cutting tools are needed to avoid the disturbance of the fibres, which produces a rough surface. For this reason it is always advisable to use plenty of soft timber in practice sessions.

These basic techniques of woodturning should be studied carefully, for the whole craft rests upon them. In discussing each I will give various approaches in common use, including those used by master craftsmen. These are, in general, the most difficult to conquer, but they have evolved over the centuries through times when men working long hours were paid by results. These were the techniques which cut down the time taken to complete a job and produced the finest surface finishes. This they still do.

Before progress can be made in woodturning, certain fundamental principles must be fully comprehended. I have always instructed my students on the basis of the following rules. Two of them are commonly quoted, and the third I put into my own words, though the principle has always existed. The first two rules, quoted in all woodturning books, refer to cutting tools only, not to scrapers. The third, which applies to all tools, I first set out in words years ago for the benefit of my students, and I am glad to see that it has since been picked up by other writers.

1.   The bevel of the tool must rub the wood

during the cut in order to support the cutting edge and prevent it from being dragged down into the wood. This does not refer to the entire bevel, just the area of the bevel which immediately surrounds the section of cutting edge actually being used. In the case of a scraper, of course, the bevel *never* rubs the wood.

2. Cutting is always done downhill, which, of course, means that wherever possible the tool moves from a large diameter towards a smaller. This does not apply to a scraper, which can move up or downhill, the finish in either case being inferior to a properly executed gouge or chisel cut.

The reasoning behind this second rule is obvious when explained, but in almost every case it is overlooked, and an entirely wrong reason is advanced. Many books suggest that cuts must always be made downhill because the cut is then with the grain of the wood rather than against it. This is quite true, of course, but the truth of the matter is that if cuts are made uphill it becomes extremely difficult, or impossible, to support the part of the edge which must be used.

This, like many other woodturning truths, can be illustrated by the excellent 'slow motion' method which I find so useful in my courses. A cutting tool - gouge or chisel - is placed on the toolrest and presented to a shaped piece of wood as for an uphill cut. A cove as shown in the sketch will prove the point as well as anything.

My students often fail to see at first why they should not make the complete cut with the spindle gouge, by cutting downhill and continuing on up. If this is tried in slow motion with the bevel of the tool rubbing as it should, and the shaving leaving the cutting edge just in from the corner, it will be seen that in order to complete the cut uphill the tool must be rolled on the toolrest, so that the

part of the edge in use becomes unsupported – whereupon a dig-in occurs. The lathe can be turned very slowly by hand while this point is investigated, and the principle applies equally to the skew chisel, which brings me to the third rule.

3. This third rule applies to all tools used on the woodturning lathe, be they gouges, chisels, parting tools, scrapers, old files, or some of the strange home-made implements I have seen in use over the years. In *every* case, the part of the cutting edge which is in use *must* be directly supported by the toolrest. It should be noted that, in most cases, it is the failure properly to understand the third rule which causes beginners so much difficulty with skew chisels. The rule deserves very careful thought.

Assuming that the tools are correctly ground with sharp edges, the wood is securely mounted in the lathe, and all clamps are checked for tightness, a start may now be made on basic turning.

CONVERSION OF SQUARES TO CYLINDERS

'Squares' in this context refer to square *lengths* of wood held between centres, not to square pieces cut from the plank and secured to faceplate or to woodscrew chuck. In the former case the grain of the wood runs with the lathe bed, in the latter at 90 degrees to it.

A method which is often advocated for dealing with the reduction of a square to a cylinder is the preliminary removal of the corners of the workpiece by hand planing, machine planing, or on the circular saw. Hand planing is laborious and time consuming. The other two methods are fairly rapid once the machine settings have been made but potentially more dangerous than the use of the roughing gouge directly on the square.

Those whose lathes have a very small swing over the bed may frequently be forced to cut or plane off the corners before mounting the workpiece to enable it to rotate without fouling the machine. If, as is too often the case, scraping methods are used throughout the turning, the planing or cutting off of the corners will speed up the job, since scraping methods are very slow.

The diagonals are first marked at each end of the square with a sharp pencil to find the centre of the wood before cutting off the corners. The workpiece is then mounted firmly in the lathe, driving-centre fangs a good ¼ inch into the wood, its height being central to the wood or very slightly above. A sharp round-nosed scraper is then employed to reduce the job, working slowly from one end to the other. The process is simple, requiring little or no skill, but it is also noisy, dusty and inefficient. The scraper edge will have to endure quite a battering, so it will need frequent attention on the grinding wheel.

Some turners use a fairly large spindle gouge, about 1½ inch or 1¼ inch, for this operation, which is better than scraping but not as efficient as the deep-throated roughing gouge. The handle of such a tool must be kept very low to avoid a dig-in. The 'nose' or central portion of the edge of a spindle gouge is almost never used in turning, most work being done with the sections of the edge which lie between the centre and the corners. This means that the spindle gouge is used not on its back, which would entail cutting with the centre of the edge, nor completely on its side, which would bring the corner into play, but midway between the two positions. The part of the edge which does the cutting will thus be at an oblique angle to the longitudinal axis of the wood, giving a slicing or paring cut.

Some points in this book have been mentioned more than once. This is deliberate and has been done because these points are very important. Typical of this is the *correct* control of depth of cut or thickness of shaving removed when using gouges or chisels, which marks the master craftsman. This point is well worth spending time on, and I can think of no better way to explain it than the method I use when instructing beginners in my workshop or lecturing to audiences at schools or exhibitions.

A gouge, in effect, is a curved chisel with a bevel on the outside only and therefore the comments here regarding chisels apply equally to gouges. A woodturning chisel is nothing more than a rather oddly shaped knife given sufficient length and thickness for its purpose. It is a piece of steel, the opposite sides of which have been ground at an angle to meet and form a cutting edge – so, of course, is a knife. The direction taken by the handle in relation to the cutting edge in either case is purely a matter of convenience – it is the edge that does the cutting.

If a child is given a knife and asked to shape a piece of wood, the first action is likely to be a rubbing of the blade flat on the wood, back and forth, increasing the relative angle until the edge begins to cut. Questioned about this procecure, the child may say that it is an attempt to 'start the cut'. What the child is, in fact, doing is to establish the correct *angle of attack* between the bevel and the material in order to produce a shaving of a given thickness. Once this angle of attack has been correctly established for the depth of cut required, the shaving comes away cleanly, with the bevel rubbing *on the surface produced by its removal*. I repeat, the bevel of a cutting tool rubs on the surface exposed by the removal of the shaving.

It is vital to note that in these circumstances additional pressure of the tool against the material cannot possibly give a greater depth of cut, because the bevel will prevent it. A heavier cut will require an increase in the angle of attack. Proper control of the depth of cut, by alteration of angle of attack, is mastered by relatively few people. Many amateurs offer the tools to the material at angles of attack which would, given sufficient pressure, produce a heavy cut – and then prevent the tool from cutting too deeply by holding off the pressure. This, of course, is a semi-scraping technique, and as such it will invariably produce rough and inferior finishes together with unwanted ridges on the wood.

If at any time a deeper cut can be obtained with a chisel or gouge merely by applying

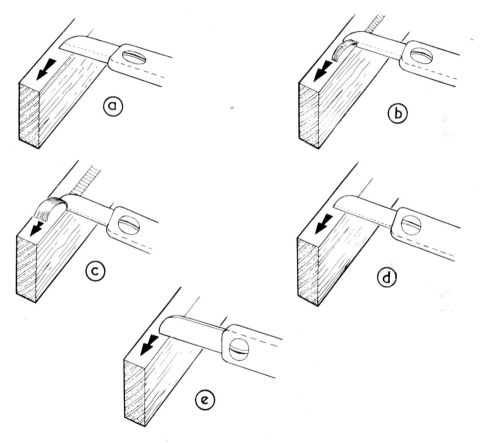

Figure 21. Fundamentals of tool use. Bevels of gouges and chisels behave in the same manner as the bevel of a knife. (a) Knife is rubbing on wood. Note that heel of bevel is making contact and edge is clear of material – no cut. (b) Angle of attack between bevel surface and material is sufficient to produce a fine shaving. (c) Further increase in angle of attack, with the same pressure against the material, produces a heavier shaving. (d) If angle of attack is increased too much the cutting edge will dig in. (e) Angle of attack drastically increased, producing a scraping action which gives a poor surface finish and dulls the cutting edge rapidly.

more pressure, the tool is wrongly presented and the angle of attack is too great. This does not apply to the use of scrapers, where the bevel never rubs the wood.

The point can be proven easily enough with the aid of a craft knife such as the Stanley type, which has a clearly defined bevel along each side of the edge. The principle is shown clearly in figure 21. In sketch (a) the knife is almost flat on the wood and cannot cut at all, the edge being clear of the material. In (b) a slight but sufficient increase in the angle of attack has produced a fine shaving, with the bevel rubbing correctly to give a smooth finish. A further slight increase in angle of attack, as in sketch (c), produces a heavier cut, still with bevel rubbing. The position of (d) causes the tool to dig in, the angle being too steep, with the bevel clear of the wood. Finally, in (e), we have a ridiculous angle of attack, giving a scraping action, which blunts the edge of the cutting tool and roughens the surface of the work. Beginners will do well to study the foregoing, which contains the basic essentials as regards the proper use of cutting tools.

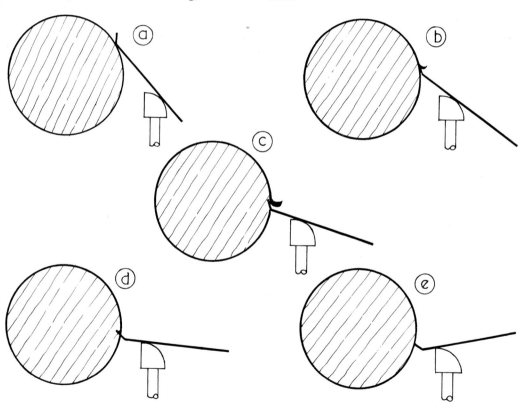

Figure 22. Tool angles. (a) Handle very low – no cut. (b) Handle raised to give light cut. (c) Handle higher – heavy cut produced with pressure. (d) Handle too high – edge likely to dig in. (e) Handle very high – edge scrapes.

Once the ideas contained in the knife procedure have been absorbed, it will be a very simple matter to demonstrate their relationship to the use of gouges and chisels in woodturning, but not scrapers, as I have mentioned earlier.

If a cylindrical piece of wood is set up in the lathe with the toolrest along it – at a convenient height, slightly below centre – it can be shown that my earlier remarks about the knife apply equally to the woodturner's cutting tools. Perhaps the best tool with which to test this theory would be a roughing gouge of about $\frac{3}{4}$ inch to 1 inch. It is placed on the toolrest with the handle very low so that the heel of the bevel touches the wood; the edge is clear as in (a) in figure 22. Turning the wood slowly by hand will not produce a cut, since the angle of attack is far too low.

Position (b) in the figure can be produced by increasing the angle of attack until a small shaving is being removed. Note here that merely raising the handle will not do, for this will cause the tool to be raised off the toolrest. To increase the angle of attack, the handle is raised as the tool is drawn backwards, bring the cutting edge lower on the wood.

In this position further application of pressure cannot produce a heavier shaving, since the rubbing of the bevel prevents the edge from going deeper. Drawing the edge down the wood still further and raising the handle will give a heavy cut if sufficient pressure is applied as in (c). It will be seen, however, that if this movement is repeated there is a danger of the bevel being clear of the wood, allowing the edge to dig in – (d) in the figure. Take the movement further still, and we have the scraping action as shown at (e), which is bad for both tools and finishes.

With a square length of wood mounted *securely* in the lathe, the three methods of roughing down can be tried, though if a scraper is to be used the corners of the work-piece should be removed before mounting in the lathe.

Taking the scraping method first, the toolrest is set up at or very slightly above centre height and positioned so that when the wood is rotated the corners will clear the toolrest by $\frac{1}{8}$ inch to $\frac{1}{4}$ inch. The clamp which holds the toolrest tight in the banjo must be firmly tightened so that the rest cannot move during the turning. Square pieces of wood are potentially more dangerous than round ones, so extra care is needed until the corners have been completely removed.

SCRAPING

The use of scrapers is dealt with at appropriate points in this manual, but it should be noted that the use of these tools should always be restricted to those occasions when cutting tools can no longer be used safely and with facility. Their use in roughing down squares is not recommended, except possibly for absolute beginners who have been unable to obtain sound tuition in the use of cutting tools.

Heavy cutting with a scraper is certain to produce poor results, causing the wood to be badly torn. When a scraper is used to convert an octagonal blank to a cylinder it is used, as always, with negative rake – i.e., the blade points slightly downward. The round-ended scraper would be used in this operation, being placed flat on the toolrest and fed forward until it is cutting lightly, then traversed from left to right or right to left. This process is repeated until the wood is round, but it is a very dusty and time-consuming business. The scraper will need to be sharpened every few minutes, since its edge has a very rough passage in work of this kind.

USING THE SPINDLE GOUGE

The use of a 1-inch or $1\frac{1}{4}$-inch spindle gouge

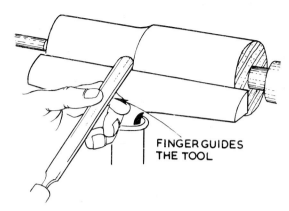

FINGER GUIDES THE TOOL

Figure 23. Use of a spindle gouge in straight cutting along a cylinder. The tool is rolled half-way onto its side and cuts with the section of the edge which lies just inside the corner.

is preferable to scraping for the roughing process, but the shape of the tool is wrong for this work and it is again a rather slow method. It should not be used on its back so that the central part of the edge does the work, but rolled partly onto its side so that the section of cutting edge between the centre and the corner can be employed.

If the cut is to be made from left to right, the tool is rolled to the right, and vice versa.

When a gouge is used, the toolrest should be slightly *below* centre, since the marked positive rake which the gouge is given – pointing up, with handle low – puts the cutting edge itself up to an inch higher than the toolrest. Light cuts should be taken, and if accidents are to be avoided it is imperative that these be achieved by keeping the handle very low.

Many beginners have the erroneous idea that holding the handle low is likely to provoke a dig in, and that holding the handle horizontally may prevent this. Nothing could be further from the truth, and the correct uses of the cutting tools can be mastered quite easily if sufficient thought is given to the fundamentals of the matter.

In more complex cuts involving convex or concave curves and combinations of the two, considerable dexterity is required as will be shown later. Little skill is needed in the use of a spindle gouge for roughing, however, since once the correct angle of attack between bevel face and work has been established, there is nothing to do but maintain the angle as the tool is moved along the rest. It takes a light slicing cut, and it will be noted that the part of the cutting edge which is in use forms an oblique angle to the wood, as should be the case in almost every cut with this tool.

X DENOTES CUTTING POINTS

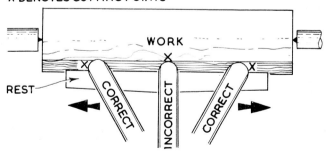

Figure 24. The correct cut with a spindle gouge gives a paring action and produces a very smooth finish. Incorrect cutting with the tool on its back, using the centre of the edge, lifts the fibres and produces a rough surface.

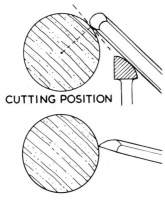

CUTTING POSITION

SCRAPING POSITION

Figure 25. If the gouge handle is kept low the bevel can be correctly presented to slice off a fine shaving. If the handle is held too high, a scraping action will result, giving a poor finish and rapid dulling of the cutting edge.

When using either spindle or roughing gouge it is safest for a beginner to divide the job up into sections, bringing a short length of the workpiece to a cylinder before starting on the next. This precludes the possibility of a badly started cut splitting off a long section of the timber, which might fly into the worker's face with considerable force and cause serious injury. My preference, developed over many years, is to cut from right to left in this operation, or towards the headstock. There is no specific reason for this, however, and if the cut seems easier from left to right there is nothing against cutting that way.

Many of my students seem to feel that they have a special cross to bear in that they are left-handed. It may be as well to dispel this myth here and now. What I always tell them is that I have the same problem – I am right-handed. Lathes are not made specifically for left-handed or right-handed turners, and all newcomers to the craft find that for a long time it is easier to make certain cuts in one direction than in the other. Practice is the only

answer here, making sure that more practice is done in the direction which is found to be troublesome.

THE ROUGHING GOUGE

This is the tool which has evolved through centuries of woodturning as the most efficient for the conversion of squares to cylindrical form, and indeed it is used for very little else. Known in the trade as a 'half-round', it is square-ended and deep in the flute, normally with a fairly short bevel. Once the use of this gouge has been mastered, it will be found efficient and extremely rapid. The tool has no vices provided the handle is kept very low, but only a highly competent turner should attempt to use it in deep hollows, where it can be treacherous. Many woodturners, myself included, use the roughing gouge not only for bringing the square block to a cylindrical blank in preparation for making a specific shape, but also for the preliminary vague outline shaping where wood is removed.

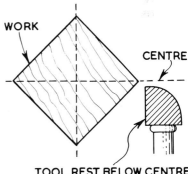

Figure 26. Basic lathe work. Diagrammatic view of toolrest positioned for roughing-down operation. The toolrest height should be slightly below centre and close to the work.

As with the spindle gouge, the toolrest will be set close to the work and a little *below* centre, and in use the gouge is inclined a little in the direction of the cut. It can be used fully on its back and square to the toolrest in the early stages if so desired, in order to make use of the central part of the edge, but in general it is rolled a little to one side, and the handle is swung round to incline the tool the way it is to go. The corners must be kept clear of the wood.

Quite heavy cuts can be taken if the tool is understood, but here again it is necessary to point out that the depth of cut must be deliberately selected by the turner in terms of just how low the handle is held – not by pressing the tool hard against the work for heavy cuts and relaxing the pressure for lighter ones.

As I mentioned earlier in terms of the spindle-gouge method of roughing down, the work is usually divided up into sections. These will be 2 or 3 inches long, but a beginner will find it best to arrange things so that at the ends of the wood the cuts run off the work rather than onto it. This means that the section at the headstock end is cut from right to left, but the section at the tailstock is cut the opposite way.

Here a very important point arises. It occurs in other cuts, too, and it will be mentioned again because it is vital for anyone hoping to attain a reasonable standard of proficiency with a lathe to understand it clearly. A common fault among self-taught turners and those who have picked up tips from other workers, which can become a real obstacle to progress, is the 'swinging' of a tool during a cut so that the business end of the blade travels faster than the handle. I have watched many people struggle to achieve a perfectly true cylinder or accurate taper with no hope at all of success. Their bodies pivoted at the hips, their shoulders swung round, and the cutting edge, instead of moving straight along the wood,

swung in an arc. When moving straight along a workpiece, blade and handle must move together at exactly the same speed. In most cases the problem is caused by the worker standing so that his body is in the way of his right hand, giving rise to a situation where the tool *must* be swung in order to complete the cut. The turner must always be sure that he positions himself in such a way as to permit the correct completion of any cut without obstruction.

It should be obvious that if a tool is presented to the wood at the correct angle at the commencement of a cut which is to travel straight along the job, that angle will change if the blade is permitted to travel faster than the handle. The cut, therefore, deteriorates right from the start, and in most cases it cannot be taken right through to the end.

I have frequently noticed when instructing complete beginners that they try to hold off pressure with the tool against the wood when it wants to cut deeply, and in doing so they relax the pressure of the blade against the toolrest. This can easily be detected by an experienced observer because it sets up a metallic rattling sound between tool and rest. This situation, if permitted to continue, can lead to a dig in. Pressure between tool and rest must be maintained during all cuts.

Another important and often misunderstood point concerns the method of gripping the blade of turning tools. This is very important indeed for anyone who wishes to achieve real mastery of the craft, and since it applies to all turning tools it should perhaps be dealt with at this stage.

The work of highly skilled woodturners, which is crisp and clear in outline because it has received the bare minimum of treatment from abrasives, owes its excellence to the manipulative skill which is exercised. Note the use of the word 'manipulative', for this is the key to the skilled woodturner's success – he holds his tools in a manner which allows him to use wrist, elbow and shoulder as required in following a shape. The exact use of the hand which holds the blade of the tool should therefore be given considerable thought.

Two grips often advocated are the 'overhand' and the 'underhand', and both should be avoided by those who aspire to a high level of skill.

The overhand grip - fist enclosing the blade, back of the hand uppermost - inhibits the smooth flowing movements needed in twisting gouges through compound curves, and chisels in the turning of beads, and in performing other manoeuvres. The difficulties

are similar to those of writing while holding the pen in a clenched fist.

When the overhand grip is employed, some part of the toolrest or its holder will frequently obstruct the movement of the hand along the toolrest. In this respect the underhand grip is as bad (the clenched fist again), but this time the back of the hand faces downward. This grip is even more likely to obstruct the free movement of the hand, and it will also prevent the smooth movements vital to good work.

For most cuts I use index finger and thumb or thumb with first and second fingers. The fingers can be below the tool with thumb on top or, as with the roughing gouge, the first

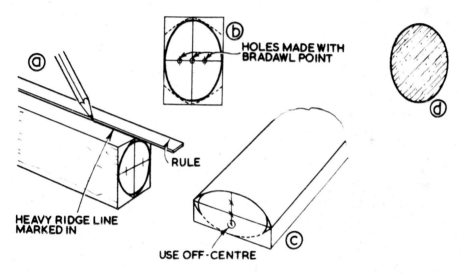

Figure 27. The roughing gouge is employed in the turning of an ellipsoidal or 'oval' shape. This process requires the use of a number of mounting points, in addition to the true centre. (a) Rectangular workpiece is marked out by bisecting the sides at each end, producing the true centre at the intersection of the two lines with two marks equidistant from those on the longer sides. Heavy ridge lines should be marked along the narrow sides, connecting the vertical lines across each end. (b) End of workpiece showing true centre and off-centre marks. (c) Workpiece is mounted on one pair of off-centres (see fig. 28) and turned to produce shape shown here. The process is repeated using the other pair of off-centre marks, giving an 'oval' shape with sharp edges along its narrow sides. (d) The final operation consists of mounting the workpiece on true centres, taking a light cut with a sharp gouge to remove the sharp edges. Subsequent sanding can be done with a strip of emery cloth, as shown in fig. 28.

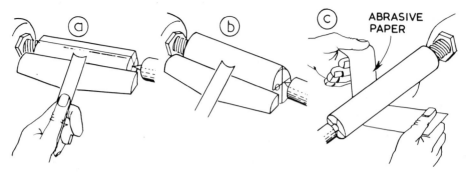

Figure 28. Turning an ellipsoidal shape. (a) After marking out, the work is mounted on one pair of axially opposed off-centre marks, and the turning is carried out using a roughing gouge until the guide lines are reached. (b) Procedure as at (a), using the other pair of off-centre marks. (c) Final sanding can be carried out with the lathe running at low speed, using a strip of abrasive paper or emery cloth.

joint of the index finger can be along the outside of the blade, pointing to the handle, with the thumb in the flute of the tool. The real point is to use only as many fingers as necessary, and to take care not to allow any part of the hand to impede its movements.

It may seem to a novice that such a grip is not adequate, but it must be borne in mind that it is the *other* hand which firmly controls the tool, and the dominant hand should be on the handle. I am always rather amused by the way in which demonstrations of woodturning points are so often obscured in photographs by large fists clasping the blade of the tool.

The grip on a turning tool, in terms of the force exerted, should be about the same as that used on the steering wheel of a car. A very common fault in the early stages is excessive tightness of grip, with bloodless knuckles and hands which ache after a few minutes. The tight grip is an affliction, and it must be overcome. I suffered from it in learning to fly, and no doubt in my days as a learner driver too, and it was not until I had learned to *relax* that I began to make progress. All beginners at the lathe grip the tools too tightly, and this is inevitable, but it must not be allowed to become a habit.

The roughing gouge will be found quite easy to use once the foregoing points have been absorbed, but frequent checks should be made to ensure that the handle is indeed being held low enough, by lowering it until the cut ceases and then raising it just enough to restart it.

The first section of the wood should always be taken right down to a true cylinder, with no flat spots remaining, before the second section is begun. It also helps to try from the very beginning to produce true straight cylinders. If this is done by watching the upper outline of the wood, the process will become instinctive, and the production of true cylinders and tapers will present no problems. Note that in raising or lowering the handle of any tool in order to increase or decrease the angle of attack, and so vary the depth of cut, the contact between blade and toolrest *must* be maintained.

There is a rapid reduction of diameter in roughing down, so it is advisable to stop the lathe at least once during the process in order to move the toolrest closer to the wood. The edge of a roughing gouge tends to become blunted more quickly than that of a spindle gouge, because it crosses the grain almost at right angles and not in an oblique position.

THE SKEW CHISELS

The skew chisel is undoubtedly the most formidable tool to a beginner, and it is difficult for anyone to achieve complete mastery of it without good tuition. It is, however, a very important tool indeed, and the effort made in learning to understand and control it will be handsomely repaid. Skews have a number of uses; probably the best-known is the smoothing cut, which removes very fine shavings and leaves a glass-like surface, even on softwoods which may be regarded as impossible to turn.

Rapid removal of wood is the function of a gouge, whereas the skew chisel is essentially a finishing tool, requiring skill and finesse of a high order, and a beginner should avoid the trap of judging his prowess by the width and length of the shavings he produces.

In good skew-chisel work the shavings are very fine, since the object is to produce a beautiful surface finish on the work, not a shaving of outstanding proportions. Over the years, many writers have been lured into the 'long shaving' trap, and quite recently I noticed an article in a woodwork magazine which showed a long shaving being produced. The inference was that this shaving indicated a high degree of skill, and in fact its vital statistics were recorded relating to its length and how quickly it had been produced. The cut by which this monstrosity was obtained is in fact

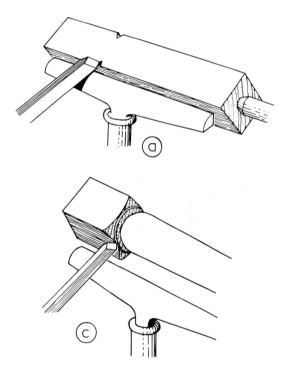

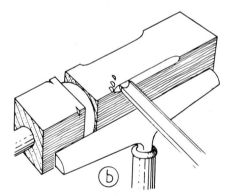

Figure 29. Cutting pummels in furniture work. (a) The long corner of a skew is used to cut pummels; only the point of the tool contacts the wood. The illustration shows the result of the first two cuts which remove small triangular chips from the corners of the workpiece. (b) When a pummel has been cut, the portion of the workpiece which is to be turned can be brought down to cylindrical form with the roughing gouge. The small nicks which have been cut in the timber to prevent splintering disappear as the curve is shaped. (c) The final shaping of a pummel with the point of a skew, which must be extremely sharp.

within the ability of an average novice, and the market for long shavings is, as far as I am aware, extremely limited.

Let us follow no false trails. The essential matters are the accuracy of shaping and the excellence of finish. On one occasion I used a photograph in a book which showed a Myford lathe festooned with great heaps of very long shavings, and I was accused by several readers of having faked the illustration. It should be understood that long shavings do not necessarily indicate supreme woodturning skill. What they do indicate is a high level of moisture in the wood. Green timber always gives long unbroken shavings if it is cut correctly. If, on the other hand, the wood is well seasoned, the shavings will be broken once or twice per revolution, across the grain, as they leave the lathe. Centrifugal force will see to that.

The skill of a turner is reflected in his ability to control with extreme accuracy the *thickness* of the shavings, by control of the angle of attack. I ask all my students why a woodturner's chisel is 'skewed', or ground with its edge at an oblique angle to the blade. A high percentage suggest that this is to enable the handle to be held at a convenient angle while executing the smoothing cut along a cylinder. Many competent woodturners erroneously believe this to be reason, but, in fact, a square-ended chisel can be used equally well for this sort of cut, the handle merely being held at a greater angle to the toolrest. The true purpose of the skew chisel's shape is to give an acute angle in one corner and an obtuse angle in the other. A square-ended chisel must, of course, have two right angles, and it would not be satisfactory for certain purposes. The corner of the skew chisel which has the acute angle is referred to as the 'long corner', and the obtuse-angled corner is the 'short corner'.

Working with the Skew Chisels

A good choice of skew chisels for the man or woman starting out in the craft would be a $\frac{1}{2}$-inch for fine work, and a $1\frac{1}{4}$-inch for general use. These can be ground to give a bevel width equal to the thickness of the blade, until experience and understanding indicate the need for longer or shorter bevels. The 'wire edge' produced in the grinding process can be removed by *one or two* light rubs on an oilstone if desired, but the rotating wood will very quickly remove this, and I do not feel this refinement necessary.

It is said that on very soft woods, the serrated edge produced by the grinding wheel will make rings on the work, and so the edge must be honed. Whilst I agree that such rings are sometimes made by a ground edge, they are very faint indeed, and by virtue of the softness of the timber they can be wiped away in seconds with very fine abrasive paper or grade 000 steel wool.

The obvious techniques of skew chisel work are discussed below. I am assuming that a piece of wood has been brought to cylindrical shape with a roughing gouge first. However sharp and skilfully used, the roughing gouge leaves a rather poor finish, and the well-known smoothing, or planing, cut with a skew properly performed will give a dramatic improvement in quality of surface finish.

The Planing or Smoothing Cut

This extremely important cut worries newcomers to the craft because, unless it is thoroughly understood, the chisel constantly digs in with some ferocity, and each such experience lowers the morale of the turner. Some struggle with this operation for several years before either giving up or seeking advice.

I have frequently stated that any normally intelligent individual can be taught to execute

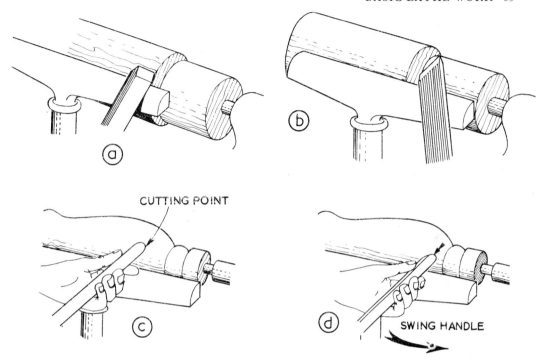

Figure 30. Basic techniques. (a) Trimming shoulder with chisel point. (b) Cut made with heel of skew can run up to vertical face. (c) Convex curve: cutting point is between centre of blade and corner. (d) A common fault. Centre of edge should not be used.

this cut in less than twenty minutes by a good instructor. I was challenged on this recently while demonstrating at an exhibition. The challenger mastered the basic technique in ten minutes before a large crowd - yet he had achieved no success in more than two years of solitary struggle. Once the basics of this cut have been grasped, practice will give full control. When the smoothing cut is correctly performed the cutting edge slices through the high spots on the wood, removing ridges and leaving hollows untouched. Two or three such cuts will bring the work to a truly level surface, and the similarity between this and the action of a smoothing plane is obvious. How-

ever, just as a heavily set plane will give a poor surface by tearing the wood, so a heavy cut with a skew chisel is inadvisable, since the surface produced will not be good. Fine shavings are needed, which will be very thin, and unless the rate of feed or movement of the chisel along the rest is quite slow, some of the wood will remain uncut.

If a pencil is placed on the toolrest and moved fairly rapidly along the work as it rotates, a spiral will be drawn. Since the shaving taken off in a good smoothing cut is not much wider than a pencil mark, it will be seen that a really slow movement is necessary to cover all the surface.

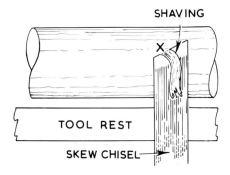

Figure 31. Skew-chisel smoothing or planing cut. The edge is presented obliquely to the timber and the longer side of the chisel is lifted clear of the toolrest. The shaving leaves the cutting edge at a point within the first third of its length measured from the short corner. The toolrest is raised up to a point just below the top of the workpiece.

The following description of the smoothing cut gives all the information needed, and constant practice will provide a satisfactory degree of competence.

Practice in woodturning, as in many other things, is of little value unless the methods in use are correct. Practice without fundamental understanding merely enables the student to become quite good at doing things badly. The essential points are set out below, followed by a discussion of them one by one in detail.

Start with a cylinder of wood (cheap softwood will do) securely set up in a lathe. For a 2- to 3-inch cylinder, a speed somewhere between 1500 and 2000 rpm will do.

1.   Set toolrest just below top of cylinder.
2.   Angle between edge of tool and longitudinal axis of work should be approximately 45 degrees.

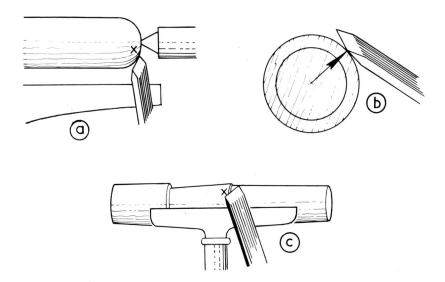

Figure 32. Basic lathe work. (a) Rolling a skew chisel round a curved surface. Long corner of skew is clear of work. Shavings are removed by the area of edge close to the short corner. (b) Sectional view of workpiece, showing smoothing cut with skew. Shaving is removed just inside short corner of chisel. (c) Start of smoothing cut along tapered section of work. X indicates section of edge which is cutting.

3. Tool should be as far forward off toolrest as it is possible to go without losing the cut, so giving a fine shaving.

4. Shaving leaves cutting edge just inside short corner, but corner itself does not cut.

5. Only short side of chisel touches rest, and other side is raised up clear of rest.

6. Chisel is moved along wood with no change in angle of presentation – in other words, blade and handle must move at same speed.

7. Start practice cuts slightly along wood and not at the extreme end, which is difficult for a beginner.

8. Practise both left-to-right and right-to-left cuts.

9. Ensure that the cut can be completed without moving the feet.

10. Aim for a fine shaving, and do not follow surface undulations.

11. Sharpen as necessary.

Point 1 is not critical, but if the toolrest is positioned high the cut is easier. I frequently leave the toolrest in its usual position just below the centre line of the wood in order to save time, but the higher position will help a lot in the case of a learner.

Point 2 is very important. The angle need not be exactly 45 degrees, in fact anywhere between 40 and 50 will do, but the edge must be positioned obliquely to the wood in order to give a slicing cut, which gives the best finish. It should be noted that really smooth finishes are the result of wood having been cut cleanly away, leaving the fibres of the job undisturbed. Only a sharp and properly presented edge can achieve this. The 45-degree angle between tool edge and wood is referred to frequently in this manual, and the above comments apply in all cases.

Point 3 is quite critical, and the juddering which is experienced by many beginners is directly attributable to its not being followed.

I find in teaching complete beginners, which means most of the men and women who come to my workshop for tuition, that they can be induced to start the cut correctly but experience judder (a bouncing action of the chisel) from a point about two-thirds of the way along the wood. There are two main causes of this, and in some cases both may be at the root of the trouble. One of these will be found in the explanation of point six; the other lies in the handle of the tool being very slightly lifted as the cut proceeds. The edge of the tool consequently moves back on the surface of the wood towards the toolrest, giving a steeper angle of attack. In effect the chisel is being asked to take a heavier cut, and judder is the direct result.

When practising this cut in the early stages, it may be found helpful to start it by placing the tool on the wood with a little too much projection over the toolrest – in other words too far up the wood for the edge to cut. If this is done with the wood rotating, the tool can slowly be drawn back a little towards the toolrest, raising the handle very slightly at the same time, until the cut is seen to have commenced. If this exact position of tool relative to toolrest and wood is maintained throughout the cut, an even and smooth surface will result. The edge must *not* be allowed to drop back towards the toolrest.

Point 4 is very important indeed, and an examination of the attitude of the chisel blade on the toolrest will show that this point relates directly to the third of the *basic* rules, which I will now repeat to save searching through the earlier pages: only that part of any cutting edge which is receiving direct support from the toolrest may safely be used. When the chisel is used for a smoothing cut the longer side is raised from the toolrest, and maximum support is at the short corner. If contact between wood and tool edge takes place in the first third of the blade edge only, nearest the short corner, and the bevel rubs, the tool cannot dig in. If any other part of the cutting edge is inadvertently permitted to contact the wood, the lack of support will result in the tool being slammed flat on the rest, digging violently into the wood as it does so. The truth of this can be established quite easily by presenting the chisel to the wood first correctly and then incorrectly while turning the wood slowly by hand.

Point 5 relates to point four as above, and it will be seen that the long side of the chisel must be raised or it will not be possible to contact the wood with any part of the edge other than the point.

Point 6 is at the root of much of the frustration suffered by beginners. I find that even when their attention is drawn to it, students are unaware that they are permitting the blade to swing, or move faster than the handle. When this occurs, the 45-degree angle between edge and wood gradually becomes greater, and in extreme cases the angle may end up at 90 degrees. The result is that the cut begins to deteriorate right from its commencement. Aim to maintain the 45-degree angle all the time.

For *point 7* it will be best to refer back to the rule which states that the area of bevel immediately surrounding the part of the edge in use must rub the work, thus supporting the cutting edge and preventing its being drawn into the wood. If a cut is started at the extreme end of the workpiece there will be no bevel support until the tool has travelled a short distance along the wood. Initially the edge itself makes the only contact, and unless there is precise and accurate presentation the tool may kick backwards or dig in.

Point 8 is important in other cuts as well as the smoothing operation. Almost without exception students find that basic cuts are easier to execute in one direction than in the other. This being so, it is necessary for self-discipline to be exercised so that more practice is done in the awkward direction than in the easy one. Unfortunately, this is not always so, and some people end up with limited ability and so must, wherever possible, try to make shapes which allow them to work in the direction they favour.

Point 9 was referred to at the start of the manual, but I am continually surprised by the large number of people whose woodturning is adversely affected by lack of attention to it. If it becomes necessary to make radical changes in body position during a cut, for example taking a step to the right or the left, there is certain to be evidence of the fact in the form of a ing or ridge on the wood. When in doubt, a 'dummy run' should be made with the tool along the rest, its edge clear of the wood. Any part of the body which obstructs the movement must be repositioned.

Point 10 is more a matter of common sense than theory, but it should be emphasized that it is always the finest correctly executed cut which produces the most satisfactory finish. It is also quite easy to make the mistake of following humps and hollows in the surface of the wood, so achieving little apart from the fact that these humps or hollows become smoother. The cutting edge must be moved in a straight path if a level surface is to result.

Finally, to *point 11:* 'sharpen as necessary' may not seem a particularly helpful piece of advice, but a chisel is blunted quite quickly in this cut. It should be borne in mind, however, that this is a *finishing* cut, so when used in the making of articles in the lathe, one or two passes may be all that is required, and a fresh edge will provide them. Practising is another matter, and in this case frequent freshening of the edge on the grinding wheel will be essential.

I am often asked how a novice can determine the moment at which a given tool has become dull. No precise answer is possible, but I tell my students that if they feel that a tool needs sharpening, they are very probably right, and sharpening will do no harm. Conversely, if it is producing a clean shaving, the tool is unlikely to be in need of attention. The brief period on the wheel which is required to sharpen a properly shaped tool removes only a minute amount of metal, so if in doubt, sharpen.

The End-Grain Trimming Cut

This cut has important variations and should therefore be practised until it can be performed without conscious effort. It is a cut which can be very dangerous if not correctly carried out, and it has been known to cause serious injuries. This should not be taken to mean that only experts can be expected to trim end grain with a skew chisel successfully. Quite the contrary, in fact – given sufficient instruction the dangers are easily avoided, and the cut becomes one of the easier operations.

Recently I read a book which stated that in this cut the point of the chisel does the cutting

Plate 4. The long corner of a skew chisel being used to clean up end grain. Note that only the point itself contacts the work.

while the rest of the edge follows and trims the surface. I hope that anyone who studies this section will understand that that such comment is dangerous nonsense and may lead to accidents.

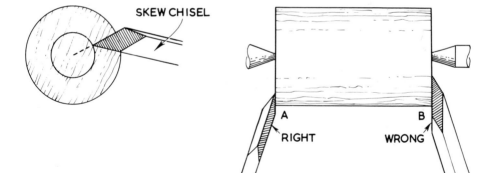

Figure 33. (Left) *Trimming of end grain with long corner of skew chisel. Only the extreme point of the tool touches the wood.* (Right) *Correct and incorrect methods of end-grain trimming with skew chisel. At the left-hand end of the work the tool is shown leaning slightly away from the timber with the point only touching the surface. Drawing of chisel at right shows an attempt to rub the whole bevel against the workpiece which will result in a savage and rather dangerous dig-in.*

Assuming that a securely mounted cylinder of wood has been prepared, the breakdown of the technique, subsequently dealt with in detail, is as follows:

1. If the ends of the wood are not squarely cut, trim them square with a parting tool.
2. Place the chisel on its side on the toolrest, long corner downward, at 90 degrees to the toolrest; then swing the handle away from the wood.
3. Select a cutting position for the point of the tool which will take off about the thickness of an average shaving.
4. With the point *and only the point* of the tool contacting the wood, push the chisel forward so that the point moves towards the centre.
5. Maintain side pressure to keep the tool in contact with the wood, with only the point cutting.
6. Do *not* swing the handle in towards the wood.

Point 1 A sharp parting tool should be used. I was amused by another statement in the book to which I have just referred, to the effect that parting tools are used in a horizontal position so that their action is a scraping one, which necessitates frequent sharpening. There are times when they have to be used in such a way, mainly in faceplate work, but normally the parting tool, like gouges and chisels, is pointed upward to allow it to cut with its bevel rubbing. Even so, the result of such a cut will be a rough surface, particularly in the case of soft timbers. In this exercise the parting tool should be placed on the toolrest firmly, inclined upward, and the handle raised as the tool is pushed forward to compensate for the reducing diameter. This means that the cutting edge describes an arc. The operation is extremely simple and hardly qualifies for inclusion as a basic cut. Note the poor quality of the parting tool finish, and

how much work with abrasive paper would be needed to bring it to an acceptable condition.

Point 2 The chisel is on its side with the long corner down, and the handle is held fairly low so that the point is presented to the wood. Since the vital aspect of this cut lies in using the point and not permitting any other part of the edge to touch the wood, it is obvious that with the point contacting the work the remainder of the edge can be kept clear by leaning the chisel *slightly* away from the wood. This inclination of the blade should not be exaggerated, or there will be difficulty in controlling the cut.

Point 3 Many people try to trim off end grain with the chisel at a 90-degree angle to the toolrest. A little thought will quickly show that it is the bevel surface nearest the wood which needs to be approximately at right angles to the toolrest, not the chisel itself, so the handle must be moved away from the work sufficiently to achieve this.

Point three seems fairly obvious, but is often not fully appreciated. In simple terms, it is possible to cut straight across the grain of wood with a saw because a kerf is produced in which the blade can move. It is not possible to do the same thing successfully with a knife or an axe, because no kerf is produced and the blade becomes jammed. If any attempt is made to cut off anything more than the thickness of a shaving in this chisel trimming cut, the point will jam, and the intense frictional heat will turn it purple.

Point 4 To explain the importance of this the third of the general rules must again be considered. With the chisel in position only the extreme point can be said to be fully supported. In order to appreciate what is involved, a simple experiment can be carried out. Turn the wood slowly by hand in the lathe while trying to push the point forward across the end of the wood with the bevel flat against the end grain, not leaning slightly away as it would be when cutting. It will be found that the tool is dragged into the wood as the unsupported part of the edge makes contact - and it is not difficult to imagine what this would be like at about 2000 rpm under the power of a 1-horsepower motor. It is clear that the rules must be obeyed if accidents are to be avoided. In this case, only the point of the chisel touches the wood.

Point 5 Side pressure towards the wood must be maintained, or the point of the chisel may skid off the work. There is, however, no need for this pressure to be excessive; indeed, there would be no advantage in that. The pressure needs to be firm rather than heavy.

Point 6 Here many people have great difficulties if no instructor is available. It is imperative that the correct angle of handle to toolrest be maintained until the cut has been completed. If the handle is allowed to swing in towards the work the cut will be lost.

The finish obtained from this cut on hard woods is quite excellent and leaves a glass-like surface.

Beads

When considering the uses of the skew chisel point, one of the first things likely to come to mind is the cutting of beads - not the sort worn about the neck, but the semicircular sectioned shape found in furniture work and on some novelty goods. Beads can be made by means of scraping techniques, and some woodturners make special scrapers with concave ends which they force into the rotating wood. The resulting finish is, however, deplorable by comparison with a properly cut bead, and those who wish to become skilled turners must make all possible effort to master the techniques.

Beads are sometimes cut with the heel, or short corner, of the skew. Quite satisfactory results can be obtained in this way, ungainly though the process looks, but it is not easy to

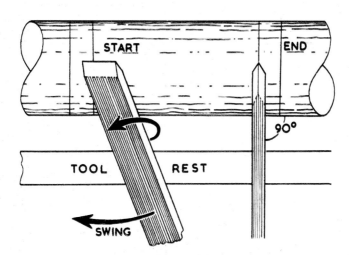

Figure 34. Skew chisel positioned at start and end of bead cut. At the start of the cut the chisel edge is square to the line drawn on the wood. The short-corner side of the chisel is just clear of the toolrest. Arrows indicate the tool movement required to produce the chisel position shown at B.

finish the cut off properly at each side of the bead, and the chisel has to be turned over so that this part of the job can be done with the point. The heel method is held by some to be easier to learn, but most skilled turners use the long corner because it gives better results. A chisel should be checked before cutting a bead to ensure that the corner or point is in perfect condition, for it may have been slightly bent by knocking against another tool.

This cut, though not necessarily the most difficult, is not easy to teach because there are a number of things which must be thought about all at once. In the early years I encountered severe problems in putting this technique over to students until I analyzed the movements and set them out in detail. Hundreds of men and women are now cutting beads quite happily, having managed to learn the rather difficult procedure from the check list as set out here:

1. On the toolrest
2. Off at the back
3. Edge square
4. Establish height
5. Along and round

Once the student understands exactly what is meant by each of these points, the cutting of reasonably well-shaped beads will become quite easy. As listed, they may appear to have little meaning, but the following explanation of each point will clarify matters. What is required, of course, is that the point of the skew be rolled in an arc so that it removes just the right amount of wood, and this is not as difficult as it may seem.

Point 1 may seem somewhat superfluous, since even the absolute novice will by this time be aware that tools must be placed on the toolrest. What is meant here, however, is that the chisel must be placed on the toolrest before it touches the wood and kept in contact with it until the cut is complete. As will quickly be discovered, the turner's concentration is almost entirely on the chisel point itself in this operation, and it is quite easy to lift the tool from the toolrest without being aware of the fact. This results in the chisel being forced

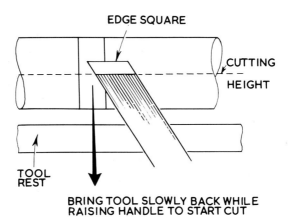

Figure 35. The establishment of the correct cutting height for the point of a skew chisel when producing beads is a problem for most beginners. The process should be carried out as shown here and the backward movement of the chisel must be stopped when the point draws a faint line on the wood.

smartly back down on to the rest, a movement which produces a severe change in the angle of attack, so chopping off part of the bead.

Point 2 is quite important in that, unless the back of the tool - the shorter side - is lifted slightly clear of the toolrest, the full width of the chisel edge will make contact with the wood, whereas only the point itself is required to do so.

In order to explain *point 3* properly it is necessary to point out that when a bead is cut, it is first marked out on the wood by incising two faint lines with the chisel point to show its intended width, and each of the two cuts which form the bead ends up on one of these lines. The expression 'edge square' means that the tool is pushed forward from the toolrest, with the handle low, until the cutting edge is above the cutting height, and square across one of the lines with its long corner at the approximate centre of the marked area.

Point 4 is quite critical. Good bead-cutting depends upon the point of the chisel being at exactly the right height above the toolrest throughout the cut. This height is established, once the first three points have been dealt with, by rubbing the chisel against the rotating wood (which it is unable to cut because it is too high up on the surface) and then drawing it very slowly back towards the body until the point is seen to scribe a faint line on the wood *and no further*. If it is brought back a mere fraction of an inch further it will be too low, too much wood will be removed, and the

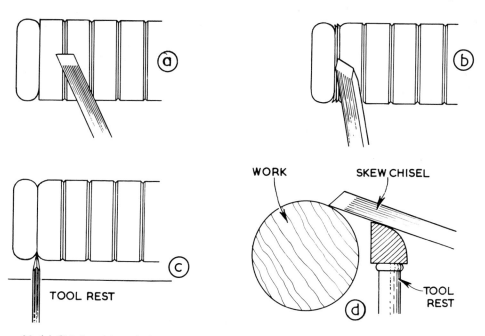

Figure 36. (a) Chisel position relative to wood at start of bead cut. Note that blade is angled so that edge is square. (b) As cut proceeds, chisel is rolled and handle is swung, so producing true curve. (c) Position of chisel at end of bead cut. Blade is completely on edge and at 90° to the toolrest. (d) Sectional view showing low handle position giving steep angle to blade cutting point, high on the work.

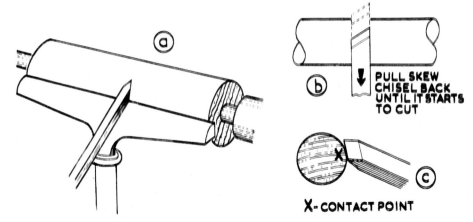

Figure 37. (a) It is most important in the cutting of a bead that the full movement of the chisel should be made. The chisel should be in the position indicated here, when the bead has been completed. It is at 90° to the toolrest in both senses, with its long corner downward. (b) The correct projection of the chisel over the toolrest when performing a smoothing cut can easily be established by starting too high on the work and drawing the chisel back until it begins to cut. (c) In the smoothing cut it is vital for the chisel to contact the work only in the area close to the short corner.

bead will be ruined.

In order to establish the cutting height correctly, it is vital that contact between chisel and wood be maintained. If this contact is broken as the tool is drawn back, the point may pass the exact position which is being sought, so that when it touches the wood again, it is too low. The cut *must* start with only the point cutting, at exactly the right height, and this height, once established, must not be lost by allowing the tool to slide down during the cut.

Once the height has been correctly established and the edge is square to the line, with the extreme point scribing a faint line on the wood, all that remains is to follow *point 5 -* along and round. In order to produce the required curve, the point must be pushed along the toolrest as the chisel is rolled from its starting position. Unless the tool moves along the rest as it rolls, small though this movement may be, the bead will be too narrow.

Note also that at the start of a bead cut the chisel is at an angle to the toolrest, with its blade almost flat. When the cut is complete, however, it is at 90 degrees to the toolrest, with the blade resting flat on its longer side. From the starting position, therefore, the blade must twist as the tool is swung smoothly round, and it is the co-ordination of these movements which is initially so difficult. The cutting of the two halves of a bead is the same but, as I mentioned earlier, it is likely to be found easier in one direction than the other. The thumb and index finger, perhaps aided by the second finger, will be adequate, and it is most important to ensure that the hand is not allowed to obstruct the smooth movement of the tool in any way.

When a wide bead is cut with a chisel there may be too much wood to be removed in one cut, and so the procedure is to make two cuts each side rather than one, taking out the corners of the bead first.

There are other less important uses to

which the skew chisel may be put, and these are covered as they arise.

THE SHAPING OF CURVES

The woodturner has only three basic possibilities open to him or her: the cutting of straight lines, convex curves and concave curves. This, of course, is an oversimplification, but nevertheless true, so the ability to produce the exact curve, convex or concave, with a near perfect finish on the wood straight from the cutting edge, can be said to constitute two-thirds of the craft.

In general, the cutting of straight lines is a simpler matter than the production of curves, the latter calling for greater manipulative skill. The shaping of curves between centres or on a chuck is the job of the spindle gouge, with its shallow flute and rounded end. This tool comes in sizes ranging from $\frac{1}{4}$ inch to 2 inches,

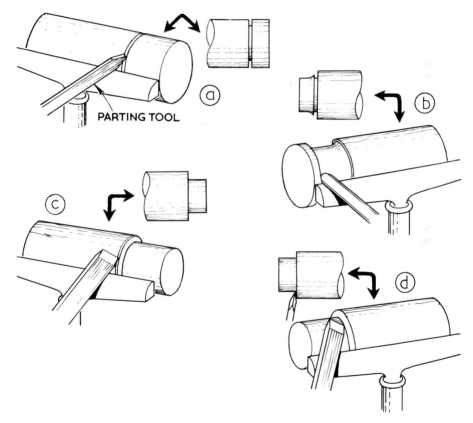

PARTING TOOL

Figure 38. Stages in the production of shouldered cylinders. (a) Diameter of pin is set in by means of parting tool, checking with calipers as the cut proceeds. (b) Bulk of waste is removed with a gouge. (c) End grain of shoulder is trimmed with long corner of skew chisel. (d) Heel of skew is used to trim the pin flush to the vertical surface.

measured across the flute. The sizes are nominal, and small variations are of no consequence.

An ideal size for a beginner to start off with is the $\frac{1}{2}$-inch, a tool which I use a great deal. It must, of course, be kept really sharp, and its fingernail-shaped end should not be allowed to develop any kind of pointed nose. Almost without exception, cutting with spindle gouges is done with the sections of the edge which lie between the centre and the corners. This tool is *never* used on its back, as most novices want to use it, since in this position the cutting edge crosses the grain at a 90-degree angle, lifting the fibres and creating a rough surface.

Convex Curves

Considerable practice will be needed before the shaping of convex curves becomes instinctive, but such practice will repay the time and effort expended. Before a newcomer to wood-turning can hope for success in combining straight lines and curves to form specific shapes, it is necessary to pass the stage of wondering whether the tools are being correctly presented or if they will dig in. The only way through this difficult period is constant practice.

If some thought is given to the rounding over of the end of a cylinder, as an example of the convex curve, it will be seen that three movements have to be combined smoothly into one, as in figure 39(c). These are: a lateral movement along the toolrest; a forward movement; and a pronounced swing of the handle.

These movements may be considered the ingredients of the convex curve technique, and they vary according to the type of curve being cut. In the quadrant type of curve, which occurs for example in rounding over the end of a cylinder or in the turning of a ball, there will be little lateral movement but

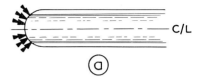

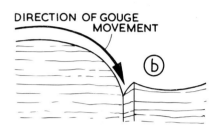

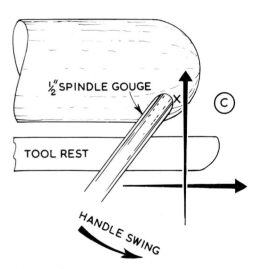

Figure 39. Basic techniques. (a) Arrows indicate areas of spindle-gouge edge which are used for left- or right-hand cuts. The centre of the edge is not used. (b) Convex curves are cut with a spindle gouge in the 'downhill' direction as indicated here. (c) This diagram shows the three movements which must be combined if a satisfactory convex curve is to be produced by means of a spindle gouge. The tool is moved laterally along the toolrest, and forward over the edge of the toolrest, and there is a large amount of handle swing.

quite a pronounced forward movement, with considerable handle swing being required in order to keep the bevel rubbing. In a long slow curve such as might occur in a section of a standard lamp, there will be considerable lateral movement with little handle swing and not much forward movement.

For the production of a curve of a given shape the three movements must be exactly co-ordinated and this is where the beginner will experience difficulties which can only be overcome by constant practice. When a curve is cut by a competent woodturner the operation is extremely fast, and there is little time for the tool to become heated by friction against the wood. In practising, however, a novice will do much more rubbing than cutting and at times will find the gouge becoming uncomfortably hot to hold. This stage soon passes, so there is no need for concern.

It is, of course, vital in this operation as in all others that the tool be kept really sharp, and it is essential for the whole movement to be studied in relation to the part of the edge

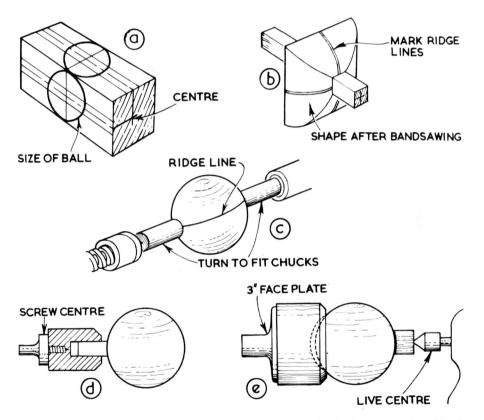

Figure 40. Sphere turning. (a) Block marked out for bandsawing. (b) Block after bandsawing, ridge lines marked. (c) Turning completed up to ridge lines. (d) One spigot removed, blank fitted into wooden chuck. (e) Sphere held between two wooden chucks for sanding.

which does the cutting. Remember that in the third rule lies the answer to many problems which beset the beginner.

In this cut, as in any other, only the section of the cutting edge which has direct support from the toolrest can safely be allowed to touch the wood. The chisel will not be on its back nor on its side but in an attitude midway between the two. The supported part of the edge will therefore be the section which lies between the centre and the corner. No other part of the cutting edge must touch the wood. If the handle is swung correctly to keep the bevel rubbing, and the common mistake of permitting the gouge to roll on to its side during the cut is avoided, there will be an oblique angle between tool edge and wood throughout the cut, providing a shearing action, which leaves a remarkably smooth surface.

A properly executed cut of this type will give a magnificent finish, even on soft pine – so good, in fact, that the burnishing effect of the bevel rubbing on it brings it up like glass, and even the finest abrasive paper is an insult to it. Many people do not believe this until I demonstrate it to them, and they are amazed by the fact that a finish of this extremely high quality can be obtained by means of a tool taken directly from a grindstone.

In the production of curves, both convex and concave, as in many other cuts, there is a marked reluctance on the part of most beginners to apply pressure with the tool during the cut. This results in the tool lightly skimming the wood, often with the bevel lifted slightly from the surface instead of rubbing firmly on it. Firm pressure should be applied throughout the cut, so that if the angle of attack between bevel and wood is too great the cut will become too deep. This situation is corrected by decreasing the angle of attack – bringing the handle slightly backward – without decreasing the pressure. Those who work with pressure of tool against material always know exactly where the bevel is and do not have to guess.

A very common problem which frustrates a beginner is the appearance of rings and ridges on the work. These are caused by having too great an angle of attack and attempting to cor-

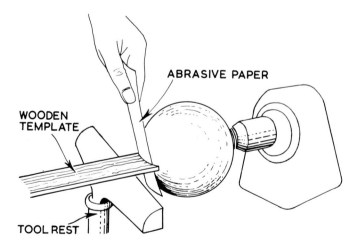

ABRASIVE PAPER

WOODEN TEMPLATE

TOOL REST

Figure 41. System for sanding spheres. Ball is still retained by one spigot.

rect the situation by decreasing pressure. A heavy cut is being offered to the tool but denied by lack of pressure, so the edge nibbles rings into the wood. The cure for this, of course, is in reducing the angle of attack so that the bevel is correctly presented, and then the edge will not cut more deeply if additional pressure is applied.

Concave Curves

The most familiar form of concave curve is, of course, the cove, which is the opposite in terms of shape to a bead. A cove, by definition, is a symmetrical concave shape, but the same technique used in the proper cutting of a cove will be used on other forms of concave curve which are assymetric.

It is important to note that at no time in the cutting of convex or concave shapes is the spindle gouge rolled onto its back with the flute facing upward. The object at all times is to keep it in a position neither on its back nor on its side, but midway between the two. If used on its back the tool will produce a poor surface, because its edge crosses the grain at 90 degrees. If used on its side, its corner will enter the wood, spoiling the cut.

In the concave curve, therefore, just as in the convex one, the cutting is done with the part of the edge that is between the centre and the corner. Cuts of this nature are started by taking out a shallow and fairly narrow cove shape by means of two cuts from opposite directions, using the gouge as described above. This initial shape can now be widened and deepened by successive cuts from alternate sides, aiming to keep the job in balance. As is the case in all shaping operations, the turner keeps his eye on the upper outline of the wood, not on the tool itself. This, once the knack has been acquired, makes it easier to achieve accuracy.

The same ingredients are present in a properly executed concave cut as in the convex one, except that in the concave cut there is a pronounced *backward* movement of the handle. It is failure to make sufficient backward movement of the handle that leads, on so many occasions, to poor results. What happens is that the handle is moved backward

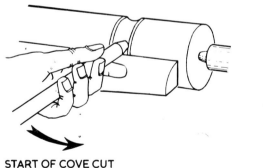

START OF COVE CUT

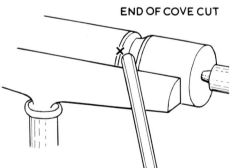

END OF COVE CUT

Figure 42. Cove cutting. (a) The commencement of a cove cut. Gouge is not on its side, neither is it on its back, but in a position mid-way between. Arrow shows direction in which handle must swing in order to maintain correct bevel contact. (b) At the end of a cove cut the gouge will still be cutting with the portion of its edge marked. The cut will finish just past the centre of the cove.

little, if at all, and what should have been a beautifully shaped curve with a marble smooth surface ends up as a 'cotton reel', with a very rough centre portion.

It may be helpful in respect of the handle movements required in the shaping of curves to take an enamelled or ceramic bowl and pass a gouge round the outer and inner surface of it, making sure that the bevel remains in full contact with the surface. The pronounced swing of the handle necessary, forward in the convex curve and backward in the concave, will be quite obvious.

One interesting point remains to be investigated concerning convex curves, and it shows up clearly in the rounding over of the end of a cylinder. When practising this cut it will be found that, at the extreme end of the cut, any further forward movement of the gouge will engage its corner in the waste wood to its right (or left if cutting from right to left).

One might perhaps say that, as it is waste wood, this does not matter, but in practical turning such curves often occur in the shape at odd points, and the only way to finish the cut cleanly is by rolling the gouge onto its side so that the centre portion of its edge finishes the cut. This can be tried out with the lathe switched off once the shape has been made, turning the wood slowly by hand.

An important fact which emerges at once is that if the handle of the gouge is lifted too high when the tool is rolled to finish the cut, the wrong part of the edge will contact the work, and the tool will climb away from the curve along the waste. If this is allowed to happen in a turning project, a deep spiral will be cut into the wood. The handle must be raised only enough to engage the centre of its edge, and no more.

Other applications of the turning tools are dealt with as they arise, notably the use of the deep-fluted gouges, frequently referred to as 'bowl gouges'. It will be seen that this description can be misleading, since these deep-fluted gouges, with their square ends, are used in the turning of discs of many kinds and not just in bowl work. Cuts such as the 'V-cut' performed with the chisel point, and the use of the chisel point for shaping small curves such as may occur on the foot of an egg cup or goblet, are also covered in their respective sections of this manual.

Continuing with considerations of turning between centres, having given detailed descriptions of the techniques involved, it may now be as well to look at some spindle-turning projects and some of the allied processes, such as the drilling of long holes to carry the flex for lamps, boring larger holes for candle holders and vases, and so forth.

A student who has practised the basic turning techniques to a point where there is no fear of dig ins or skids is ready to undertake some simple turning projects. The urge to make a spinning wheel, should it arise, must at this stage be restrained. Work as complex as this can come later.

Beginners often find that simple shapes are far harder to achieve than they had thought. An example of this, which enables some of the basic techniques to be tried out, is the old-fashioned rolling pin with a knob at each end and a curve on the main portion. It appears to be an extremely simple project to anyone who has done no turning, but a well-made version of this demands some skill.

Certain points will pose problems. For the finished exercise to look right, the main portion of the job must be symmetrical. Care will be needed in shaping the curve, and the second general rule must be borne in mind – that the cutting must be downhill wherever possible. One problem therefore is how to avoid a nasty ridge or hollow at the centre where the right- and left-hand cuts start. At any two points equidistant from the centre the diameter will have to be the same. At the ends of the exercise there are convex and concave cuts which must flow smoothly into each other without the necessity for protracted use of abrasives.

If the timber selected for the operation is exactly the length of the finished project, centre marks will be left in the wood, and it will not be possible to complete the shaping of the knobs properly without risking contact between the gouge and the lathe centres. By no means least among various problems is the shaping of the coves between the knobs and the body of the rolling pin, because the gouge, if improperly used, is likely to skid back along the work and plough a spiral furrow. This particular problem is one which bedevils most beginners, and although I did not deal with it when discussing the cutting of concave shapes, its fundamentals will be dealt with in this section.

Altogether there do seem to be rather a lot of difficulties in the making of this simple object, but they will soon be overcome by the keen student who has been putting in plenty of basic practice. This little project is intended purely as an exercise, and it is in fact a very valuable one as a start to the serious business of turning, so it deserves more than cursory attention. As with all woodturning projects there is a logical sequence which, if followed, will make the whole operation much easier. Many jobs are spoiled by being tackled in the wrong way, but the logical sequence of operations soon becomes obvious to a turner who has begun by obtaining instruction of good quality. In the final analysis of course, plain common sense is the best guide.

The exact size of the timber selected for a job of this nature, or indeed the exact size of the finished project, is not of paramount importance. What matters is proportion, balance and symmetry, plus a satin-smooth finish on the work *before* it is sanded. A first-class woodturner does not sand a job of this kind in order to achieve a silken finish – this will have been produced by the tools – but fine garnet paper may be useful, as fine grade as 320, to remove any tiny stray fibres or minute lines on the wood which the average observer would find hard to see. In most cases I do not sand spindle work with the lathe running, but turn the wood slowly by hand while I rub very fine paper back and forth *along* the grain.

This point is important. Anyone who doubts this should take time to examine a few table lamps or candle holders, or any type of spindle turning, which is hand turned rather than machine-made. The amount of work spoiled by the presence of vast numbers of scratches running across the grain is hardly credible. Poor turning requires copious sanding with relatively coarse paper, and the damage done by this is seldom entirely eradicated. In view of this, and quite apart from the present high cost of good-quality abrasive paper, the student must practise until surface finishes can be achieved direct from the tools which are at least as good as those expected from a razor-sharp plane.

For the turning of this exercise the choice of timber is by no means critical, but it is as well to avoid wood which is either very hard or very soft, since these present problems which I will deal with later. A fairly soft timber such as sycamore will do, or beech, which though harder turns very well.

The use of the roughing gouge having been mastered by sufficient practice, a square piece of timber can be used for the job, but in order to overcome the problem of shaping the knobs and leaving them without centre marks the wood will need to be roughly 2 inches longer than the overall length of the project, so that there will be a waste section at each end.

This square length of wood is mounted securely in the lathe and reduced to a cylinder fractionally larger than the required finished diameter of the exercise piece using the roughing gouge, with the handle held as low as possible. The next step is to mark out the length of the rolling pin on the workpiece, leaving roughly equal amounts of waste at each end. A medium-grade pencil should be used while turning the wood by hand, which will leave a clear black line.

Measuring inward from each line, the work can now be marked as shown in the sketch, and parting tool cuts are made as indicated. These cuts are made to a depth which leaves a diameter fractionally greater than the size of the knobs, to allow for final smoothing cuts and sanding.

The accepted procedure for this process is quite simple and should be practised on scrap timber prior to using it on an actual workpiece. A pair of spring calipers is set to the appropriate size and held in one hand, while the parting tool – which if sharp can be controlled easily and safely by one hand only – is held in the other. As the tool goes into the wood the calipers rest against the rotating wood at the rear. When the correct size is reached, the caliper jaws will slip over the wood, whereupon the cut is stopped immediately. The calipers are held firmly but are not pressed hard against the work.

Spring calipers should always be used for work of this type, rather than the variety which operates purely by friction, since the bumping of the wood against the jaws of the latter type may cause the setting to alter during the cut.

The waste wood which remains to be removed when the parting tool cuts have been accurately completed can be removed by means of a series of further cuts with the parting tool – which, of course, is held with its handle low, thus permitting its bevel to rub the wood.

Some turners, myself among them, keep a square-ended chisel expressly for the removal of waste. Its performance is frequently a source of amusement for those whose experience is slight, as with many timbers the cut gives a long, wide shaving. Little skill is required, in fact; the square-ended chisel is used as a wide parting tool. The toolrest is set high, and the edge of the chisel is square across the work with the blade flat on the toolrest. Keeping firm contact between toolrest and full width of blade, the tool, with its bevel rubbing, moves forward as the handle is raised. The edge is kept as far forward from the toolrest as possible without losing the cut. The essentials here are to maintain contact with the toolrest throughout and not to raise the handle any more than necessary to keep the cut going.

Once this waste has been removed, the workpiece will appear as a cylinder with a round pin projecting from each end, with a

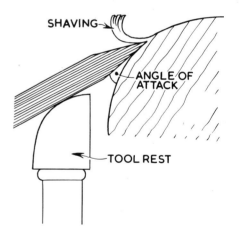

Figure 43. The frequently expressed idea that the parting tool should be used in a horizontal position is entirely wrong, though there are odd occasions when it may have to be held thus. The tool is used with the toolrest fairly low, so that it can point upwards and its bevel rubs to support the cutting edge in the same fashion as that of a chisel – which of course it is.

disc of waste at the end of each pin. This waste can be removed with chisel or parting tool, being careful to avoid contact between tool and lathe centres.

Further work with parting tool and calipers is now required to produce the shape shown in the sketches. The shaping of the knobs and the coves which connect them to the body of

the rolling pin is then carried out by means of sharp spindle gouges. These are used as described earlier, taking smoothly controlled paring cuts and working 'downhill' all the time. The spindle gouge is also used to shape the ends of the main section of the job to a gentle curve, and the tiny curves at the ends of the coves are put in with the long corner of a skew

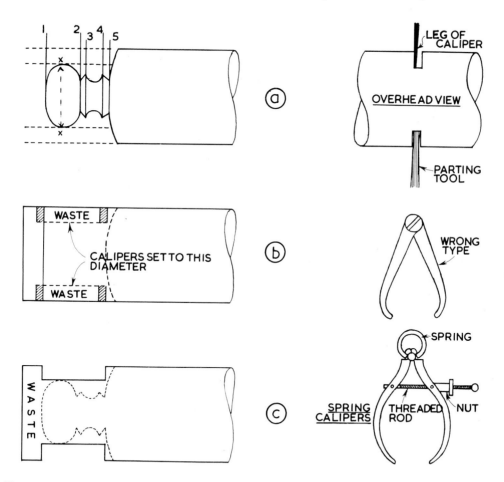

Figure 44. Use of parting tool and calipers in the making of a rolling pin. (Only one end is shown.) The area marked waste in (b) is removed first, and the waste marked in (c) is removed when all the rest of the turning has been completed. The sequence of the shaping is shown by numbers in (a).

chisel, rolling the point as in a bead cut and allowing nothing but the extreme point to contact the wood.

Final cleaning up after careful inspection of the job is done by light *cuts* - not scrapes - with freshly sharpened gouges and chisels. Pressure of bevel against wood is essential, and shaving thickness is controlled by handle movement to alter the angle of attack between bevel and wood as necessary. Definite shavings must be produced, though they may be as fine as a hair. The work can now be sanded with very fine, open coat garnet paper, about grade 340, or possibly grade 000 steel wool.

A final burnish with a handful of soft shavings completes the work, but care is needed to ensure that no shavings harder than the wood in the lathe are used or the job will be scratched. It has been known for small metal objects such as screws or nails to be inadvertently gathered up with shavings to be used for burnishing, and the adverse effect of such an error upon the workpiece is not difficult to imagine!

The final stage in an operation of this kind is the reduction of the diameter at each end to about $\frac{1}{4}$ inch using a cutting action with the point of a skew. The workpiece is then removed from the lathe, the waste portions are cut away by means of a hacksaw blade, and the sawn area of the job is sanded by hand. A hacksaw blade is used because its very fine teeth leave the end grain undisturbed, and I keep one near the lathe at all times.

This has been a description of an interesting elementary exercise in spindle-turning, and the methods used would serve to make quite a number of objects. Further exercises of various kinds are given at the end of this manual. All of them will be extremely valuable to anyone endeavouring to master the craft correctly.

5 Chucks and their Uses

In the early days of woodturning, a novice would be best advised to work on wood which is securely mounted between centres until reasonably competent in the proper use of tools, leaving chuck work and bowl-turning to be tackled when ready for them.

In general the expression 'faceplate-turning' is used to describe work which is supported at the headstock only, the tailstock not being used. The important division in this craft, however, is between the turning of discs and the turning of workpieces where the grain runs roughly parallel to the bed of the machine.

The former is dealt with later in this manual, and it will be seen that the turning of discs presents its own special problems. Chuck work is mainly concerned with work where the grain runs the same way as the lathe bed; in other words, the end grain of the wood faces towards the headstock and tailstock.

The variety of chucks freely available to the woodturner from lathe manufacturers and machinery suppliers is not wide, though there are a number of wooden types which can be made by the turner from odd scraps of timber – or indeed in metal, if the necessary knowledge and equipment are possessed. Some of these are more efficient than others as regards both the length of wood which may safely be turned on them and their ability to support this wood firmly even under possible adverse circumstances, as when the tools are not expertly used.

In this chapter most of the various types of chuck likely to be encountered today are dis-cussed, together with the problems which may arise. Before going into this, however, I must try to clear up the issue which bothers so many beginners when they begin to find their feet as woodturners, or indeed as wood-workers of any kind. Among my own students as well as those who have attended my many lectures, I have found an attitude which verges on defeatism in respect of the acquisi-tion of true skill. At the root of this is the modern tendency to abuse the word 'crafts-man'. A typical comment is, 'Of course, I don't expect to become a craftsman, but per-haps I can be fairly competent in time.' Some seem almost to regard a craftsman as a semi-deity, and the 'craftsman cult' is further fostered by some magazines to the detriment of the craft itself. By definition, a person who follows a craft is a craftsman; he or she may be a good craftsman, a very bad craftsman or per-haps a master craftsman, but the word itself has little meaning without qualification. The very important point, so often ignored, is that the struggling beginner of today is the good, bad or indifferent craftsman of tomorrow.

Just how good a beginner may become is dependent on effort, determination and enthu-siasm – and just how much others are pre-pared to share their knowledge. Take heart, therefore, for the person who began wood-turning only last week is a craftsman and, given help and encouragement by those who know how to help, may well, with effort, be-come a highly skilled one. Those who attempt to surround any aspect of woodwork with mystique can safely be ignored.

WOODSCREW CHUCKS

Taking the various chucks used by the wood-turner individually in rough order of importance, the woodscrew chuck is a natural starting point. Some discussion on chuck work as such follows at the end of the chapter.

The majority of lathes offer as basic equipment or as optional extras one or more wood-screw chucks. These are invaluable aids and are considered essential by many turners. I work with two sizes and always have several of each size around the workshop, so that partly turned work which needs to be temporarily laid aside for some reason does not have to be separated from the chuck. This avoids the common situation where work removed from a chuck is not exactly centred when replaced. It is useful to have several faceplates for the same reason.

The common sizes of woodscrew chuck are $1\frac{1}{2}$-inch and $2\frac{1}{2}$-inch, metrication having failed at the time of writing to gain much of a hold on lathe and woodturning tool manufacturers. Naturally, metric sizes approximating these will do equally well; the size is by no means critical. It is the measurement taken across the circular face of the chuck, its diameter in fact, which is used to describe it, and both sizes will be needed. The smaller of the two can be very useful for small-diameter objects such as chess pieces or knobs for furniture, which are awkward to deal with on the larger version since they are smaller than the chuck diameter.

Woodscrew chucks are made without sufficient consideration for their purpose, like many items of equipment for the woodturner. They have completely flat faces, whereas if they were made so that the face was very slightly lower at the centre than at the edges – or slightly concave – a far better grip would be obtained on the wood in most cases. With a perfectly flat face a problem is often caused by the wood immediately adjacent to the screw swelling when the screw is forced in, so that there is no contact around the rim of the chuck and the workpiece wobbles under pressure from the tools.

The smaller of the two chucks has one central screw. No provision is made for the use of further supporting screws due to lack of space at the rim. A length of roughly 3 inches is as much as most people can manage on a single screw, but this will cover a surprising amount of small work.

The chucks are similar in design, being threaded to fit the lathe mandrel, and they are usually provided with a simple means of changing the central screw. Two or sometimes four holes are provided in the outer part of the larger version, to permit the use of additional screws. A $2\frac{1}{2}$-inch woodscrew chuck can be used for the turning of many forms of disc and will cope quite well with small bowls.

CUP CHUCKS

Cup chucks are not available for many makes of lathe, though users of Arundel machines are fortunate in being able to obtain them. They offer a very secure method of holding quite large pieces of wood at one end only, as required in the making of biscuit barrels, tobacco humidors, tankards and similar items. I prefer the type shown at (a) in figure 46 though this has largely been superseded by the pattern at (b) on grounds of safety. Ideally the turner should possess at least one of each.

In the case of lathes whose manufacturers do not offer cup chucks, it will be necessary for the turner to have one or two made by a competent metal worker.

Type (a) should be used as its original designer intended – exclusively for workpieces whose diameter is greater than the chuck by an amount which will guard the bolt beads, so

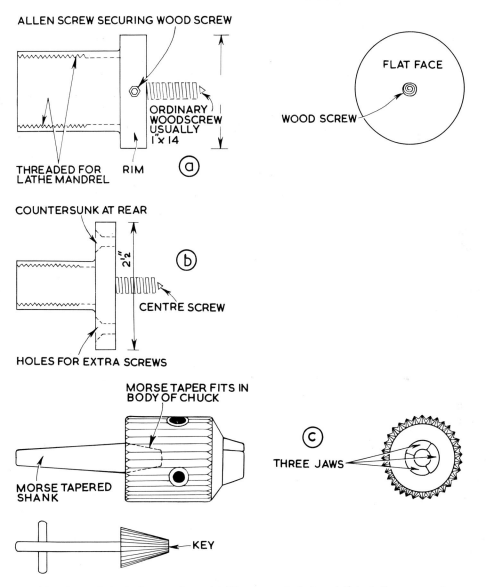

Figure 45. Manufactured chucks in general use. (a) Diagrammatical view of 1½-inch-diameter woodscrew chuck. (b) Large version of chuck as shown at (a) with 2½-inch-diameter face and provision for the fitting of additional screws. (c) Jacobs pattern three-jawed chuck. Similar to the chuck of an electric drill, but considerably larger. Note the Morse tapered shank which enables the chuck to be used inside headstock or tailstock.

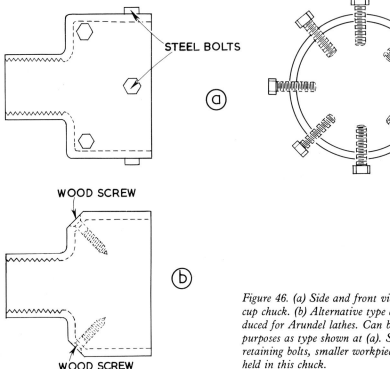

STEEL BOLTS

(a)

WOOD SCREW

(b)

WOOD SCREW

Figure 46. (a) Side and front view of a functional cup chuck. (b) Alternative type of cup chuck as produced for Arundel lathes. Can be used for similar purposes as type shown at (a). Since there are no retaining bolts, smaller workpieces can safely be held in this chuck.

that they cannot cause injury to the hands. In other words, the diameter of the workpiece must be greater than that of the chuck, including the projection of the bolts.

The square block of wood to be used is first turned to a cylinder between centres, with a pin cut on its end which will fit closely inside the chuck. The pin should be of sufficient length to reach almost to the bottom of the hole, and it can be cut quite easily with a sharp parting tool, using a pair of calipers as described in chapter 4.

The first cut is made at the end of the wood, after which a series of further cuts is made until the pin length has been achieved. Note that the pin should be a good fit in the chuck; any attempt to hold and turn workpieces

whose pin is appreciably smaller than the internal diameter of the chuck may well lead to an accident. The bolts on a chuck of this kind must be tightened firmly with a spanner.

The pattern shown at (b) is not as positive in its grip on the wood as the other, but it should be used for jobs where the wood is an exact fit in the chuck or has a maximum diameter equal to the internal diameter of the chuck. The pin, or the section of the wood which fits into the chuck, is waste. It is cut off the workpiece after turning is complete by means of a parting tool, or with a saw after the wood has been taken from the lathe.

In connection with the parting off of work in cases like this, where the waste has to be cut away, an extremely dangerous practice is sometimes advocated – namely the use of a handsaw while the lathe is running. This should *never* be attempted, for two very good reasons. Firstly, should the saw jam in the cut, it could be thrown back at the operator with considerable force with results which do not bear contemplation. Secondly, even if the practice were safe, which it assuredly is not, it would be worthless because of its sheer inefficiency. A moment's thought will show this to

be the case. A handsaw is made to be used in a manner which allows its teeth to follow one another through the wood, the waste particles dropping from the gullets as they emerge. This cannot happen if the saw is held against rotating timber, and frictional heat will destroy the temper of the steel.

I am often asked to state exactly what length of wood can be turned with a specific type of chuck, bearing in mind that one end has no

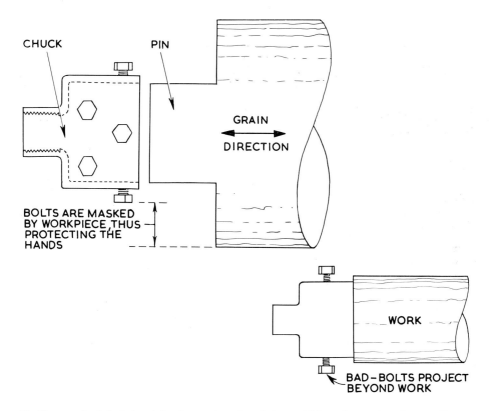

Figure 47. The cup chuck is designed for the turning of workpieces which are larger than the overall diameter of the chuck, including the projection of the retaining bolts, and should not be used for workpieces smaller than this. The grain of a piece of wood turned in a cup chuck should always run in the same direction as the lathe bed, rather than across it, and the pin which is on the end of the workpiece should reach almost to the bottom. It will be seen from the lower drawing that, if the workpiece is smaller than it should be, the worker is in danger of injury to his hands by contact with the moving bolts.

support. The answer in every case is that the length will depend upon the excellence or otherwise of the attachment - the care which has been taken - and the skill of the turner. Even a solid workpiece, correctly fitted to a chuck, will 'whip' when the extreme end is being cut if it projects far enough, and considerable skill is needed to cope with such situations.

Ingenious woodturners may devise ways of supporting the end of the workpiece by means of home-made devices, but at the present time there are no such supports on the market.

THE ENGINEER'S CHUCK

The best advice which can be given to woodturners concerning the engineer's chuck is that it should not be used on a woodturning lathe. It is intended, as its name suggests, for use by engineers on lathes which are designed for the turning of metal. Such chucks are massive and extremely heavy. The three or four jaws which project from them have sharp corners, and serious hand injuries are likely,

since the jaws are virtually invisible when the chuck is rotating at woodturning speeds.

This is bad enough, but there is yet more potential danger. Engineer's chucks are designed to grip metal, not wood. When they are tightened onto wood they compress it, and regardless of how much they are tightened, the wood will still give way. If a heavy workpiece is held in such a chuck by means of a pin on its end, it may well be secure when the lathe is started but is quite likely to fly from the machine during the turning.

JACOBS PATTERN THREE-JAWED CHUCK

This chuck is in common use by woodturners everywhere, and it is a valuable asset. Its main uses are in drilling small holes, boring large ones and holding odd items such as drum sanders. In essence it is a larger and heavier version of the chucks which are fitted to electric drills, having jaws which are opened and closed by means of a toothed key.

It is supplied complete with a shank tapered

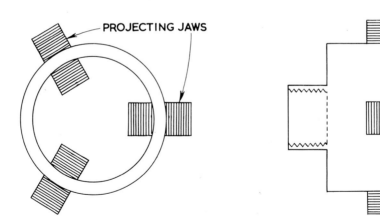

PROJECTING JAWS

Figure 48. The danger involved in using an engineer's chuck on a woodturning lathe. The jaws have considerable projection beyond the chuck itself and are almost invisible at high speeds.

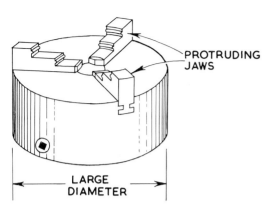

PROTRUDING JAWS

LARGE DIAMETER

Figure 49. Engineer's chuck designed for metal-turning, and not to be used on woodturning lathes. It is very heavy and can be dangerous.

to number one, two or three Morse to suit the lathe for which it is purchased. One end of the shank is also tapered to fit into the chuck body, though in practice this tends to become so firmly jammed as to be almost impossible to move. The capacity of such chucks is normally $\frac{1}{2}$ inch or sometimes $\frac{3}{4}$ inch. Half-inch chucks are quite adequate for the woodturner's purposes.

The normal function of a Jacobs pattern chuck in woodturning is the holding of drill bits and boring cutters, and the pressure applied during the boring sets the tapered shank firmly in its hole in the headstock or tailstock. Care is needed if these chucks are used for purposes where such pressure is non-existent, however, since it is then possible for the tapered shank to work loose, causing both the chuck and the tool held in it to be thrown violently from the machine. The correct procedure when using drum sanders or similar objects in a Jacobs chuck is to 'set' the taper when fitting the chuck by giving the nose of the chuck a sharp tap with a piece of wood, then to remove the tailstock centre and bring the tailstock itself up, so that the end of the

poppet barrel is about $\frac{1}{16}$ inch from the sander.

Some very tiny jobs, such as the reproduction antique doll's house furniture which I have made over the years, can be turned from short lengths of dowel stock, and this can be held quite satisfactorily in a Jacobs chuck. This is a relatively expensive item of ancillary equipment, but is well worth the money since its quality is very high.

COLLET CHUCKS

These are not generally popular with experienced woodturners, but they do have their uses in holding small pieces of wood. The principle is similar to that used in the chuck of a router, the jaws being moved by screwing up or unscrewing part of the outer casing; they are not provided by lathe manufacturers, presumably because there is little demand.

'Three-in-one' Chuck

A chuck known as the 'three-in-one' is manufactured by the Myford Engineering Company for its lathes, and it is, in fact, an ingenious and quite useful device. It is a combination of backplate, flange chuck and woodscrew chuck; the functions of the first two can therefore be dealt with here.

The body of the chuck has a flat face in which several holes are bored. These holes pass right through and are countersunk at the back to accept woodscrews. Used without the screw plate or outer ring, the chuck is a backplate used as a small faceplate. It can be used in this way, but the larger woodscrew chuck is generally preferred because it is easier to mount work centrally when there is a centre screw.

When the chuck body and outer ring are

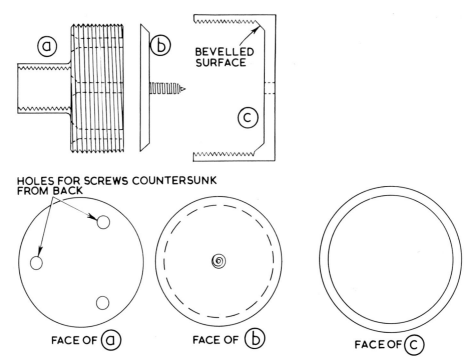

Figure 50. 'Three-in-one' chuck as supplied for Myford ML8 lathe. This chuck is in three parts and can be used as a backplate, a woodscrew chuck or a flange grip chuck to hold fairly long items securely.

used together without the screw plate, the assembly becomes what is often referred to as an 'egg cup chuck'. The inner side of the face of the outer ring is bevelled, and the chuck body has a fine thread around its outside onto which the outer ring fits. Wood to be used in this sort of chuck must first be placed in the lathe between centres and turned to a cylinder which will just pass through the hole in the outer ring, and a flange is left on one end to match the inner bevel of the chuck ring.

The workpiece is then passed through the ring so that its flange fits snugly, and the ring is screwed onto the chuck body. A special tool is provided to enable the ring to be pulled up really tight. Quite long workpieces can be handled in this way without much trouble, and the chuck is excellent up to a point. The main snag is that the maximum size workpiece which can be turned is governed by the diameter of the hole in the ring. Naturally, there is a waste portion left in the chuck after the turning is complete which can be removed when the job has been parted off.

When all three parts of the chuck are used, the bevelled edge of the screw plate fits the bevel of the outer ring, and the assembly becomes a woodscrew chuck. Unfortunately, it has only the centre screw and it is not possible to fit others, a fact which rather diminishes its usefulness.

THE COIL-GRIP CHUCK

This type of chuck has come into use in recent years, and it has gained some popularity in spite of being very expensive. It is in some ways similar to the three-in-one chuck, from which it presumably derived, but it has overcome the limitation that the maximum diameter of the workpiece is that which will pass through the outer ring. At first sight this chuck looks like a large version of the normal 'three-in-one' chuck, and certainly it is a good deal bigger. The system of chuck body, screw plate and outer ring is the same, but the difference lies in a coil spring which fits inside the outer ring.

The work is turned to a cylinder with a pin to fit the chuck, and a groove is cut in the pin with a sharp parting tool. The exact measurements for this are given in the instructions, which are supplied with the chuck. The idea is that when the ring is tightened, the spring is forced into the groove, which locks the workpiece in the chuck. This system works quite well.

Note that, with chucks of this type, the wood being turned needs to have the grain running lengthwise, not across as would be the case if a bowl was held by a pin cut on its base. In such a situation there would be little strength in the pin, which could easily break, especially if a gouge should dig into the wood.

WOODEN CHUCKS

One or two forms of chuck which can be made easily in the home workshop are worth mentioning and can be very useful. They have been known for a great many years, probably for longer than is generally realized.

One of these is the cotter chuck, which works in very much the same way as the securing of the crank of a bicycle. A cylinder of wood is turned up on a woodscrew chuck and hollowed out, either with a parting tool or by boring with a saw tooth pattern bit held in the tailstock. This is then drilled through at right angles, as shown in the drawing, to take a tapered wooden pin.

The workpiece is turned between centres with a pin left on one end to fit the wooden

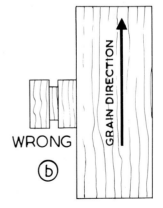

Figure 51. (a) Work to be mounted in a coil grip-type chuck must have grain running lengthwise as shown. If such a chuck is used to support material which has the grain at right angles to the lathe bed (b), there is a danger of the main portion of the workpiece splitting away from the projecting pin.

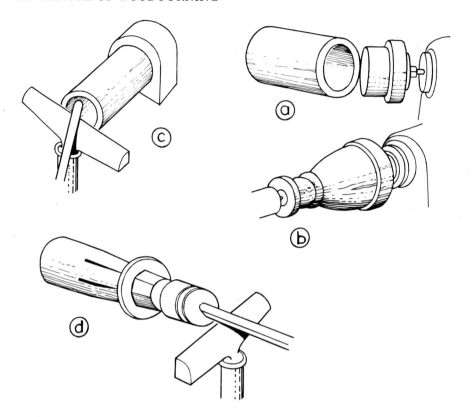

Figure 52. Various home-made wooden chucks. Small wooden chucks, such as shown at (a) can be used to secure a variety of workpieces, which are driven over or on to the chuck. Tailstock support should be used where possible. The chuck shown at (d) is made by the turner from scrap timber to a tapered form, drilled out to about two-thirds of its depth, its length slotted by means of a saw, and will hold small objects very firmly. A wooden or metal ring is tapped up the taper to close the jaws.

chuck, and a groove is cut across this pin with a round file or Surform tool. When the workpiece is fitted into the chuck the tapered hardwood pin is driven home, and the job is securely held. Only dense hardwoods such as beech or yew should be used, and these must be free from splits or cracks.

The wooden collet chuck is also easy to make and very effective for small jobs. Here again a cylinder of wood is turned up on a screw chuck and hollowed out.

A series of holes is drilled around the chuck, as shown in the sketch, and saw cuts are made, with a handsaw, from the edge into each hole. The forward part of this chuck, as the drawing shows, has a slow taper on the outside. The work is fitted into the chuck, and a metal or plywood ring is driven up the taper, closing the chuck onto the work quite tightly.

Some workers like to fit a metal ring round the base of this type of chuck to prevent it from splitting.

PLUG CHUCKS

Nothing could be simpler than a plug chuck. They are available in metal and are much like a cup chuck without the retaining bolts. The better types have a very coarse thread cut on the inside, so that if the wood to be turned is a good fit, it can be literally screwed into the chuck, cutting its thread as it goes.

Wooden cup chucks are simply pieces of wood mounted on woodscrew chucks, with a hole bored in them. They are useful for holding small jobs for final polishing or sanding, for example, in the turning of napkin rings (see pages 201-3).

The opposite form of this, of course, is the bayonet chuck, which consists of a piece of wood on a woodscrew chuck with a pin turned on it, over which a hollow workpiece can be driven. The principle is useful for various jobs; these last two chucks are used in the making of circular picture frames or wooden rings.

In my own workshop I frequently use a chuck which was at one time manufactured by the Coronet Tool Co. Ltd., of Derby, for use on its lathes. It is shown in fig. 55, and it will hold wood very firmly indeed if care is taken in the fitting. In essence it is a small faceplate

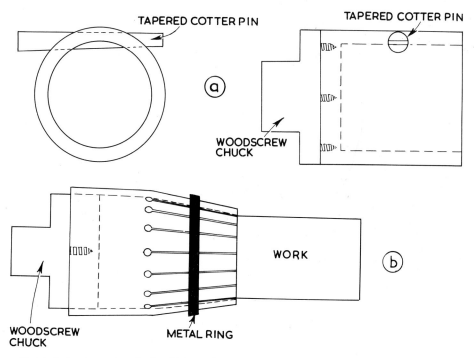

Figure 53. (a) A simple wooden chuck which can be turned on the lathe, for holding small items. Timber to be gripped in a chuck of this kind will have a flat cut on its end after it has been reduced to a cylinder, to engage with the cotter pin. (b) Tapered wooden chuck with saw cuts is tightened into workpiece by driving a metal or plywood ring up the taper.

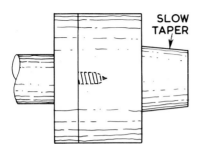

Figure 54. Small pieces of scrap wood, turned as shown here, will be found extremely useful for securing open-ended workpieces between centres. Short workpieces can be turned on a 'chuck' of this nature, if care is taken.

with a projecting nose, or pin, which has a coarse thread. A hole is bored in the end of the workpiece, which is then forced over the nose of the chuck with a twisting motion, so that it cuts its own internal thread. By the time this manual is published, I hope to have similar, but slightly modified chucks for sale – the chuck would be greatly improved by increas-ing the diameter of its flat plate and providing four holes, countersunk at the back, to permit the fitting of screws.

I am convinced that such a chuck would offer an extremely strong mounting for many operations, and I am currently having a proto-type made up for testing. Many jobs on the lathe have to be held by means of screws into the end grain of the wood, which is not, unfor-tunately, the best place for screws in terms of holding power. There is no doubt in my mind, however, that a workpiece held by four screws plus the strong grip of the threaded nose would be very firmly held indeed.

Those who do not have all the chucks des-cribed here should not lose heart. A very wide range of jobs can be tackled with the large and small woodscrew chucks alone. It must always be borne in mind, however, that work secured only at one end is not normally as safely held as it would be between centres, and that the security of such jobs decreases with the length of the workpiece.

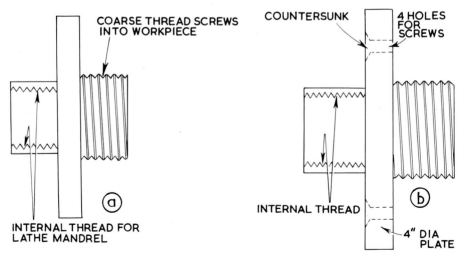

Figure 55. (a) A small backplate with coarse-threaded 'nose'. No longer obtainable, but used years ago to support heavy workpieces for deep-box turning.

The turning tools should be used on spindle turnings until practice has made almost perfect, and the correct presentation of bevel to material has become instinctive, before chuck work more than about 3 inches in length is attempted. A mistake on a spindle turning which results in a dig in, especially if the drive belt is kept slack, is not likely to have dangerous potential. Such an error made near the end of a long workpiece held only at the headstock end can quite easily cause the wood to be ripped from the screws and thrown violently from the lathe. The woodturning lathe, used with common sense and correct methods and after proper initial instruction, is perhaps the safest of all woodworking machines, but it does not suffer fools gladly!

Some of the more popular jobs which are turned on a chuck are egg cups, vases, goblets and tankards. There are others, of course, but the methods used in making these four can quite easily be adapted to cope with most situations. As is the case with most woodturning projects, fewer difficulties will be encountered if a logical sequence is followed.

EGG CUPS

These are firm favourites with many turners. They require little material, can be made in a very short time, and are readily accepted by novelty and gift shops. From a beginner's viewpoint they also represent an extremely useful exercise in basic cuts and a simple stepping-off point on the road to well-turned goblets and vases.

The design shown here provides for holes through the stems of the cups so that they can be mounted on a simple stand. The base of the stand is made from a disc of wood, and those who may be unfamiliar with the turning of discs should refer to the instructions given in pages 125-44 of the manual. It is not really necessary to turn the dowel over which the egg cups are fitted, though this would certainly provide a fair test of skill. An ordinary piece of machine-made dowel will serve quite well.

In this instance the egg cups themselves are the real object, inasmuch as they represent a simple form of woodscrew chuck work. Most turners would use the smaller of the two woodscrew chucks for this job, since although the hold on the material is not as secure as that offered by a flange chuck or 'egg cup chuck', there is less preparatory work, and from a production viewpoint the screw chuck enables far

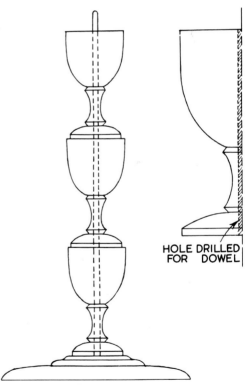

HOLE DRILLED FOR DOWEL

Figure 56. Sets of egg cups can be made in the manner indicated here. They slip over one or two dowels protruding from a suitable base.

more items to be produced in a given time.

The blocks from which the cups are to be made should first be cut to length either by hand or with a circular saw, and it is helpful to have the stock truly square. A block $2\frac{3}{4}$ inches by $1\frac{7}{8}$ inches will do very well, but this can be varied to suit individual taste. It is as well to ensure when cutting the blocks to length that the sawblade is at exactly 90 degrees to the stock.

Two commonly used centring methods are shown in figure 57. The first, and more exact, requires the accurate drawing in of the diagonals, with a bradawl mark made at their point of intersection. The second, though less accurate, is adequate for many jobs. A pencil is used to draw four lines near the middle of the wood, parallel to the sides; the distance from the edge is controlled by allowing the finger-tips to run on the outside of the wood as a guide. This is easy enough to do, and the centre point of the wood can be taken to be the central point of the small square.

When fitting work to a woodscrew chuck, it is helpful to predrill a hole $\frac{1}{16}$ inch to $\frac{1}{8}$ inch in diameter, which will serve to guide the screw and assist its penetration. If no hole is bored the wood will tend to swell around the screw, giving rise to a situation where the strongest contact with the face of the chuck is at the centre, there being little or no support around the edge. This permits the workpiece, when under pressure from the tool, to rock slightly on its mounting.

Small blocks of this type, or indeed any other workpiece, must NEVER be fitted to the chuck by placing them against the point of the screw and pressing the 'start' button of the machine. A sensible person may feel that no one would do this – and I wish this was the case – but I have seen it many times. It may look clever, but it is extremely dangerous and incredibly stupid. Serious hand injuries are possible. The block for the egg cup should be mounted by hand with the lathe switched off; it should be screwed on steadily and kept square to the face of the chuck.

Just how tightly should it be screwed on? This is a common query, and the true answer can only be found by experience, but the block should be screwed up tightly. Over-tightening may strip the thread inside the wood and so defeat the whole object.

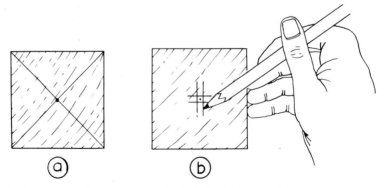

Figure 57. Marking squares prior to mounting in the lathe. (a) Diagonals drawn across: centre point is at intersection. (b) Mark a small square in the centre of the large square with a firmly held pencil, guiding its point with pressure from the finger tips. The centre of the small square can be determined by eye.

Plate 5. A pair of egg cups. This is the point at which the beginner should approach the problems of copy turning.

It is quite common for those with limited woodturning skill to advocate the use of the tailstock for support during the reduction of the square block to a cylinder, and even in later stages of the work. Beginners would be better advised to perfect their tool handling so that this kind of crutch becomes unnecessary. Egg cups and similar objects should not need tailstock support at any stage if the turner is competent. Sharp edges and correct bevel presentation will ensure success. The shape shown in the illustrations can be varied; it has been used here to bring in a reasonable number of basic cuts.

As usual, the first operation is the removal of the corners of the blank, reducing it to a cylinder. The roughing gouge is used, with its handle kept as low as possible, and the cuts are made from right to left along the full length of the wood. Cutting in this direction tends to push the work onto the chuck rather than pull it off, and there is no need to do the job in sections as would be done with a spindle turning, because it is very short and not of large effective diameter.

It may seem strange to use the word diameter in relation to a square piece of wood, but to a turner the effective diameter of a square is the length of its diagonals – which is,

of course, the same as the diameter of the circle through which the corners of a square turn when it rotates on accurate centres. It is the diameter of this cutting circle which has to be considered when deciding upon the correct angle of presentation for a gouge.

There should be no difficulty in removing the corners of the square with a sharp roughing gouge, but the job should be stopped while there are still some flat areas left on it. At this stage a sharp parting tool is taken across the face of the block, with only the corner of the tool cutting, making sure that a little more wood is removed from the centre than at the outer edge, so that the face of the block is left with a very slightly concave surface.

When this has been done, the end grain is trimmed by cutting across it with the long corner of a sharp skew chisel in the manner described earlier (see page 67). This should leave the surface very smooth and with the appearance of having been polished. The cut is more effective with some timbers than with others, as will soon become apparent, but any close-grained hardwood can be used for egg cups.

The exact centre of the block must now be located by supporting a skew chisel on the toolrest, which is set across the face of the work, and pushing the long corner into the wood. The chisel is placed flat on the rest, and the point makes a conical depression. A bradawl is now pushed into this depression as the wood rotates, to a depth of about 1 inch. I prefer this type, which has a square-sectioned blade, to the round variety. The square type is the old birdcage maker's awl, designed for the cutting of holes through thin wood close to the edge to take the fine round bamboo, but it is now more generally known as an auger awl.

When the hole has been made the lathe is stopped, and the workpiece is reversed on the chuck. The slightly concave shape of the surface which is now against the chuck ensures that there is contact between chuck and work all round the outer edge of the chuck, and that the finished egg cup will stand on a flat surface without wobbling.

The roughing down is now completed, leaving the wood $\frac{1}{16}$ inch greater in diameter than the maximum required in the finished job to allow for the final sanding. The wood is now marked out to indicate the area taken by the foot, the stem and the cup. This will normally leave a section of waste at the right-hand end, which can now be removed by means of a parting-tool cut.

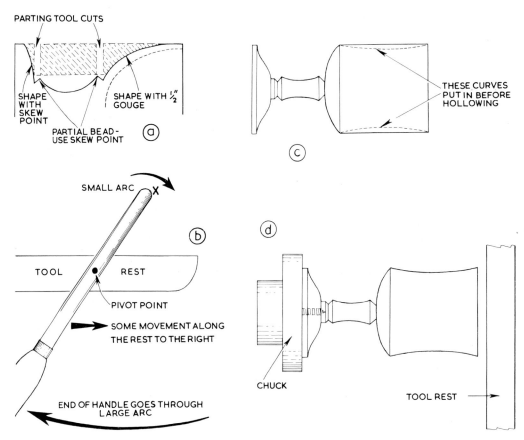

Figure 58. Stages in the shaping of an egg cup. (a) Hollowing is completed before the outside is shaped. (b) Note that in the production of a cove, such as that occurring at (a), the cutting edge must move through a small arc. Since the tool is pivoting on the toolrest a short distance from its cutting edge, the handle must obviously move through a far larger arc. Failure to swing the handle sufficiently will preclude the possibility of a satisfactory result. (c) The internal shape must be completed before any work is undertaken on the stem section. (d) The toolrest must be kept as close as possible to the end of the workpiece.

No shaping should be done before the cup is hollowed or the wood will be weakened, and it will be difficult or even impossible to hollow (depending, of course, on how much it has been weakened). One or two books on wood-turning contain the rather amusing suggestion that egg cups should be made between centres on a 'stick' of four or five at a time, on the grounds that in this way it is easier to compare the shapes. The writers have carefully avoided the questions of how items made in this way can be centred exactly on the lathe after they have been separated, and how they can be hollowed with the stems already shaped. In fact, it would be difficult, if not impossible, to complete either operation successfully. The only shaping which may with advantage be done before hollowing is as shown in figure 58(c), where a very slight concave curve is required.

The procedure for hollowing an object of this nature is quite straightforward, but a little practice on scraps of hardwood is advisable before the project itself is attempted. In order to achieve exactly the desired depth it can be helpful to drill a small hole into the exact centre of the end grain, to a depth about $\frac{1}{16}$ inch less than is required for the finished article. This hole acts as a guide during the turning, and sufficient wood will be left to allow for final finishing cuts and sanding.

The bulk of the waste is removed by means of a small spindle gouge, but due to the depth of the hollow in relation to its width, a point will be reached beyond which the gouge cannot safely be used, and a scraper must be employed to finish the operation.

The procedure for hollowing out small objects of this kind, where the tools are working directly into end grain, is set out here in detail, and the technique can be used for a wide range of articles.

The toolrest must be set square across the face of the wood at a height which permits the gouge to work at or about the centre line. This means that the rest will be slightly below centre; the exact position will be obvious after a few hours of practice, but a beginner may need a trial-and-error approach at first. The small gouge should not have a pronounced 'nose' or point but a fingernail shape, and for the procedure in question its bevel should not be too long. The gouge is not used on its side nor on its back, but in a position midway between the two. The first cut is made from a point about $\frac{1}{8}$ inch in from the edge, through to the centre, and the handle must be swung steadily throughout the cut to permit the bevel to rub, so preventing a dig in. Since the gouge is supported by the toolrest midway between the centre and the corner, the part of the cutting edge in use is that section which lies between centre and corner. The centre of the gouge is *not* used. Note also that the cutting edge must not be permitted to pass the centre of the job, or it may be lifted from the toolrest and slammed back with considerable force, possibly injuring the operator's fingers.

The key to success in this technique is a smooth and continuous swing of the handle throughout the cut; the distance covered by the handle will be considerable. If this swing is not smoothly executed through a sufficiently wide arc, the bevel will leave the surface of the wood, and the tool will dig in. This must not be allowed to occur, since it is certain to destroy the grip of the chuck screw in the end grain to some extent.

There are a number of situations in wood-turning where this very pronounced handle swing is required, and the process must be mastered. In considering the shape which is being produced inside the work relative to the 'pivot point' of the gouge on the toolrest, some practice movements with the lathe switched off will show that the handle of the tool must be swung through a very wide arc in order to produce a small arc with the cutting edge. Many turners have trouble in hollowing end grain with a gouge, because they make some handle movement during the first part of the cut and then stop the handle swing and push the tool along the rest towards the centre.

The long corner of a skew chisel is employed to form the small curves which connect the stem to foot and to cup. The technique is exactly the same as for cutting a bead, rolling the chisel round so that only its extreme point is used.

In many turning projects it will be found that the more awkward operations come when the job is almost complete, and highly skilled turners come very close to the point where a skid of the tool could ruin the job completely, rather as a skilled sailor comes very close to the wind. Practice, however, eventually gives a beginner the necessary confidence to tackle the awkward jobs.

The exercise piece described here, like all woodturning projects, should be examined very carefully at this stage for any faults, however small. If any are found they must be corrected with sharp gouge or chisel before any sanding is done.

The starting point for this hollowing cut must also be considered. In bowl turning, the hollowing of most projects begins at the centre of the wood, working back towards the outer edge with each successive cut. This works well with a square-ended gouge working on the face grain, but when a gouge with a curved edge is used on end grain there is difficulty in starting each cut, since the gouge can easily be thrown sideways. If the first cut is made near the outer edge, however, there will be firm support for the bevel in each cut thereafter.

Scrapers should be used only when it becomes difficult or dangerous to continue with a gouge or chisel, the finish produced by a scraper being relatively rough. In this sort of job a point will be reached where the handle

swing can no longer be made completely, because the back of the tool strikes the rim of the job. No attempt should be made to continue with the gouge beyond this point, or a dig-in is almost certain to occur.

The hollowing is completed with a round-nosed scraper held flat on the toolrest. The best edge for the type of job under discussion will be produced by grinding the bevel once only on the carborundum wheel, with sparks showing along the edge. This produces a 'burr' or 'wire edge' which works very well. The tool should remove shavings from the wood, not dust.

If undue pressure is used with a scraper the wood will be badly torn; in this case, the single screw mounting must also be considered, and any rough work with the scraper is likely to weaken it so that the workpiece begins to run out of true.

When using a scraper in a hollow, cuts can be made either from the centre to the edge or vice versa. When resharpening the scraper, the old burr is removed on the flat side of the grinding wheel before the new one is produced by re-grinding on the curved face of the stone.

When the hollowing has been completed, some turners put a small shaped piece of softwood in the hole and bring the tailstock up to support the job while the shaping is done. This is not necessary, however, and it is as well not to use too many 'crutches' of this kind when learning – they can be difficult to discard later.

The shaping of the rest of the job is done with the $\frac{1}{2}$-inch spindle gouge and the long corner of a skew chisel. Two parting-tool cuts are made first, as in figure 58(a), and the waste wood between them is removed. This can be done either by a number of similar parting-tool cuts or by raising the toolrest almost level with the top of the work and taking the waste out in one movement, with a square-ended chisel used flat on the toolrest and operated in the same way as a parting tool. Its edge goes forward and down in an arc towards the centre of the wood, and the handle is raised.

When this waste has been removed, the cup section of the job is shaped, using a $\frac{1}{2}$-inch spindle gouge as described earlier, with a paring action. The surface so produced will, if the edge is really sharp, require no sanding.

The foot is shaped either with the same gouge or with the long corner of a skew chisel, using a slicing action. I prefer the chisel point for this, and the cut is a variation of the end-grain trimming cut. Only the extreme point of the chisel touches the wood throughout the cut, and the rest of the edge is unsupported and is therefore leant slightly away from the wood. If this is not done the chisel will dig in violently, probably breaking the foot of the job and ruining the whole project. If the handle is swung smoothly during this cut, a curve will be produced.

Plate 6. A set of four egg cups turned in yew. If sufficient care is taken in the turning, sets like this can look very attractive.

There should now be a nicely shaped cup and foot, separated by a rough area which is turned into a cove with a partial bead at each end. The cove shape is made first, working exactly as described on page 77, and care must be taken to keep the bevel rubbing with some pressure or a very ridged surface will result.

6 Further Chuck Work

The small woodscrew chuck with its single screw is used in many operations, such as the making of wooden buttons for coats or cardigans and the production of finials and small knobs for use on furniture. The three items mentioned will serve as examples, and the turner will see that with slight variations of method the small chuck can be used for numerous purposes.

Wooden coat buttons, often made in yew or walnut, are popular and easy to make. A small square sectioned length of suitable timber is mounted on the chuck and reduced to a cylinder with a diameter to suit the buttons. The shaping is done on the end of the workpiece, using cutting tools where possible and sharp scrapers where necessary. For work of this kind the turner may need to make specially shaped scrapers from old chisels or suitable pieces of steel. The rim of the button can be treated as a small bead and cut with the chisel

point, and the central flat area can be trimmed smooth with a very sharp square-ended scraper.

When the button is complete and has been sanded, it can be parted off from the stock with a sharp parting tool, taking the cut right to the centre and catching the button in the left hand as it falls clear. A narrow parting tool can be used to avoid waste. Final cleaning up of the back of the button is done by hand or on a belt sander. Backgammon or draught pieces can be made in the same way. Drilling of the thread holes for the buttons can be done with an electric drill mounted in a stand.

Finials are a common requirement for various forms of furniture, particularly for wall clocks. Usually the turner is required to copy a specimen or to work from a drawing. Unfortunately, the problems of the turner rarely seem to be considered by designers, and finials can call for small details requiring pre-

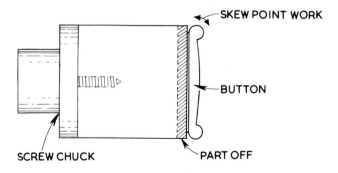

Figure 59. Wooden coat buttons can be produced quickly and easily on a lathe. With a little practice, identical buttons will result.

cise and delicate cuts. The shapes will often force the use of scrapers, and of scrapers which have to be made for the purpose by the woodturner, but these must be razor sharp. As much work as possible should be done with gouges and chisels.

Care must be exercised in using the scrapers or small pieces may be knocked out on the fine edges. The sanding of such items also needs care or the crispness of the design may well be lost.

Chessmen are a similar proposition. All items of this nature are best made individually on the small woodscrew chuck and parted off from the waste section when completed. They can be done in units of four or five in a 'stick' between centres, but there are problems with this method which are likely to cause frustration for beginners.

As the items are shaped the wood becomes unstable and progressively more difficult to control, as its diameter decreases. A chain is only as strong as its weakest link; one must therefore remember that a job of this kind is as strong as its narrowest section. The turning has to be supported with one hand while the other operates the cutting tool; the free hand applies pressure to the rear of the job to counteract the pressure of the tool. This sort of work should not be attempted until a fair level of competence has been reached.

Small woodscrew chucks invariably have only one screw to support the work, and workpieces turned on them are in general no more than 3 inches in length. The larger woodscrew chucks have more than one screw; in fact, the best examples have five including the central one. When a battery of large woodscrews is used like this, the support even into end grain is remarkably good, and the workpieces can be up to 8 or 9 inches in length. If longer workpieces are to be turned with support at the headstock end only, some form of flange chuck is required.

The larger of the two screw chucks is, therefore, suitable for the turning of many items which are outside the scope of the small one, such as vases, goblets, wooden drinking vessels, biscuit barrels, tobacco humidors, and so on. This type of work is apt to worry beginners, who are not too happy about fairly long and rather heavy workpieces which are not supported by the tailstock, but if the woodscrews used are in good condition the grip is excellent, and if the tools are sharp and correctly used there should be no more problems than when working between centres. The use of a large woodscrew chuck for small bowls is mentioned in the appropriate section of this manual, but typical uses are the making of a goblet and a tankard.

Goblets are very popular with most skilled turners. They can be very attractive if carefully turned and finished, and they are always

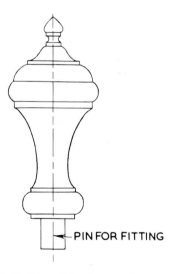

Figure 60. Finials and furniture knobs are a common requirement. They are normally turned on a woodscrew chuck, leaving sufficient waste to permit the parting-off of the workpiece when completed.

a good line for those who are interested in selling their work. Sets of goblets on trays call for some copy turning ability, and good examples command high prices. At one time I made a large number in yew, in the shape of a brandy glass, and they sold very well indeed.

The making of this wooden 'brandy glass' goblet is worth looking into, and those who succeed in making really good specimens will be delighted with the results. Yew is a very good wood for this kind of work if it can be obtained in a suitable thickness and without the many tiny cracks which are so common in this timber. A good goblet of this kind takes a long time to produce by comparison with many other projects, and it is a pity to find at the end of it that the timber is split or cracked.

The exact size chosen for the goblets is a matter of personal choice for the individual, and a glass version can be used for reference as regards proportion.

The first step, of course, is to select the timber and mount it as securely as possible on the chuck prior to running it down to a cylinder with the roughing gouge. Note should be taken of the length of screw which projects from the chuck, with reference to the thickness of the foot of the project. It is easy to forget this point, and the rattling sound produced as the gouge finds the screws is not pleasant. The tool can quite easily be resharpened, but the job is spoiled. To avoid this, a waste piece is provided, and the goblet is parted off when complete just beyond the screw points as shown in the sketch.

Once the wood has been brought to a cylinder slightly larger than the required maximum diameter of the finished goblet, using a sharp roughing gouge with its handle held as low as possible, the hollowing can be done. As with the egg cup, it is important to complete the hollowing before cutting into the wood to form the stem.

The $\frac{1}{4}$-inch spindle gouge is used for the removal of most of the waste, working in the same manner as described for the egg cup, but here again the round-nosed scraper will have to take over after a while. The shape of the brandy glass goblet is such that the internal shape cannot be completed with a gouge (see fig. 61. Scrapers used for work of this kind must be extremely sharp, and they must be used lightly. Any attempt to hurry the hollowing by exerting extra pressure on the scraper will result in the surface of the wood being torn, and damage so caused may be very difficult or even impossible to repair with abrasives. The internal shape when finished will need to be checked thoroughly for ridges. It must be completely smooth, as scraper ridges are extremely difficult to remove with abrasive paper.

It is quite possible for a competent turner to complete a goblet like this without tailstock support, but those in the early stages of learning the craft will find it helpful to insert a tapered wooden plug in the opening and bring the tailstock up, to help steady the work while the external shaping is done. If this procedure is adopted the tailstock pressure must be kept very much in mind during the turning, or the job may be ruined at the last minute.

The tapered plug will have been turned on a woodscrew chuck, so the centre will already be located and the positioning of the tailstock centre will present no problems. At this stage there is a fair thickness of wood around the rim of the goblet, and normal tailstock pressure can be used. This *must* be reduced as the turning proceeds, however, or the wood will be split as its thickness decreases and the tapered plug is forced in. Goblets are turned quite thin around the edge, and in the final stages there should be virtually no pressure on the plug.

The procedure for shaping the outside of the goblet is along the lines laid down for the egg cup. No scraping should be done – the whole job should be carried out with a $\frac{1}{2}$-inch spindle gouge and a $\frac{3}{4}$-inch skew chisel. Paring cuts must be used, removing shavings throughout, not dust. Those with sufficient skill can roll a sharp skew chisel over the cup

section working downhill from the centre, of course, to take off a fine shaving. The cut is the well-known smoothing cut, but it is very difficult for an inexperienced person to perform over a sharply curved surface. The cut

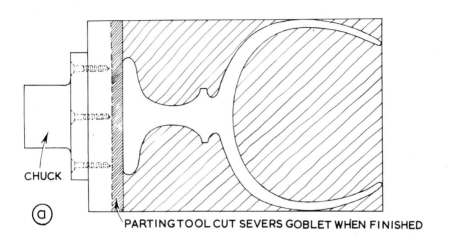

CHUCK

(a) PARTING TOOL CUT SEVERS GOBLET WHEN FINISHED

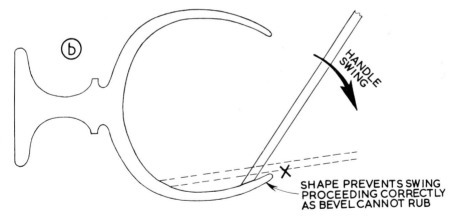

(b)

HANDLE SWING

X SHAPE PREVENTS SWING PROCEEDING CORRECTLY AS BEVEL CANNOT RUB

Figure 61. Production of goblets. (a) Blank is mounted on woodscrew chuck with sufficient waste at the chuck end to permit parting the job off, when complete, without striking the screws. The hollowing is done first and support may be given, while turning the outside, by fitting a tapered plug to the open end and bringing up the tailstock. (b) It will be seen that a gouge cannot be used to complete the hollowing of a shape like this, since if the tool is taken further than the position shown by the dotted lines, it will strike the rim of the goblet, and any further cutting must be attempted without bevel support.

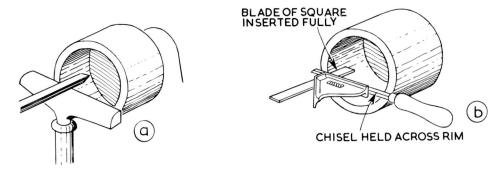

Figure 62. (a) Blanks can be hollowed by enlarging a pre-drilled hole with a heavy-duty square-ended scraper pushed straight into the work. (b) A woodworker's combination square can be used to check depth, making the necessary allowance for the thickness of the chisel.

produces a beautiful polished surface, if done properly, especially on a dense timber like yew.

When the goblets have been parted off, the bases are sanded smooth. Self-adhesive green baize can be stuck on if desired. A polyurethane finish is often used, but the best results will be achieved with a two-part catalyst resin such as Rustins plastic coating.

The making of vases is rather similar, but usually they do not have the stem section. Vases are in general cheaper than goblets. To make the hollowing easier most turners bore a hole with a large cutter almost to the depth intended for the vase. The processes of boring in a lathe are discussed on pages 187–92 in full, but in brief a saw-tooth pattern bit is used in a chuck in the tailstock and fed into the wood as it revolves at low speed. The hole so produced is opened out to the required size by means of a square scraper, finally being shaped with a round-nosed version of the same tool.

The opening out of a hole of this type can present some problems, because a scraper of normal thickness can flex or whip when projected as far over the edge of the toolrest as is

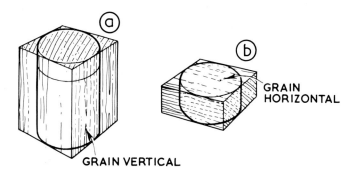

Figure 63. (a) Boxes can be made from 'sticks' with the grain running vertically in the finished job. (b) Small boxes can be made from 'discs'. The grain runs across the boxes.

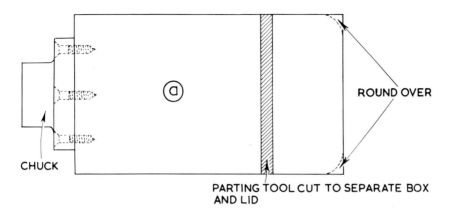

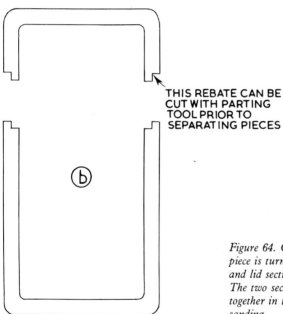

Figure 64. Construction of small boxes. (a) Work-piece is turned to a cylinder, outside of lid is shaped and lid section is separated from box section. (b) The two sections after turning. They can be fitted together in the final stages for cleaning and sanding.

necessary in a deep vase. This flexing is very hard to control, even for an experienced turner, and it has been known to cause accidents. For this reason I designed the deep hollowing tool, which is manufactured for me by Ashley Iles Ltd, and is now in use all round the world. It is in fact a replica of a tool which I made up for my own use many years ago to overcome the problems involved in hollowing out a deep tea caddy, the design of which called for a narrow opening with parallel sides. The tool is a very heavy scraper, ground to a shape suitable for the job.

Once the hollowing has been done, the tapered plug system can be used to provide tailstock support for the shaping of the out-side, and the turning presents no special problems. Finishing can be done with a resin, as with the goblet, and this does give a com-pletely waterproof job. Some turners, how-ever, still use the older paraffin wax method. The source of this is usually candles, of course. These are melted down, and the hot wax is poured into the vase. It penetrates the wood, making it quite waterproof, but must be poured out again before it sets, which it does very quickly.

Small boxes are turned on a screw chuck, sometimes on the smaller chuck but normally on the larger if they require the support of more than one screw. The square block from which the box is to be made is mounted firmly on the chuck and turned down to a cylinder slightly greater in diameter than the required outside measurement of the box, as usual, to allow for final cleaning up with a sharp skew.

When this has been done, the lid section is marked out on the wood, its top is rounded over, and a parting tool cut is made right through the work, separating the lid section from the piece which is to form the box. If both lid and box are to be rebated, as is norm-ally the case, a rebate can be made on the out-side of the lid section before the parting off is done.

Rounding over the top of the lid is not a difficult operation. Best results will be obtained by using a $\frac{1}{2}$-inch spindle gouge rolled partly onto its side so that the cutting edge has a slicing action.

When the lid and box sections have been separated, the block for the lid can be laid aside until the box itself is completed. It is helpful to open up boxes in the manner des-

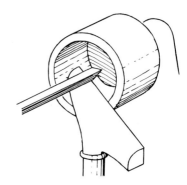

Figure 65. When levelling the bottom of a box with a square-ended scraper, the toolrest can be swung into the aperture. A careful check must be made to see that the toolrest clamp is tight.

cribed for the vase by boring a fair sized hole first with a saw tooth pattern bit, but if no facilities are available for this, the boring can be done by pushing in with a square-ended scraper.

As the drawing shows, there must be a re-bate on the inner edge of the rim of the box, so care must be taken in the hollowing to allow for this. Making this rebate an accurate fit with the one on the lid is a matter of trial and error. The lathe is stopped while the fit is tried, and light cuts are taken between trials. A fairly tight fit should be the aim, which will be relieved by sanding at a later stage.

When the inside of the box is smooth and correctly shaped, and the rebate satisfactorily finished off, the inside is sanded. Having been scraped it will require thorough treatment with several grades of abrasive paper, but there is always an element of danger in put-ting fingers into small holes like this while the lathe is running. To avoid possible injury it is best to wrap abrasive paper round an odd cylinder of scrap wood and use the result as a sanding stick, keeping the fingers well clear. Sanding sealer should be used, applying two or three coats and allowing each one to dry before it is sanded.

When the internal finish is completely satisfactory, the box can be removed from the lathe and set aside while the lid is made. All woodturners discover quickly the value of having several chucks of the same size and several faceplates. If the turner has more than one large woodscrew chuck, he can leave the box on while another is used in making the lid. This is not merely a question of saving time. The fact is that due to the well-known perversity of inanimate objects, projects which are removed from a chuck or a faceplate can rarely be exactly centred when they are replaced, no matter how much care is taken.

Beginners are often worried by jobs which have to be held without the aid of screws. There are many occasions where screws cannot be used because of the holes which would be left in the finished job, but there is always a way round such situations. The answer is generally some form of home-made wooden chuck, and these can give more than adequate grip if care is taken in their construction. The types required in dealing with box lids are ex-tremely simple and well within the scope of a novice.

In order to hold the lid blank while the internal shaping is done, a piece of scrap wood can be mounted on a woodscrew chuck and hollowed with a sharp parting tool to accept the lid as a push fit. If the hole has been excavated correctly it should only be necessary to tap the blank into position with a mallet or a piece of wood. If the fit is too slack, the inside of the wooden chuck can be soaked with water, which will cause the grain to swell and so improve the fit. Alternatively, a sheet of brown paper can be used to give an adequate grip.

A point which sometimes escapes people who use methods of this kind for the first time is that the job has to be removed from a chuck of this nature when the turning and sanding have been done without damaging the surface. To facilitate this, such chucks should have a central hole bored right through before they are mounted on the screw chuck. When the job is done, chuck and workpiece can be removed together from the screw chuck. A

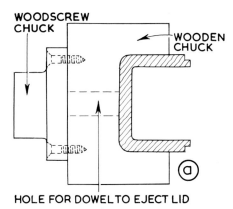

WOODSCREW CHUCK

WOODEN CHUCK

HOLE FOR DOWEL TO EJECT LID

(a)

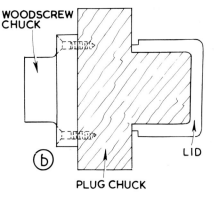

WOODSCREW CHUCK

LID

PLUG CHUCK

(b)

Figure 66. Lids for small boxes. Items such as small box lids present considerable problems for the beginner as regards safe handling of mountings for the turning of both outside and inside.

piece of dowel rod pushed into the wooden chuck from the rear and given a sharp tap should dislodge the workpiece quite easily.

The lid section, having been turned and sanded in this way, can be given any final external attention it may require by means of a plug chuck, as shown in the sketch. Hard or soft woods can be used for most forms of home-made chuck. For final finishing purposes, the chuck with the box attached to it is returned to the lathe, the lid is fitted to the box, and the tailstock is brought up with a small disc of scrap wood between its point and the work. Do not apply too much pressure.

With the lathe running the outside of the box and its lid can be sanded ensuring a perfect join. If the box has been made with a waste section at the base to take the screws, it can now be cut away from this waste section with a parting tool, but tailstock and lid must be removed first. If the waste section method has not been employed, the box is taken from the chuck, and the base is covered with self-adhesive green baize.

When the lid of a box is to have a knob, this can be turned from the solid wood as part of the lid. There will be no problem about fitting the lid into a wooden chuck for any reason if the ejection hole for the dowel is made large enough to accommodate the knob. An alternative method, often used, is to make the knob as a separate item with a small pin turned on the end to fit into the hole in the centre of the lid. A simpler approach still is to fit the lid

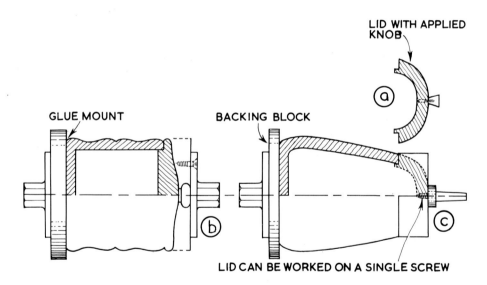

Figure 67. (a) If the box lid is to have a separate knob, it is applied after turning. The screw hole produced by the woodscrew chuck can be used in the fixing. (b) Lathes which will accept a small faceplate screwed on to the nose of the tailstock can be extremely useful. Here the completed lid is held in position on the box for final sanding by means of a shaped piece of wood screwed to the tailstock faceplate. (c) The type of small woodscrew chuck which has a Morse tapered shank can be used as shown here. The lid is turned in the normal manner, being then removed from the lathe complete with chuck and replaced at the tailstock end. The two sections can now be finished and sanded together.

section onto a woodscrew chuck using the centre screw only. The hollowing is then done with a parting tool, working carefully around the screw. The knob can then be fitted to the lid by means of a spot of glue and a brass screw passing through from the inside of the lid. A countersink tool should be used to let the screw head in flush with the surface.

PICTURE FRAMES AND RINGS

The finer points relating to the turning of discs are dealt with on pages 125–44, but the making of circular picture frames, particularly in the smaller sizes, is very much a chuck operation and so is best covered in this section. For the purpose of explaining the procedure, I will assume the use of a scraper for the actual shaping of the project.

Circular picture frames are used not only for pictures, but also for framing such items as dried flower and sea shell arrangements, Victorian pot lids, good-quality circular tiles, and so forth. Small circular frames of good quality are almost unobtainable, at least on the British market, so this is a good opportunity for the skilled turner.

The method may seem complicated, but it presents no real problem, and with practice the frames can be produced quite rapidly. It is possible to make several frames in diminishing sizes from one disc, and even then the small disc left at the centre need not be wasted. It can be used for a table lamp base or perhaps a small ashtray.

A disc of suitable diameter and thickness is first prepared by marking out a circle on a flat piece of hardwood. Then a small hole is drilled through this wood at the exact centre, which will have been marked by the leg of the dividers. The disc from which the frame is to be made can now be cut out with a coping saw, or better still on a bandsaw. This latter

machine, if of good quality, is likely to be one of the most important purchases a woodturner can make apart, of course, from his lathe.

When the disc has been cut out it is mounted on the larger of the woodscrew chucks, using the centre screw only. If the material for the frame is thin the screw point may protrude through it, but this is of no consequence. If the frame being made is fairly large, it may be necessary to use a faceplate rather than a woodscrew chuck, to provide more support. As I remarked earlier, I will assume the use of a scraper for this job, but a good turner will of course use a gouge. The use of gouges in the turning of discs is dealt with later on in this manual (see pages 127–8).

The toolrest is now set up ready for work on the outside of the disc, which, however carefully sawn, will not at this stage be a true circle. The scraper is held horizontally or pointing slightly downward, flat on the toolrest. A number of light cuts across the edge of the disc will soon bring it to a true circle, and the work is continued until the disc is of the precise diameter required.

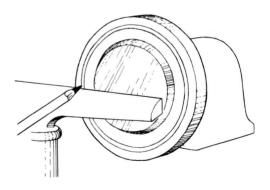

Figure 68. Circular picture frames. When the shaping of the front of the frame has been completed, the work is reversed on the machine and the position of the rebate must be marked accurately with a pencil.

If the cut surface is now examined carefully two areas of poor finish will be found in the quarter grain – the grain area which lies between the end grain and face grain. This problem is covered in the section dealing specifically with the turning of discs. In this case it will be rectified by repeated applications of shellac sanding sealer, which are allowed to set hard before sanding.

With the disc trued up to a circle of the required diameter, the overall width of the frame is marked by carefully measuring in from the edge. If a pencil is placed on the toolrest with its point against the wood at the mark, the lathe can be turned by hand to mark the inner edge of the frame.

The next step is to make a parting-tool cut just inside this marked line. The toolrest is set across the face of the disc, about $\frac{1}{4}$ inch from it and just below centre, and the parting tool,

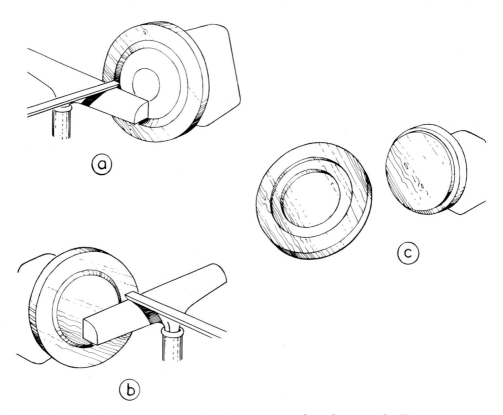

Figure 69. (a) Work of this nature can be shaped with square- or round-nosed scrapers, if sufficient competence has not been achieved with the deep-fluted gouges. (b) Areas which are intended to be flat can be trimmed with a square-ended scraper after a gouge has been used to remove the bulk of the waste, so removing any high spots. (c) If the rebating on the back of the picture frame is done first, the workpiece can then be forced over a suitable disc on the headstock which will support it while the face of the job is shaped.

pointing upwards a little, is pushed in to a depth of little more than half the thickness of the wood.

When this operation is completed the shaping of the frame itself can be attended to, in this case using a very sharp round-nosed scraper and working with light cuts. Although scrapers are notoriously inefficient as regards the production of smooth surfaces, they are necessary for some operations, and if care is taken with the sharpening the results will normally be acceptable. It must be noted, however, that work done with a scraper must necessarily take far longer than the same operation with a gouge, and any attempt to speed up the job by pushing the scraper hard against the wood will be fatal to the surface finish. The grain of the wood will be savagely disturbed, and any time saved by heavy scraper cuts will be lost completely in the subsequent attempts to rectify the tattered surface finish with sealer and abrasive paper. A very poor surface finish, as produced by heavy scraper cuts, will also tempt the turner into using coarse grades of abrasive paper, which will scratch the wood deeply. The removal of these scratches then becomes a problem in itself.

Once the frame has been shaped, it can be sanded thoroughly, having first been given a generous coat of shellac sanding sealer. It is important for the sealer to be allowed to dry completely before any attempt is made to use abrasive paper, or it will pull up into dirty rings on the wood. Most proprietary sealers take only a few minutes to harden off in a warm room.

The job is checked after this first treatment with sealer and abrasive, and if necessary a second coat of sealer is applied. Very little sealer is needed for the second coat, the wood having been sealed effectively by the first one. It is the initial application of sealer which must be generous, as the wood absorbs the liquid rapidly, particularly on the end grain.

Under normal circumstances I do not use abrasive paper on the second coat of sealer but rub this down with steel wool of grade 000. Coarser grades should not be used in woodturning, as they may scratch the work badly. The rotating wood is now rubbed with a soft cloth and the resulting surface examined. It should be ready for the application of wax, friction polish, polyurethane or any other finishing medium.

At this stage the workpiece is removed from the woodscrew chuck, and a piece of scrap material is mounted in its place. This will be used as a chuck to hold the job while the back is attended to, so it needs to be larger than the workpiece and about $1\frac{1}{2}$ inches thick. A piece of softwood will do, provided it is free from cracks.

When this is securely mounted, the toolrest can be positioned across the face of the wood and a little below centre. The object now is to take out a recess (using a parting tool) which will accept the workpiece as a firm drive fit. The depth of the recess should be roughly equal to half the thickness of the workpiece.

Operations of this nature are a frequent requirement in turning, and some degree of precision is called for, as it is very easy for an inexperienced turner to end up with a recess which is fractionally too large. It must never be forgotten that a cut of say, $\frac{1}{16}$ inch in width, will produce an overall increase in diameter of the recess of $\frac{1}{8}$ inch. It is therefore best to make a recess which is too small to accept the workpiece and then to extend it by minute amounts, stopping the lathe after each tiny cut to check progress.

A wooden chuck like this which does end up a little too large can be soaked with water inside the recess, which has the effect of swelling the grain and improving the fit. Alternatively, a sheet of brown paper can be placed across the chuck before the workpiece is tapped into position, and in most cases this will provide the necessary packing.

When the job is firmly held in the wooden chuck, work on the back of the frame can commence. Many beginners do not like the idea of separating parts of a job when there is a chance of one section flying from the machine, which is perfectly natural. With experience, accurate judgements of potential dangers can be made, but in the early stages certain precautions can be taken.

In this case, the centre part of the disc must be separated from the ring which forms the frame, and those who feel the procedure to be desirable can pass a screw through the centre of the job into the wooden chuck. When the two parts are separated the screw will hold the waste disc in place. I never bother to do this, having discovered years ago that the disc will merely drop onto the bench, but there is no harm in being over-cautious.

The overall width of the frame is now measured in from the edge and marked accurately in the same way as for the front. The rebate to hold the glass and picture with backing is now cut to the required width and depth, using a freshly sharpened parting tool. The

tool is held horizontally for this cut, which must, of course, be made on the *outside* of the marked line. It will probably be necessary to extend the initial cut by further light ones to achieve the desired width.

If the measuring and marking has been done accurately, a steady parting-tool cut on the inside of the line will meet the one made from the other side and neatly separate the two parts, at which stage the lathe can be stopped and the centre disc removed. This leaves the ring clear for sealing and sanding, care being taken to check thoroughly for any rough patches, which must be corrected.

Those who are interested in the production of picture frames will be able to obtain the necessary fittings from a local art shop. The most useful items are the tiny pear-shaped brass plates, drilled with a small hole, which are pinned to the frame so that they can be swung to project over the inner edge to retain the backing. Small brass plates, as shown in figure 70, are useful for frames which are to be hung on a wall. They should be let into the frame by taking out a recess with a sharp wood chisel which will allow the plate to fit flush with the surface of the frame.

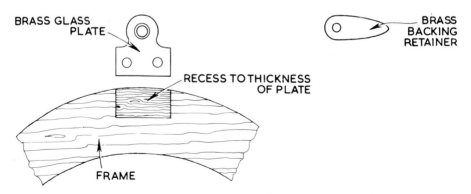

Figure 70. Circular picture frames can be fitted with brass 'glass plates', as used for hanging mirrors. Small brass backing retainers can be purchased to hold the hardboard backing in position. Alternatively, these can be made in the workshop.

The making of wooden rings calls for little explanation, since the procedure follows closely the making of a picture frame. The problem for an inexperienced turner will be the production of rings with a cross section which is truly circular. This can be achieved with practice, and there are no satisfactory short cuts. Rings are often needed for use in games or for curtain poles – this method of hanging curtains has come back into popularity in recent years.

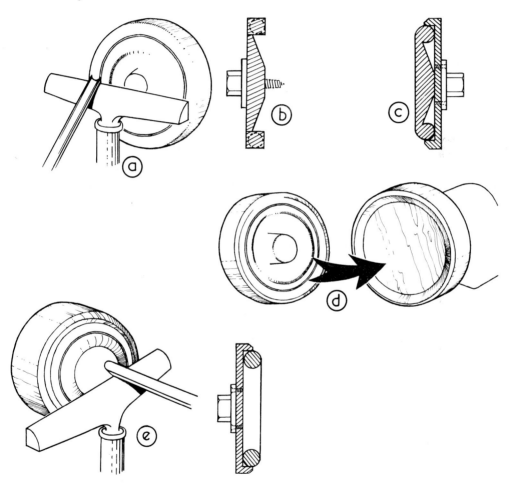

Figure 71. (a) Stage in the turning of a wooden ring. The work is mounted on a woodscrew chuck and the shape is begun with $\frac{3}{8}$-inch-deep fluted gouges. (b) Sectional view of work at stage shown in (a). (c) Sectional view of workpiece after partial shaping, reversed and tightly fitted into recessed wooden disc. (d) Workpiece with ring partly shaped is reversed in hollow block of headstock. (e) Final stages in production of ring. Sectional diagram shows centre cut away.

DEEP BOXES

The procedures outlined in this section are those required for making tankards, biscuit barrels, large vases and other deep and fairly large box-type structures, where the grain runs vertically in the finished job. This is a very important part of the craft and covers a wide range of projects.

There are two basic approaches to work of this kind, and both need to be practised until a high standard is achieved. In the first a solid block of wood is used, and a considerable amount of work is needed to hollow out the interior. In the second the blank itself is built up from rectangular staves, and the assembled blank, being already hollow, needs relatively little work to finish the interior.

Both approaches are useful for certain jobs, and both are fully dealt with here. Consideration is also given to the various ways of holding work of this kind securely in the lathe, which is very important, particularly in view of the fact that some of these jobs are large and quite heavy. As a fairly extreme example, I have made vases 30 inches tall with a maximum finished diameter of 12 inches. The weight of a job like this can be imagined, and the mounting of the blank needs to be very secure indeed.

For obvious reasons, a job as large as this should not be tackled by an inexperienced turner – but if a start is made on small projects, it is not difficult to work up gradually to big ones. It is the internal shaping that bothers the beginner, who can see that there is potential danger in this kind of work if it is not carried out with care and a good working knowledge of the procedures.

Chucks

In general, the turner is concerned mainly with jobs of the biscuit barrel or tankard type, which require fairly small blanks. Larger blanks and the specific problems relating to them are covered at the end of this section. Most of the many tankards, tobacco humidors and so forth which I have turned have been mounted on a 2- to 3-inch diameter woodscrew chuck using a total of five screws. This has always proved entirely satisfactory, even though the grip of a woodscrew in end grain is by no means as secure as when mounting a disc.

A flange chuck of the more sophisticated type can be used with a pin turned on the end of the blank to fit into the chuck, the split ring of which fits into a groove turned in the pin. A small faceplate can also be used. The faceplate, of course, needs to be smaller in diameter than the workpiece so that it cannot obstruct the free movement of the turning tools.

Centring a blank of this kind exactly to a

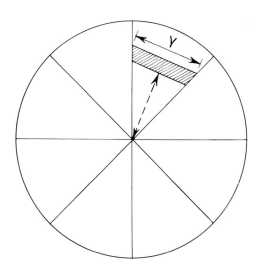

Figure 72. Built-up work. When constructing blanks for tankards, biscuit barrels, etc., a full-size drawing can be made, as shown here, to give the dimensions of the staves.

faceplate can be a problem which is usually overcome by turning a small pin on the end of the blank which will fit exactly into the centre hole of the faceplate. Faceplates for some lathes have specially designed centring devices built into them, however, making this procedure quite unnecessary.

Old or worn screws should not be used for faceplate or chuck mountings. Only screws which are in first-class condition can be considered safe. It is also advisable to ensure that the ends of blanks to be used for work of this kind are quite smooth, and that they are cut at exactly 90 degrees to the sides.

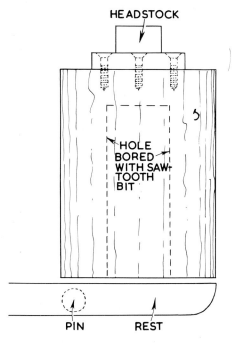

Figure 73. Deep-box construction. The blank is opened up with a large saw-tooth bit which rotates at low speed and is held in a chuck at the tailstock. With the toolrest positioned as shown, the aperture can be enlarged with a scraper or deep-hollowing tool.

The length of the screws will need to be considered in relation to the length and weight of the blank, bearing in mind the tool pressures which will be used at the further end of the workpiece where the leverage on the screws is greatest. The holding screws should project through the chuck as far as the workpiece will permit.

Solid Blanks

These should be mounted as firmly as possible on the chuck, all screws being pulled up very tight. It must be borne in mind that a solid blank is heavier for its size than a built-up one. For those who tackle this work for the first time there is an element of apprehension, and the approach can in fact be *too* cautious. The danger in deep hollowing is that a dig in with a tool which is projecting some distance over the toolrest is obviously more difficult to cope with due to the leverage factor, and the real answer, of course, is to prevent such an occurrence by correct tool manipulation rather than trying to control it when it happens. For this reason the hollowing techniques are best practised on shallow vessels, working gradually up to deeper ones. Since scraping methods are used throughout the hollowing however, the process is really quite safe and by no means difficult to master.

When the blank is safely mounted on the chuck, a large saw-tooth pattern bit is fitted in a chuck in the tailstock and fed slowly into the revolving wood by means of the tailstock handwheel. A 1½-inch diameter bit will be about right, and chapter 7 of this manual, which deals with drilling and boring, should be studied.

The hole is bored to a depth just short of the required depth of the project, and the tailstock is removed, clear of the work. On most lathes the complete removal of the tailstock from the lathe is a quick and simple job and is a help to the turner. If the tailstock cannot easily be

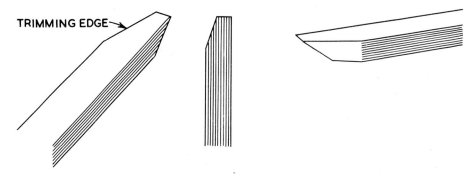

TRIMMING EDGE

Figure 74. The 'Stokes' deep-hollowing tool, designed for working into deep-end-grain structures, such as biscuit barrels and tea caddies. This is, in effect, a very strong, heavy-sectioned scraper which cuts with its right-angled end, the side being ground back to clear the wood.

removed, the chuck and bit should be removed from it, which will prevent injury if the worker's arm is brought back sharply for any reason.

The hole produced by the saw-tooth bit has now to be widened, and it was for precisely this work that I designed the deep-hollowing tool, which is now in use in many countries. This specially shaped scraper makes light work of what would be a heavy job for ordinary tools and reduces the risks involved. In the absence of a tool of this kind, a heavy duty square-ended scraper can be employed. It must, of course, be sharp and should be flat on the toolrest at all times while cutting, not lifted off at either side. All scrapers must be pointed slightly downward or be horizontal. If they are pointed upward, serious accidents are probable.

During the initial stage of opening out the inside of the blank the toolrest will be across the face of the workpiece, a little below centre and as close to the wood as possible. The usual mistake made by novices is in attempting to remove too much wood in one cut – in other words, using too much of the scraper edge. This can cause the tool to 'snatch', in an incipient dig into the wood, the result of which is often a loosening of the work on its mounting. Only about $\frac{1}{8}$ to $\frac{1}{4}$ inch of the scraper edge should be used, pushing the tool steadily forward into the job, with a reasonably firm grip on the handle. It may help in the case of a beginner if the lathe speed is dropped to about 1000 rpm until the initial widening of the hole is complete, and the drive belt of the machine is fairly slack, so that it can slip if the tool should dig in.

When the interior has been widened sufficiently many workers turn the toolrest so that its end projects into the job, but some badly designed toolrests do not lend themselves to this. In any event, if the method is used, the lever which clamps the rest in its holder must be tightened as firmly as possible. The Stokes pattern toolrest, which I now supply to users of most makes of lathe, is ideal for this, and, of course, the job is much easier and safer if the tool can be supported close to its cutting edge throughout the entire operation. The cutting of the final shape when the hole has been widened is done with a sharp round-nosed scraper, taking light cuts and working from the bottom of the hole towards the top in smooth steady movements.

When the inside is finished it will need a thorough sanding, bearing in mind the fact that where a scraper has been used the surface will be relatively rough in places. As with goblets and vases, the fingers cannot safely be used, so the abrasive paper is wrapped round a cylindrical piece of wood.

For the external shaping the workpiece can, if desired, be supported by the tailstock, using a wooden plug with slightly tapered edge as shown in the sketch. The job then becomes a spindle-turning operation, the shape being

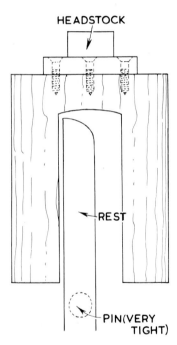

HEADSTOCK

REST

PIN(VERY
TIGHT)

Figure 75. If ordinary scrapers are used in situations where they project several inches over the toolrest, they may 'whip' and create problems. It may be possible to position the toolrest inside the job, so providing support all along the cut. If this method is adopted the toolrest must not be allowed to move while the wood is rotating. The clamp which secures it must be tightened very firmly.

produced with a roughing gouge, and the surface cleaned up by smoothing cuts from a very sharp skew chisel.

If the project is a tankard, a suitably shaped handle is cut out with a fretsaw and then filed and sanded by hand. If small tenons are cut on the handle at the points where it will fit to the tankard, these can be fitted into little mortises cut with a tiny chisel. The handle is fixed with Araldite. For biscuit barrels special liners can be obtained through specialist suppliers of woodturning fittings.

The alternative approach in the making of deep box-type articles is the built-up blank. This method is widely used, though beginners are discouraged by the extreme accuracy which is required in the preparation of the staves. The turner who has access to good-quality circular saws or planing machines will have little trouble in this respect if he goes about the job in a sensible manner, but it cannot be too strongly stressed that a very high degree of accuracy indeed is necessary in any form of built-up turning. No error can be tolerated in the preparation of the staves if a satisfactory standard of work is to be achieved in safety.

Those who have made picture frames will appreciate the degree of accuracy required to produce a neat job, and this has only four sides. A blank prepared for the turning of a biscuit barrel or a tankard may have eight, twelve or sixteen staves – and in large flower tubs made from oak I have used sixty-four. However many staves are used, each one will contain two angles whose accuracy will affect that of the finished job – in other words, any error in setting the machine which cuts the angles will be doubled in each stave. It will be seen, therefore, that a quarter of a degree error will produce a total error of four degrees in an eight-sided figure, six if there are twelve sides, and so on. The prime prerequisite, then, is extreme accuracy in cutting the angles.

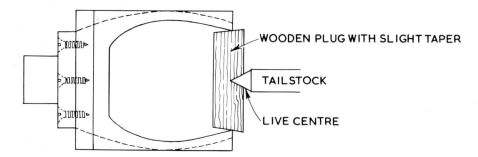

WOODEN PLUG WITH SLIGHT TAPER

TAILSTOCK

LIVE CENTRE

Figure 76. Use of tailstock and tapered plug to shape timber, to support objects such as vases and cups while outside shaping is done. Tailstock pressure must be light.

The turning itself, in the case of a built-up blank, is very much the same as with a solid version. The aspects to be examined carefully regarding the built-up system are the initial preparations and the mounting of the finished blank in the lathe.

Built-Up Blanks

Preparation Whilst it is quite possible to build up one blank the best approach is the production of a fair number as a batch. This is really the only way if the turning is a commercial proposition, since the making of individual blanks is completely uneconomic. The hobbyist will also find it advantageous to follow this system so that he has a store of built-up blanks in various sizes on which he can draw as required.

In order to achieve satisfactory results the utmost care must be taken throughout the whole process of building up these blanks, since there is no room whatsoever for error. Hand tools can be used if sufficient skill is possessed, but the use of woodworking machinery can give a high degree of accuracy and will speed up production considerably.

There is little point in building small blanks. By far the best idea is to cut the staves into about 2-foot sections, and the blank when built up can be cut to the required lengths for turning by means of a bandsaw or, if necessary, by hand.

For a straight blank, that is, one which is not tapered, the procedure is quite simple. Having decided upon the thickness and width of the material to be used in the staves,

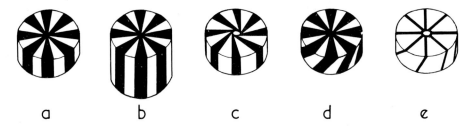

a b c d e

Figure 77. Some built-up blanks. (a) Pie wedge – grain horizontal. (b) Pie wedge – grain vertical. (c) Face spiral. (d) Edge spiral. (e) Edge spiral with spacers.

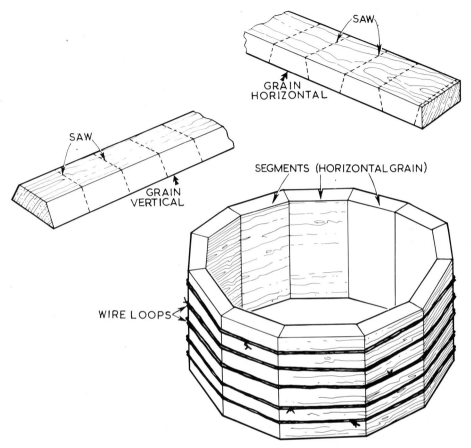

Figure 78. Built-up turning does not necessarily require timbers of differing colours. Quite large objects can be constructed by the methods shown here, even to log boxes and flower tubs for the garden.

these are ripped accurately to the required width on a circular saw using a very sharp blade. The sharpness of the blade is not important from the point of view of finish on the sawn surface, since this will subsequently be planed to give the requisite angle for the assembly of the staves into a cylinder. It is, however, important in as much as blunt circular saw blades can cause the wood to move away from the rip fence during the cut and,

although this movement may be tiny, it can create inaccuracies.

I find that the most satisfactory method is to cut the staves up without tilting the saw table to give the required angle for assembly, then produce this angle along the edges of the staves by means of a powered planer. If the saw table is tilted and the circular sawblade is used to produce the angle for build-up, the finished surface of the angled edges is unlikely to be as smooth as that which would be produced on a planer, and this can give rise to an unnecessarily thick glue line in the finished job.

One point which is important and should be brought out is that timber to be used in built-up work should be accurately thicknessed before being ripped into staves. It is also important not to mix up batches of timber which have been thicknessed, since there may well be small variations between the batches.

When the timber has been thicknessed and ripped to width it must be passed over the planer in order to produce exactly the required angle for the build-up. The problem here is that no error whatsoever can be tolerated in the setting of the tilt of the planer fence.

Most machine planers are equipped with scales showing the tilt of the table fence in degrees by means of a small pointer. The degree of accuracy required for built-up work is such that this scale and pointer cannot be

satisfactorily used, and it is necessary to set the tilt of the planer fence by means of a template.

Templates for this purpose can be manufactured in the workshop provided sufficient care is taken in their construction. They must be absolutely accurate or they will be worse than useless. On a trial and error basis, it is possible to produce satisfactory templates from plywood, oil-tempered hardboard, Tufnel or metal. Once such a template has been constructed and proved to be accurate in use, it should be kept in a drawer or on a nail in the workshop so that it can be used over and over again.

As an example, if the angle required is 22.5 degrees, as it would be in an eight-sided figure, then a template is needed which will, when placed upon the table of the planer, produce an exact angle of 22.5 degrees when the planer fence is brought over to lie flush with it. When carrying out this procedure I normally place a strong torch behind the tem-

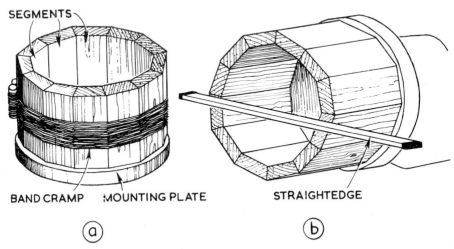

SEGMENTS

BAND CRAMP   MOUNTING PLATE   STRAIGHTEDGE

ⓐ   ⓑ

Figure 79. (a) Segments for built-up box structures can be cramped by means of a steel band cramp, or by winding around them and tightening by twisting with a stick 'Spanish windlass' fashion. (b) A careful check must be kept on the end surfaces throughout the process of cutting and re-assembling.

plate and make certain that the planer fence is completely flush with the edge of the template with no light showing through. The locking knob on the planer fence must, of course, be firmly tightened.

Because so many people have complained to me over the years of problems in the setting up of their planers to produce the exact angles required, and with regard to the difficulty of making templates which were themselves sufficiently accurate, I have for some time now been selling sets of metal templates which are specially made for me for the purpose described here.

The planing of the edges of the staves is not a difficult matter, but familiarity must not be allowed to breed contempt where powered planers are concerned, since they have proved to be statistically more dangerous than circular saws. The guards which are provided should be used at all times.

It will not be possible to produce the full bevel on the edge of a stave in one pass over the planer. The machine should be set for the normal $\frac{1}{16}$-inch depth of cut, and the first stave should be passed over the blades until the bevel has been achieved, counting the number of passes necessary. If, for example, this should be four passes, then the same number will be required on each edge of all the staves.

When the planing is finished, the edges of the staves can be brushed with adhesive, the cylinders assembled, and some form of pressure applied to keep them correctly clamped together while the adhesive hardens. There is no need to use large quantities of adhesive,

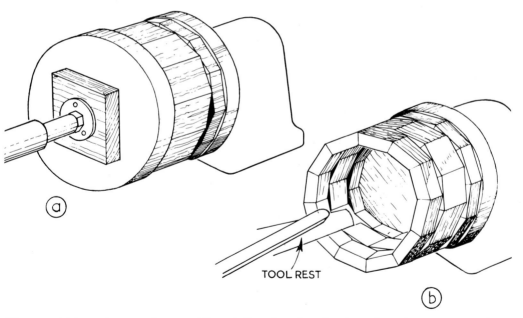

TOOL REST

Figure 80. (a) In cutting up and re-assembling a built-up box, the tailstock can be used as a pressure pad to hold the assembly while the glue sets. (b) Shaping of the inside of a box-type structure is best carried out with a sharp round-nosed scraper.

since most of this will be forced out of the joints while the staves are clamped, making quite a mess.

Many people use PVA adhesives, which are satisfactory, but I have always preferred to use Cascamite or Aerolite 306. Clamping cylinders of this nature can be done quite satisfactorily with large hoseclips, which are available in sizes up to 6 or 8 inches in diameter. If the hoseclips available are not large enough, they can be opened out and joined together.

An alternative method is to use wire wound round the assembly, through which a stick is pushed. When the stick is twisted, pressure is applied to the staves. Too much pressure is a mistake, since it forces most of the glue out of the joints. The assembly, after clamping, should be kept for twenty-four to thirty-six hours at room temperature before any attempt is made to cut it up and turn it.

The description above refers to the making of straight cylinders, rather than tapered ones, but tapered staves assembled into a tapered cylinder will produce blanks from which sets of articles can be made, for example, a set of three drinking tankards. If this process is chosen, the staves are first ripped to required width and then tapered prior to planing. It is not, however, necessary to taper both sides of each stave. If, for example, on a stave 2 feet in length the overall taper is $\frac{3}{4}$ inch, it will be found quite satisfactory to taper one side of each stave to give a $1\frac{1}{2}$-inch taper. The planing is then carried out as described above, and when the staves are assembled into the cylinder it will be seen that they go together perfectly well, but that the ends of the cylinders are uneven. Once the assembly has dried thoroughly, these ends can be trimmed flush on a bandsaw. The system described here can, of course, be used to produce quite large cylindrical blanks for the making of flower tubs and other similar items.

So far we have discussed in detail the building up of blanks of this kind from staves, but it will be noted that when these are cut into lengths suitable for turning they are open at both ends. Because of this, there is often some difficulty for a beginner in mounting such a blank in a lathe ready for turning. It is actually quite a simple operation, and it brings in the use of tapered wooden discs, or plugs, which are used for turning a wide variety of hollow blanks on the lathe. When a tapered plug has been made for any given job it should not be discarded after use, since it will sooner or later be found to be of a suitable size for some other piece of turning. Any suitably sized piece of timber can be used for the making of plugs, and softwood will do quite well.

Having cut off from one of the main blanks a suitable length for the project to be undertaken, the first step is the turning of a tapered disc to fit into one end of the blank. The taper should not be too steep. The turning of the plug is done on a woodscrew chuck using a deep-throated gouge. When the fit has been tried and found to be satisfactory, the plug is removed from the woodscrew chuck and laid aside while a second plug is turned, so there is one for each end of the blank. The blank itself is now mounted in the lathe supported by the two plugs, one of which is attached to the woodscrew chuck, the other by the tailstock centre.

It is now necessary to cut a rebate in the end of the blank nearest to the tailstock, so that a base with a matching rebate can subsequently be glued into position. In order to do this, the toolrest is swung round so that a sharp parting tool can be pushed into the end grain, taking about a $\frac{1}{16}$-inch width of cut each time. The tool is held in a horizontal position and pushed straight forward. No attempt should be made to take a wide cut, since this may cause a minor dig in, which can shift the blank on its temporary mounting. If the parting tool is sharp and the work is done carefully, there should be very little difficulty.

When a suitable rebate has been cut, the lathe can be stopped and the blank removed. A disc of hardwood is now mounted on a woodscrew chuck, trimmed to a suitable diameter using a $\frac{3}{8}$-inch deep-throated gouge, and a rebate is cut on the edge of this to fit that which has been cut in the blank itself. Care should be taken to achieve a really snug fit, and it will be necessary to stop the lathe frequently to try the two pieces. Once a satisfactory fit has been achieved, the woodscrew chuck is removed from the lathe mandrel complete with disc, adhesive is applied around the rebate, and the base is fitted to the blank. The assembly can be held lightly in a vice until the glue is hardened or it can be propped up on the floor with a weight on it.

Once this stage has been reached the turning is quite straightforward and should present no problems. Having given sufficient time for the adhesive to harden correctly at room temperature, the blank can be remounted in the lathe. The first operation should be the shaping of the inside. This is best done with a round-nosed scraper which has been ground to a fine edge, and if it is possible to get the toolrest inside the blank while the internal shaping is done, greater support will be available for the blade of the tool. If for any reason this is not possible, it will be observed that considerable projection of the blade over the toolrest is necessary, and this can give rise to snatches and dig ins unless the turner is fully experienced. In any case, no real pressure should be used on the tool, and it may be found best to start at the bottom of the recess, bringing the tool back to the outer edge in smooth easy movements. The best advice for this sort of operation is to hasten slowly, since any attempt to hurry the work is likely to result in some form of dig in.

When the inside of the blank has been brought to a suitable shape, the resulting surface must be thoroughly sanded. Here it must be emphasized that, on small blanks, no attempt should be made to put the hand or part of the hand inside. The best approach is to find a scrap of cylindrical wood, which should not be difficult in a woodturning workshop, around which abrasive paper can be wrapped. This can then be used as a sanding stick, and the inside of the job can be finished off using two or three grades of abrasive paper. Note that, wherever a scraper has been used, it will be necessary to use more abrasive paper than when the wood has been sliced with a cutting tool.

Once the sanding has been completed and the inside of the job is considered entirely satisfactory, a wooden plug can be placed in the open end, and the tailstock can be brought up to give some support. This is not absolutely necessary, but certainly for a beginner it is worth considering.

With the plug in place under light pressure from the tailstock, the job is now, to all intents and purposes, a piece of spindle-turning, which can be completed by means of a $\frac{3}{4}$- or 1-inch spindle gouge. Many workers, myself included, use a roughing gouge for most of the outside turning, finishing off with a very sharp spindle gouge and if possible one or two fine paring cuts with a freshly honed skew chisel.

BOWL-TURNING

The Turning of Discs
Almost all beginners - and I have met a tremendous number of them over the years - seem to be possessed with a burning desire to get to the turning of wooden bowls at the earliest opportunity. One woodturning authority has even been known to suggest that bowl-turning is the ultimate as far as the craft is concerned, and that when a really first-class

wooden bowl can be made the turner is qualified. This, in my opinion, is a fallacy, since a bowl can be turned by means of just one deep-fluted gouge and possibly a scraper.

Spindle-turning and chuck work, on the other hand, call for considerable skill in the use of almost all the tools, some of which in fact have various duties to perform.

In the turning of a bowl with a deep-fluted gouge the tool is required to perform two cuts, one which is used in the shaping of the outside and an entirely different cut which is used for hollowing. Both of these will be described fully in this chapter.

Many beginners seem to have the idea that the trunk of a tree can be sliced crossways and the resulting slices used for the turning of bowls. This is not impossible, but it is certainly not a process to be recommended, since the heartwood contained in such slices is almost certain to split. Even if it does not, the blank itself will be extremely unstable, and after turning it will distort badly. Making a bowl by hollowing into end grain, as would be required in such circumstances, is an arduous and time-consuming business.

Bowls are almost invariably turned from discs which have the grain running across them rather than through their thickness, as would be the case with a slice taken across a tree trunk. In other words, the blank from which a bowl is made is normally a circular disc cut from a plank. Since bowl blanks are in fact discs, they have a great deal in common with smaller discs such as those used in the making of ashtrays, bases for table lamps, butter dishes and so on, and before going deeply into the subject of bowl-turning, it will be as well to consider the subject of discs as such.

For a very long time indeed woodturning has been arbitrarily divided by writers into two parts – faceplate turning and spindle-turning. To my mind this is not a sensible

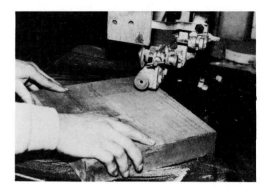

Plate 7. Preparing a disc from a square. Note that the bandsaw guides are set just above the work to reduce the risk of accident.

division, even if a case could be made for splitting the craft into two parts at all. Faceplate turning is, by definition, the turning of workpieces which are supported at the headstock only, without assistance from the tailstock. Spindle-turnings, on the other hand, are supported by both head and tailstock. A faceplate turning, therefore, need not necessarily be attached to the faceplate – it may be mounted on a chuck.

Work held in a chuck may have the grain running across it, as is the case with a disc from which a bowl is to be made, or it may have the grain running through it in the same direction as the lathe bed, as is the case with spindle-turning. Some confusion arises because of this kind of subdivision, and it does seem that there is a case for an alternative, which would be to refer to the turning of discs or to the turning of 'sticks'.

This point is quite important, because the turning of a workpiece on a chuck which has the grain running parallel to the lathe bed will be very similar to normal spindle-turning, whereas the turning of any form of disc brings totally different problems. Of the many people who write to me or telephone with queries concerning bowl-turning, the vast majority are concerned not so much with the use of the tools in the shaping of the outside and inside of the object, as with the production of a satisfactory finish. This will be dealt with in full later in this chapter, but it should be noted that, since a disc has the grain running across it, the problems of finishing are considerably greater than in spindle-turning.

Let us consider the turning of a simple disc into which a circular tile is to be fitted, perhaps to make a stand for a small pot plant. It is probably safe to say that anyone who is not capable of the satisfactory completion of a job of this nature is not ready for the turning of a bowl.

Students on my courses are taught to use the square-ended deep-fluted tools, which are commonly referred to as 'bowl-turning gouges', for the turning of all forms of discs. This is because, if properly ground and handled, they work extremely well, and the use of a square-ended gouge in disc turning is considerably easier for a beginner than the handling of a spindle gouge, which is ground to a curve.

It should be noted, however, that many competent woodturners frequently use spindle gouges in the turning of bowls, because in certain situations a far superior finish can be achieved. Many novices seem to labour under the delusion that the deep-fluted gouges, or bowl gouges as they are commonly called, are something special and have a mystique of their own. Nothing could be further from the truth; these tools are very simple and extremely easy to use. They are subject to the same rules as any other gouge. In other words,

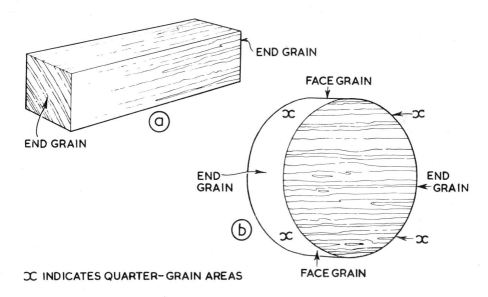

ɔC INDICATES QUARTER-GRAIN AREAS

Figure 81. The most sensible division of the craft of woodturning is into blanks which are 'sticks' and those which are 'discs'. Diagram (a) shows a 'stick' in which the grain runs roughly parallel to the bed of the lathe. In (b) it will be seen that the grain problems which the cutting tool must face in a disc will vary continuously as the blank rotates.

all cutting must be done in a downhill direction wherever possible, the bevel of the tool must rub the wood during the cut to support the cutting edge, and only that part of the cutting edge which is receiving direct support from the toolrest can safely be used. Anyone who has learned how to handle a spindle gouge by assiduous practice of turning between centres will have little difficulty mastering the deep-fluted variety.

The making of a stand for a pot plant is basically the same as the turning of a cheeseboard, which is merely a larger version of the same thing. This sort of project appeals very much to beginners because it is easy, and the artefact which results is very attractive. The first step is to mount a suitable disc of wood on a woodscrew chuck of about $2\frac{1}{2}$ inches diameter, using short thick screws which have consider-

able holding power with relatively little penetration. For a disc such as we are considering here, the central screw of the chuck alone will provide sufficient grip.

In the turning of thin discs, as distinct from the turning of bowls, there is an inherent danger which must be pointed out clearly at this stage. Because the grain runs across the disc there are two very vulnerable points which, in fact, lie in the quarter grain. Unless the handle of a deep-fluted gouge is held sufficiently low, there is every possibility that the tool will dig into the wood. Should this occur, the dig in is most likely to be in the quarter grain area, and just as an axe will easily split a short length of board, so a dig in of this nature can easily split the disc apart.

If the entire disc were to fall from the chuck while rotating it would simply fall, pos-

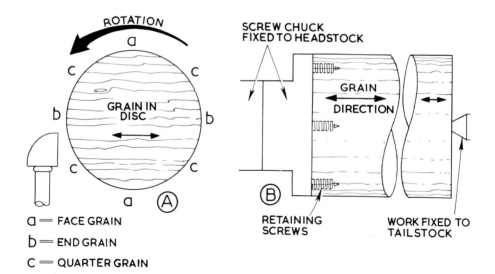

Figure 82. (A) Grain problems in turning a disc. Face grain (a) and end grain (b) will cut well. Two of the quarter grain areas (c) are likely to have the ends of the fibres lifted by the gouge unless the edge is very sharp and the tool is correctly manipulated. (B) It will be noted that where the grain runs roughly parallel to the lathe bed in workpieces which are mounted between centres, the problems shown at (a) and (b) will not occur.

sibly striking the lathe bed or bench and jumping a little sideways due to its spin. An object rotating on its axis is gyroscopically stable and subject only to the force of gravity. If a section of such an object rotating at a fairly high speed should become detached, on the other hand, it will be subject to centrifugal force and will fly from the lathe at high speed. Serious accidents have occurred through this, and it is not impossible for a serious injury to result. Workers who are in the initial or intermediate stages of the craft, who have not reached the point at which they can be quite confident of controlling the gouge and avoiding dig ins, would be well advised to wear a pair of high impact goggles, or better still a lightweight face visor. This is not intended to put anyone off the turning of small discs, but it is easy to see how anyone who has not been warned of the danger might sooner or later find out the hard way.

With the disc mounted on a screw chuck and the toolrest in position across the edge of the work, the project can be brought down to the required diameter using a $\frac{3}{8}$-inch deep-fluted gouge with the handle held low. It is best to get the feel of this sort of tool before starting work, if it is being used for the first time.

Apply the tool to the surface of the wood so that the heel of the bevel is making contact while the edge itself is clear. If the tool is now drawn gently backwards and the handle raised slowly at the same time, a point will be reached where the edge makes contact with the surface of the disc and the bevel is rubbing. This should produce a fine shaving if the lathe is turned slowly by hand, and it will be noted that any further backward and downward movement of the tool, minute though it may be, will increase the thickness of the shaving or the depth of the cut.

If the lathe is now started this process can be repeated, and it will be obvious that, unless

the tool handle is raised too much or the tool is lifted clear of the toolrest, there will be no danger of a dig in. The rule, therefore, is that in the turning of any form of disc the handle of the tool must be kept as low as possible throughout the operation. Since this type of gouge is square ended, almost all parts of the edge can be used at some stage. Like most gouges, these work best when rolled slightly onto their side, but, for the initial rough cutting required to bring the disc to the correct diameter, many turners would use the tool on its back with the flute facing upwards to take advantage of that section of the edge.

When the diameter of the disc is as required the toolrest can be moved away, and the area to be recessed to accept the tile can be roughly indicated in pencil. The trick in operations of this kind is always to ensure that the recess is initially made too small so that it can be enlarged by means of gentle cuts at the corner by the parting tool, until the fit is correct.

Timber to be used for operations of this kind should be sawn into discs and subsequently stored at normal room temperature for a week or two if possible. This point is frequently overlooked, with the inevitable result that the wood loses moisture after the tile has been fitted and shrinks across the grain, so breaking the tile. This is a disappointing end to an interesting project and must be avoided at all costs.

It is as well to leave a very slight gap between the tile and the edge of the recess, and some thought must also be given to the fixing of the tile itself. If, as is sometimes the case, the tile is glued firmly into position with a powerful adhesive, any subsequent movement of the timber will break it. The method which I have used for many years in projects of this nature and have found to be entirely satisfactory is the fixing of tiles by means of three or four blobs of impact adhesive. Since this does not harden fully but remains slightly

Plate 8. Recessing cheeseboards by means of a parting tool. In this particular operation the tool has to be held horizontally which gives it a scraping action and rapidly destroys the cutting edge.

Plate 9. Deep-fluted gouge in use on a cheeseboard. Some turners use a round-nosed version as here, but the square-ended type is more common.

Plate 10. Cutting the middle of the cheeseboard. Note that the gouge is on its side with the bevel rubbing the wood.

rubbery, the tile is in effect mounted on a number of small shock absorbers, which allows for any small movement of the timber.

With a stand for a pot plant or a cheeseboard, some shaping may be required around the edge of the project. This can normally be done with a gouge, but if the shape is complex some scraper work may be necessary. Provided the scrapers are freshly sharpened and undue pressure is not used, there should be no serious problems.

When the shaping has been completed, the work can be given a thorough sanding. If the turning has been of a high standard, little or no abrasive paper as such will be required, and a good rubbing with fine steel wool will be sufficient. The tile can now be fixed in place, the job removed from the chuck, and the back of the workpiece covered with self-adhesive green baize.

The turning of a small disc is a simple and straightforward operation. Problems arise, however, when the size of the disc increases, as in the turning of a bowl or a table top. I frequently receive queries from turners who are experiencing great difficulty with the production of items such as circular tops for small tripod tables. The problem always seems to be the virtual impossibility of achieving a smooth surface. Although, as stated earlier, the rpm as such is not a critical factor, the speed in linear feet per minute at which the tool is to cut at any point of a workpiece is of extreme importance.

If a disc of, say, 18 inches is to be turned, it will be a relatively simple matter to reduce the speed of the lathe to a point where the outer edge of the disc is moving at a speed which will suit the cutting tool. It is not, however, possible to achieve a suitable cutting speed right across the disc, from edge to centre. If the outer edge is moving at a satisfactory cutting speed, the centre will be rotating very slowly. Any attempt to take a cut from the outside edge through to the centre is doomed to failure, since the speed of the material relative to the cutting edge decreases as the cut proceeds. Workpieces of this nature are best prepared completely flat on both sides before mounting on the lathe. The only turning then left to be done is the shaping of the edge itself.

In the turning of a bowl this problem, whilst it still exists, is not so severe and can be coped with, since the vast majority of bowls are less than 18 inches in diameter. Having said this, however, I must point out that here an entirely different problem arises, in that the thickness of the blank for a bowl is often quite considerable. The weight is also fairly great, and it will be seen that the momentum of a hefty bowl blank is a force to be reckoned with. Whereas the average spindle-turning will stop dead if a dig in occurs – provided, of course, that the drive belt is slack – this cannot happen with a large and heavy bowl blank. Furthermore, unless the piece of wood from which the bowl is to be made is of even density, it will remain out of balance throughout the entire operation. This sort of situation arises where a blank has sapwood at one side and heartwood at the other, which will cause vibration, and this vibration will continue until the job is finished. Such vibration can be reduced by lowering the speed of the machine, but there is obviously a limit if a suitable cutting speed is to be maintained.

In view of the points outlined, it is always best for beginners to start their bowl-turning with small blanks, working gradually up to the larger and heavier ones. The cuts involved are the same in both cases, but the problems of vibration and surface speed are greatly diminished in the case of the small blank.

The Procedure for Bowl-Turning

Tremendous satisfaction can be obtained from the turning of a bowl, provided that the results are of a high standard. In the early stages of bowl-turning there is frequently a strong desire to turn very large bowls, but this desire should be resisted until a satisfactory example of a small bowl can be produced. We have, up to this point, been discussing the turning of discs, and a bowl is of course a disc. Bowl-turning, however, exercises a strange fascination over many people, some of whom devote a great deal of time to this aspect of the craft. In view of this, I have provided as much information about it in this manual as space permits.

When a large blank is attached to a machine, an inexperienced turner will feel some degree of apprehension. In view of this, it may be as well to point out that if a bowl blank is securely attached to the faceplate and rotated at a reasonable speed, and provided all normal safety precautions are observed, there is remarkably little danger. As with any other form of woodturning, practice is the key to success, provided sufficient information regarding the correct use of the tools has first been absorbed.

Leaving aside for the moment the use of scrapers, which are necessary in the turning of many bowls, and restricting our thoughts to the use of bowl-turning gouges, i.e. the square-ended, deep-fluted type of gouge, there are only two specific cuts which must be mastered. Once the turner understands these two cuts, a period of time should be devoted to practising their execution without necessarily trying to produce a bowl. Small circular blanks of softwood which are free from splits and knots are excellent for this purpose; a suitable size is a 6- or 7-inch diameter by 1-inch thickness. Blanks of this size can best be dealt with on a woodscrew chuck, since a faceplate will normally be too large and will interfere with the free passage of the tool.

The gouge can be a $\frac{3}{8}$-inch or $\frac{1}{2}$-inch version, and it must be very sharp, particularly for the turning of softwoods. While I have previously stated that it is not strictly necessary to use an oil-stone, it may be advantageous to do so when soft fibrous materials such as pine are being worked. Practice should be restricted for a few weeks to producing various bowl shapes on small discs without hollowing them, working down until the disc is too small to be of any further use. This should be followed by practising the second of the two bowl-turning cuts, which is obviously the one used in removing the interior.

Many turners begin their careers without the advantage of a bandsaw, and I am often asked it it is safe to use a square blank rather than a disc, mounting this on the lathe and bringing it to a disc shape by means of gouges and scrapers. The answer is that, whilst a fully experienced turner could get away with an operation of this kind, a beginner might have trouble.

It is, in fact, dangerous for an inexperienced worker to start with a square blank. If no bandsaw is available, the corners of square blanks should be removed, thus converting the square to an octagon, and the initial turning should be done with a heavy scraper until the blank is circular. Once sufficient skill has been acquired, this part of the job can safely be done with a gouge, which, of course, works far more rapidly.

Blanks for the turning of bowls, in common with those for any other form of turning, must be thoroughly examined to ensure that no cracks or other faults are present. It is always best to have material which is to be used for bowl-turning planed on both sides, preferably making sure that both faces are parallel. Those who intend to make quantities of bowls will be best advised to purchase material in the form of blanks, and the mill which supplies these blanks will pass them through a thicknessing machine for a nominal fee. The wood can be stored in the plank or cut into squares and bandsawn to discs for storage. If the latter procedure is adopted, the edges of the discs must be protected or they will split as they dry out. The best form of protection is a double layer of wax, but if this is not available, paint will serve the same purpose.

The wax used in the timber trade throughout the world to protect the end grain of sawn timber is not easy to obtain but there is no difficulty regarding its application to the timber. It has a relatively low melting point but should be kept away from a naked flame. An old roasting tin which is shallow and flat can be heated on an electric hotplate, and in this a few lumps of wax can soon be reduced to a colourless liquid. The blanks can be dipped into this, and the wax will harden off very rapidly so that a second coat can be applied.

It is, of course, vitally important that blanks for bowl-turning should, like any other form of blank, be very securely attached to the machine. Most faceplates are made of some form of alloy which is relatively soft, and if such a faceplate is screwed tightly to a surface which is not in fact flat, it is highly probable that distortion of the faceplate will occur.

The marking out of discs prior to bandsawing is best done with a large pair of dividers. If such a tool is used the centre of the disc is clearly marked by the leg of the dividers, which will greatly facilitate the subsequent mounting of the blank on the faceplate.

At this juncture, I would like to point out that a woodturner who is considering the purchase of a bandsaw should take time over the selection of a machine and be prepared for the fact that the cheaper versions will be of little use, since much of the cutting will be carried out on thick and hard timbers. A good bandsaw is an investment and will pay for itself over the years. It will be properly guarded and will give excellent service. Cheaper models will be a constant source of frustration and

irritation and will break blades with monotonous regularity. Since bandsaw blades are now a fairly expensive item, the purchase of a cheap machine represents a false economy.

It is frequently suggested that the table of a bandsaw should be tilted for the cutting of bowl blanks, thus reducing the amount of turning required in the shaping of the outside of the bowl. While this may be a good idea for a complete beginner, it is doubtful whether it has any real value to an experienced woodturner, who will rough out the shape of the outside of a bowl in a very short space of time using a large gouge.

The vast majority of lathes currently available are provided with faceplates which have a hole roughly 1 inch in diameter at the centre. As a result of this, many people complain of the difficulty they experience in centring the blank to the faceplate. It would be extremely helpful if centring devices were provided for faceplates. In the absence of such a device, the blank must be roughly centred by eye when it is fitted to the faceplate, or a series of concentric circles can be drawn on the face of the disc by means of a pair of dividers so that the lines which result can be viewed through the screw holes in the faceplate. Neither system is, of course, as simple or as accurate as the use of a centring device.

Various methods by which bowl blanks can be attached to faceplates, and the ways in which the problems which arise can be surmounted, are discussed in this chapter. It is of paramount importance that the screws used in fixing the blank do not penetrate the wood any more than is strictly necessary, and that the holes which accept these screws are drilled to a carefully predetermined depth. While it is extremely annoying to take one final cut on the inside of a bowl and find that the tips of the screws have been uncovered, it is even more aggravating to find that, although the tips of the screws have escaped the attentions of the gouge, the holes themselves, having been drilled too deeply, are exposed.

The ideal size of woodscrew for the mounting of blanks on chucks or faceplates is 1 inch by number 14. Unfortunately, this is a size screw which is extremely difficult to find, having little use in everyday woodwork. The 1-inch by 14 screw had its heyday when iron frames were screwed to the wooden structures of beds, where it gave great holding power. Since the construction of beds has changed drastically in recent years, some serious detective work may be needed to trace this particular item.

Most faceplates are provided with eight holes for screws, and where it is desired to hollow out a hole to maximum depth, the penetration of the screws can be reduced by interposing a disc of hardboard or plywood between blank and faceplate. The reduction in holding power can be compensated for by using eight screws instead of the more usual four. When a blank has been attached to a faceplate, the assembly should be examined carefully to see that the faceplate is in contact with the wood all round its periphery. Any gaps which appear between the edge of the faceplate and the wood will obviously mean that the screws have not been fully tightened and that, at some stage during the turning of the bowl, movement of the blank on the faceplate is likely.

Although this movement will be very small, it can give rise to problems in achieving a satisfactory finish. There are a wide number of variations on the theme of mounting blanks for bowl-turning, but the simplest and most common is when the disc is mounted directly onto the faceplate and is not disturbed until the bowl is finished. This is the method which I use myself for most of the bowls that I turn, and in most circumstances it is entirely satisfactory.

Very few lathes are equipped with a 4-inch faceplate, which I consider an essential part of any good lathe. The reason is that the 4-inch faceplate fills the gap between a large woodscrew chuck, which is normally about $2\frac{1}{2}$ inches in diameter, and the 7- or 8-inch faceplate, which seems to be the standard issue. The point is that the size of the chuck or faceplate used in the mounting of a bowl disc is important, because the chuck or faceplate must not be so large as to interfere with the passage of the cutting tool when the outside of the bowl is shaped. In the absence of a suitable small mounting device, such as a woodscrew chuck or 4-inch faceplate, the turning of, say, an 8-inch diameter bowl on a 7- or 8-inch faceplate will be difficult or impossible unless a fairly thick disc of scrap timber is positioned between the blank by means of four screws. A further four screws, which will, of course, need to be longer, are passed through both faceplate and disc into the bowl blank. By this method, it will be quite a simple matter to form the shape of the outside of the bowl without any fear of the gouge striking the metal faceplate. As the curve of the bowl sweeps round towards the faceplate, the gouge will be able to cut into the scrap timber.

Having mounted the blank by one of the methods described above, it will be necessary to trim it up with a few light cuts so that it is perfectly circular and runs as far as possible in balance. The security of the toolrest must be carefully checked, and the handle of the deep-fluted gouge must be kept as low as is commensurate with the removal of a satisfactory shaving. At this stage the tool can be used on its back with the flute or hollow part vertical, and a few passes from left to right or vice versa will clean up the edge of the blank in preparation for the subsequent shaping.

When this has been done, the surface produced should be examined. At this point the beginner meets a problem which bothers a great many turners who have not been correctly instructed – the lifting of the ends of the fibres of the wood in two places around the bowl. The examination of the blank will reveal the fact that at two points on its edge there is end grain, and at two points there is face or side grain. It is at the point where the tool leaves the end grain and runs through the quarter grain that the trouble arises. The ends of the fibres will tend to lift as the tool reaches the face grain, and if the roughing out of the disc with the gouge has been done with a blunt edge or with heavy cuts, there will be two rough patches axially opposed on the blank.

This can be ignored in the early stages, since it is quite easily rectified as the job proceeds. A beginner can demonstrate this quite easily, having once produced such rough patches, by sharpening the gouge and taking a few carefully controlled light cuts which remove fine shavings. It is important to note, however, that light cuts are not the result of light pressure with the tool against the wood, which is a common misconception. A properly executed light cut removing a fine shaving should be performed with firm pressure of the bevel against the wood. The thickness of the shaving is controlled by slight alterations in the angle of attack of the bevel to the surface of the work.

The most common fault with beginners who find that the tool is cutting too deeply is that they reduce the pressure of the tool against the work in order to reduce the thickness of the shaving. Except in situations where scrapers or scraping methods are used, depth of cut should be controlled by alteration of the angle of attack, not by reduction or increase of pressure. A few controlled cuts removing a fine shaving will almost invariably correct the fault in question.

In shaping the outside of a bowl, the rule which says that all cutting must be done in a downhill direction – or, in other words, from a large diameter towards a small one – must be observed. The handle of the tool is kept as low as possible and the curvature of the outside of the disc is achieved by commencing at the extreme left or right of the work, taking off a little material at a time. Control of the shaping will be facilitated if the upper outline of the work is watched rather than the point at which the tool is cutting.

A further difficulty which arises both in spindle-turning and in bowl work is that, because all cutting has to be done in a downhill direction, a bowl with a strongly curved shape will require some cuts to be executed from left to right and others from right to left. The difficulty here for an inexperienced worker is the blending of these cuts so that no unsightly ridge or hollow results. The mistake made in many cases is that the tool is allowed to start with a definite cut, whereas it should be placed with its bevel against the wood and the heel of the bevel making contact, so that the edge is clear. If this is done, contact with the wood can be maintained while the position of the tool is gradually changed until the edge contacts the work, and the start of the cut will be smooth, leaving no sign of the point of commencement.

In some bowl shapes no definite base is used, the curvature of the outside flowing smoothly round to the point where it joins the bottom of the workpiece. In others, however, a distinct base may be required, standing proud of the bowl itself by perhaps $\frac{1}{4}$ or $\frac{1}{2}$ inch. This base can be formed by using a parting tool or with the aid of a square-ended scraper; the shape of the bowl itself is adjusted so that it meets the base correctly. In the subsequent sanding, after the bowl has been completed, careful attention should be paid to the base, since the use of a parting tool or scraper is likely to produce rough areas.

Skilled turners frequently use spindle gouges in the final stages of shaping the outside of a bowl, but the process definitely requires a fair degree of skill if accidents are to be avoided. The curved shape of the end of a spindle gouge will, if the tool is used on its side rather than on its back, permit an oblique relationship between the part of the edge which is cutting and the wood. This gives a paring action, and if the tool is sharp the surface so produced will be of a high quality. The danger lies in the fact that with the tool working on its side in this fashion, contact between the cutting edge of the wood must be restricted to that section of the edge which is receiving support. This, of course, is the area close to the corner. A slight mistake in the handling of a spindle gouge when working like this may result in the centre of the edge touching the wood, which will flip the tool over onto its back and cause a fairly spectacular dig in. It goes without saying, of course, that firm contact must be maintained between bevel and wood throughout the cut.

Hollowing

The hollowing of a bowl is carried out with the same tool as used for the shaping of the outside - the $\frac{3}{8}$-inch or $\frac{1}{2}$-inch deep-fluted pattern. There are, however, one or two points which merit consideration before the physical act of hollowing is described in detail.

In the case of a small bowl, that is, up to 9 or 10 inches in diameter, most workers prefer to start at the centre, working gradually back until the final cuts produce the finished internal shape. While this does seem a commonly accepted method for small bowls, there is no valid reason why the operation should not commence at the outside edge so that all cuts start at the same point and run through to the centre. It is a matter of preference, and the individual turner will soon adopt a suitable method.

There is, of course, a major difference between the hollowing of a bowl and the excavation of a project such as an egg cup, in that a bowl is turned from a disc of wood which has been cut from a plank, whereas the egg cup or vase is made from a piece of wood which has its grain running in the same direction as the lathe bed. Where the hollowing is being done into end grain like this, the start of each hollowing cut with a gouge offers the possibility that an incorrectly applied tool may skid violently. For this reason it is customary to start at the outside edge when hollowing into end grain, so that after the first cut has been made there is a surface which can be used to support the bevel of the tool in subsequent cuts.

Whilst the height of the toolrest in spindle turning is not critical, in working on the face of a disc the toolrest height must be exactly right so that the tool, with its bevel rubbing the wood, can be taken through to the centre of the work without difficulty. If the toolrest is too low, assuming the tool to be correctly applied to the wood, the cut will finish below the centre point of the job, leaving some material uncut. If, on the other hand, the toolrest is too high, the cut will pass above the centre point, giving the same result.

When setting up a toolrest for the hollowing of a bowl, place it across the work about $\frac{1}{8}$ inch clear of the wood, and then turn the bowl by hand. Even when the workpiece is rotated slowly in this fashion, the exact centre will be obvious to the eye. The toolrest is positioned slightly below this point, so that the cutting edge itself will run as required. Before any attempt is made to hollow out a bowl, the clamps on both the saddle and banjo must be checked for tightness.

As a result of many years of woodturning and woodcarving, I have acquired a large selection of gouges and chisels, many of which would, upon examination, be found to bear little resemblance to the tools described in this manual in terms of bevel angle. This happens to most workers as their experience grows, bevel angles being very much a matter of shaping the ends of the tools for specific purposes. The controlling factor, of course, is that whatever angle is ground on a gouge or a chisel it should permit the execution of a given cut with complete bevel support.

Many turners, in fact, like to have gouges for use in bowl turning and in spindle work which are of the same size and type, but ground with slightly different angles which they find suitable for specific operations. When I have any large amounts of bowl-turning to do I use gouges for outside shape which have longer bevels than the ones I use for hollowing. This is a personal idiosyncrasy, but readers may like to try the idea.

One of the most satisfying experiences in the craft of woodturning is without doubt the hollowing of a large bowl with plenty of power by means of a large bowl-turning gouge. If the tool is sharp and correctly applied to the wood, huge thick shavings will snake away across the workshop, and the woodturner's ego will be considerably inflated. Do not, however, become too excited by this, since the use of a deep-fluted gouge in hollowing a bowl is a very simple matter once the basic principles have been grasped.

The first cut at the centre of the workpiece will produce a small dimple-like hollow. The second cut, of course, will widen and deepen this dimple, which will become progressively wider and deeper as cut follows cut. In hollowing a bowl with a square-ended gouge, the tool is on its side on the toolrest with the flute facing towards the centre of the workpiece. It is the supported edge which does the work, and the upper, unsupported edge does not come into contact with the wood.

Having taught hundreds of students over a long period of time to handle the gouge correctly in the hollowing of a bowl, and

answered queries from hundreds more, I can state quite confidently that the most common fault lies in insufficient swing of the gouge handle. The arc through which the handle moves in a correctly executed cut is very long indeed. As soon as the cut begins the handle must be pushed backwards relative to the flute of the tool, and this backward movement must continue until the cut is completed. Difficulties in hollowing bowls arise with astonishing frequency due to the simple fact that the amount of handle movement a turner is prepared to give to the tool will, in most cases, depend upon confidence and experience, the former being derived from the latter.

If, as is frequently the case, the cut starts well but the handle movement is insufficient, the cut will become deeper as the tool moves along the wood. The one factor that will definitely produce a dig in is a movement of the gouge which breaks the contact between bevel and wood. A typical situation is one in which the bevel of the tool contacts the wood during approximately the first third of the cut, but the turner does not continue to swing the handle backward, attempting instead to push the tool bodily along the toolrest. This brings the bevel away from the wood, and a dig in is almost inevitable. Such mishaps are a strain on the nerves, since in the latter stages of hollowing there will be considerable projection of the gouge over the toolrest, and consequently the leverage exerted by a dig in may take the tool from the hands of the operator.

Some lathes are equipped with toolrests which have a curved section designed to be swung into a bowl, thus enabling a cut to be completed with maximum support for the blade. I have tried these out in the past and found them to be of little value, but they may be helpful to some people.

A point worth noting is that, although many inexperienced turners do no feel happy about making what they consider violent or extravagant movements with the tool handles, the only possible result of swinging the handle back too far is the loss of the cut. In other words, if the handle moves back too quickly or too far, the edge of the tool will be pivoted up clear of the wood, and the heel of the bevel will be rubbing. I once saw this happen at an exhibition, and the reaction of the turner was to apply more pressure in the hope of recovering the cut. The friction so produced generated tremendous heat, and in a matter of seconds clouds of smoke were drifting across the stand. Without passing comment, I took the liberty of examining the gouge while it lay on the bench, and the end of it was a most attractive shade of purple; obviously the temper of both tool and turner had suffered badly.

The internal shape of a bowl will determine the percentage of waste material which can be removed with a gouge. Some bowls can be hollowed completely from start to finish with a gouge, their shape being such as to permit the bevel to rub the wood throughout. Others, however, are undercut, by which I mean that the wall of the bowl curls in towards the top. With a bowl of this shape it will not be possible to remove all the waste with a gouge, because the back of the tool will strike the rim of the bowl as the handle is moved backward and it will not be possible to maintain correct contact between bevel and wood.

In such cases the bulk of the waste can be removed with the gouge, which is a very rapid and efficient method, but a point will be reached where the full handle movement required is not possible because the tool strikes the bowl rim. At this stage the gouge must be laid aside and the hollowing continued with a sharp round-nosed scraper. Scrapers used in bowl-turning are in general made of stouter sectioned steel than those used in other forms of faceplate work because of the degree of projection over the toolrest which is involved.

It is most important that scrapers are sharpened as soon as the cut is seen to be deteriorating. The cutting action of a scraper depends entirely upon the wire edge which is formed during the grinding, and this edge will disintegrate fairly quickly when used on hard timbers. Although a scraper is a very simple tool and easy to use, a fair amount of practice is required in order to get the feel of it and to be able to use it in smooth sweeps, without creating ridges and hollows in the surface. It must also be noted that a properly sharpened scraper should be removing shavings, not little piles of dust. If shavings are not coming from the edge of the scraper, it must be sharpened.

Beginners frequently complain that they find difficulty controlling a scraper when hollowing a bowl, because as the waste is removed and the bowl becomes deeper, the leverage factor causes the tool to rock up and down with a kind of seesaw action. Most people experience this in the early stages, but practice will provide a sufficient degree of control to overcome the problem. Under no circumstances should heavy pressure be used with a scraper at any point during the cut. Undue pressure will cause the surface of the wood to be torn and badly damaged, and such damage is difficult to repair.

When the inside of the bowl is almost completed there is a case for ticketing the end of the scraper as described earlier. This produces a better cutting edge which, though it is less durable, is preferable for the final finishing cuts.

Having tried out, in the course of my woodturning career, all the procedures for finishing bowls which I have either read about or dreamed up for myself, I have ended up with a simple formula which guarantees success. I would not claim it to be the quickest way to achieve a good finish, but it has the merit of certainty, so I offer it here in the confident hope that it will help many people to overcome their difficulties. Before describing the process however, I would like to mention one small point. In turning a bowl, no matter how sure I am of the moisture content of the timber, I always like to stop just short of the final finishing cuts and leave the bowl if possible for a couple of days, so that the finishing cuts will correct any distortion which may occur.

In the light of considerable experience I will not now undertake bowl-turning in any shape or form unless I have to hand a supply of suit-able sanding sealer. This is the key to success, provided always that the work done up to the point where the sealer is used has been of a high standard. A shellac sealer such as that manufactured by Messrs. Rustins Ltd. is in my view as good as any other. Pure cellulose lacquer can be used, but some people may find the smell objectionable, and the fire risk involved in storing cellulose around the workshop must be considered. We sell large quantities of Rustins sanding sealer every week in our Bath showroom, and we have a large number of customers who would not

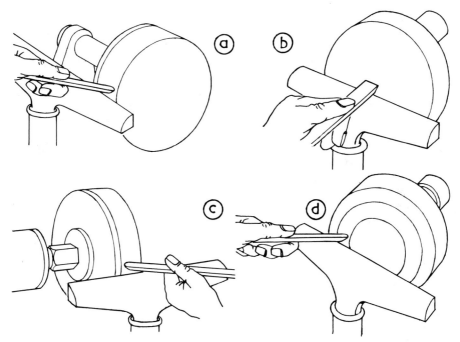

Figure 83. The scraper in disc turning. (a) Scrapers are always presented to the workpiece with negative rake or, in other words, pointing slightly downwards. Horizontal presentation is acceptable, but these tools must never be pointed upwards. (b) When a scraper is used, the edge must be sharp and the pressure light to avoid undue tearing of the surface. The blade of a scraper should always be kept flat on the toolrest. (c) A square-ended scraper presented at right angles to the surface of the material is traversed gently from side to side in order to produce a flat surface. (d) The hollowing of bowls and shaping of discs in general can be done with a sharp scraper but the process is slow and the resulting finish poor.

consider working without it either on spindle or faceplate operations.

Before any sealer is applied the bowl is given a preliminary sanding. Whenever abrasive paper is used, care must be taken to see that the surface of the wood has been brought to as smooth a finish as possible with the tools so that only fine grades of papers are required. If coarse grades are used they are likely to put deep scratches into the wood, and these can be extremely difficult to eliminate.

This brings me to the vexed question of the merits and demerits of reversing switches. Various newcomers to the woodturning scene have recently been advocating the use of reversing switches. The message seems to be, 'Don't worry, the work will not fall off the lathe while it is running'. This is a remarkably optimistic viewpoint, but I must take leave to doubt its veracity. The facts are simple. The lathe mandrel is equipped with either a right- or left-hand thread according to its direction of rotation, on the same principle as the nuts and studs which secure the wheels of motor cars. If the thread is correct for the direction of the rotation, the wheelnut or faceplate becomes self-tightening in use.

The woodturner must always bear in mind that if the lathe is run in reverse, the thread immediately becomes self-loosening. It is possible to start a lathe in reverse, if the workpiece is small and relatively light, and it is equally possible to sand such a workpiece and finish it completely without its parting company with the lathe. There is, by the same token, a distinct possibility that it will unscrew itself and fall off. If the workpiece is large and heavy its initial inertia will be such as to effectively preclude any possibility of its running in reverse on the mandrel. As soon as the button is pressed to start the lathe, the rotation will separate the mandrel and faceplate.

Certainly there is little danger in such a situation, but in nine cases out of every ten the bowl, upon which much care and effort has been expended, will in falling strike some part of the lathe and so sustain damage.

The point of a reversing switch, of course, is that in sanding a workpiece the fibres of the wood are brushed backwards and after a short time will all be lying with their ends pointing in the same direction. An observant woodturner will soon note the fact that abrasive paper produces satisfactory clouds of dust for a minute or so, and that the dust removed decreases rapidly in quantity from this point on. If the direction of rotation is now reversed, and the abrasive paper is transferred to the opposite side of the bowl, the fingers can trail on the wood safely and the cutting action of the abrasive paper is vastly improved.

The idea is to alternate the rotation of the blank on the machine, so cutting down the time required for abrasive work. This is helpful but by no means essential. For nearly thirty years I managed very well without any facility for reversing, and now that I do have this facility, I find that I use it only very infrequently.

Once the sanding has been satisfactorily completed the bowl should be given a generous coat of sanding sealer, which is then allowed to dry. In a warm room the sealer will dry and harden in ten to fifteen minutes. No attempt should be made to carry out any further work with abrasive paper until the sealer is completely hardened, or the action of the abrasive paper will lift the sealer, causing it to form rings on the surface of the work. If this happens, the only really satisfactory remedy lies in further cuts with a sharp gouge, after which, of course, one is back to stage one of the sanding.

Assuming that the sealer has dried and hardened thoroughly, the bowl is then given a very thorough sanding using an open coat garnet paper of a grade no coarser than 240. If the bowl is now rubbed with a handful of fine shavings as it rotates the turner will be able to switch off the lathe and examine the surface. Already a marked improvement should have taken place, but unless the turner has been extremely fortunate in the choice of timber, further treatment will be necessary.

I often feel that in the average woodturner there is a trace of masochism indicated among other things by a strong desire to turn bowls from such timbers as mahogany. Whilst I would agree that a nicely turned mahogany bowl can be extremely attractive, there is no doubt that this timber is among the most awkward to work. The grain of mahogany is soft and woolly, and whereas a bowl made from ash or beech may come to a beautiful finish after only two coats of sealer, it is not unusual to find that five or six coats are necessary on woods like mahogany.

Sealer, being wet, causes the grain of the wood to swell up. It then dries and hardens, locking the raised grain in position so that a thorough sanding will remove most of the sealer together with the swollen grain, leaving a very much improved surface. The further function of the sealer is the obvious one, in that it seals the surface of the wood so that any polish or finish subsequently applied will remain on the surface rather than being driven into the wood on the end grain.

When the first coat has been thoroughly sanded a second can be applied, but less sealer will be required this time since the surface has already been sealed, and none of the second application will soak into the wood. When the second coat has hardened it can be given a thorough treatment with fine steel wool, followed by another burnish with a handful of soft shavings.

Examination of the surface is now likely to show a dramatic improvement, and with luck it will have reached the stage at which it will be impossible to tell where the grain is if the

Plate 11. Bowls and table lighters are very much in demand. End-grain finishing, both inside and out, needs careful work on any kind of bowl.

fingers are run round it with eyes closed. This is a very good test for the bowl-turner in that, when this stage has been reached, any desired form of finish can safely be applied. For best results a third coat of sealer should be applied and allowed to harden. It is then cut back with fine steel wool and burnished lightly with soft shavings. This process can be repeated as many times as desired, so that a shell of sealer is built up around the bowl. After this has been done a smear of wax polish, buffed up with a soft cloth, will finish the job off nicely.

With the turning and polishing completed, the bowl can be removed from the faceplate and some attention given to the underside. If the blank has been secured to the faceplate by means of four screws, the resulting holes will be neatly positioned. These can be plugged with small scraps of wood and the base of the bowl can then be thoroughly sanded and several coats of sealer applied to it. Sand between coats in the same manner as for the rest of the bowl. Rather than apply self-adhesive green baize, for which I have a personal antipathy, I prefer to fix a small rubber disc over each of the plugged holes, thus forming four feet which will protect the furniture on which the bowl is placed. Green baize can look beautiful when first applied, but it deteriorates rapidly if the bowl is in daily use.

It is often suggested that the blank from which a bowl is to be made should be mounted onto the faceplate, and the outside of the bowl complete with its base should be shaped and finished. The idea is that, when this has been done, the blank is removed from the faceplate and reversed upon it, so that the recently formed base goes against the faceplate. When the bowl has been reversed and securely replaced, the hollowing can be carried out. The only reason which has ever been advanced to me for this rather surprising process is that it is said to be possible to cut more with the grain by this method than if the whole bowl is turned at one mounting. It may be that some people do find this sort of procedure helpful, but I can see no reason whatsoever for changing the position of the bowl halfway through the turning.

If this system of reversing the bowl on the faceplate halfway through the job is tried, the main snag will immediately become apparent. This is that, whilst it is quite easy to replace the bowl on the faceplate securely, it is by no means easy to replace it so that it is truly centred. Even if the utmost care is taken over this, the tightening of the screws is almost certain to move the bowl slightly, and bowls turned in this way frequently have walls which are of varying thickness. Those who feel they must follow this method will find that they have rather more work to do than is strictly necessary, since in order to be certain of accurate centring in the remounting of the blank, it is necessary first to screw a disc of wood to the faceplate and form a recess in this disc with a parting tool which will accept the base of the bowl as a push fit. Four screws are then passed through faceplate and scrap disc into the bottom of the bowl. This will ensure accuracy in centring, but the performance seems hardly worthwhile.

It seems to me that if a turner is going to take all this trouble, it would be as well to go the whole hog and turn a bowl which has no screw holes in it when complete. In order to do this, the blank is mounted on the faceplate, and the outside of the bowl is completely formed with a base which projects from the bowl by $\frac{1}{4}$ to $\frac{3}{8}$ inch. The bowl blank is then removed from the faceplate, and a scrap disc is attached and recessed to accept the base of the bowl as a really tight fit so that the hollowing can be undertaken without the use of any screws at all. This, of course, means that there is no need to hide screw holes, and it removes any possibility of the screws being uncovered by the gouge during the hollowing. If a bowl is made by this method it can be hollowed out so that it is quite thin, but the turner must take care that one final cut does not cut the bowl into two pieces.

Many turners, beginners in particular, do not really like the idea of hollowing out a bowl which is held on purely by the tightness of the fit of its base in the home-made wooden chuck. It should be borne in mind, however, that provided there are no dig ins, the action of hollowing is in fact pushing the bowl into the chuck rather than pulling it out, and I have made a great many bowls in this fashion without any untoward incidents whatsoever.

A belief quite widely held is that expert turners in days of old used a peculiar kind of hooked tool with which they removed the centre of a bowl in one piece, this piece being used for the making of a smaller bowl. This I consider to be impossible, though I am quite prepared to be proved wrong. The misconception probably arises from the fact that there was once a fairly widely used system whereby a *slightly* curved tool was fed into the face of a bowl disc to a reasonable depth. When this had been done the blank was removed from the faceplate and the central portion was split away from the main body of the job, usually by driving in a heavy chisel. The piece so removed could have its bottom planed flat and then be used for the making of a bowl. This, or course, is quite a different matter, and is perfectly possible, although I have yet to meet anyone prepared to show me how to do it.

Bowls with lids are quite attractive and seem to be readily saleable. There is very little difficulty attached to the turning of a lid, but one or two points must be watched if the result is to be satisfactory. One of the most important is that, when a bowl is to have a lid, the materials to be used for the bowl and the disc from which the lid will be made should be stored indoors for a week or two in the same sort of conditions in which the bowl is likely to be kept when it is finished. This will permit shrinkage to take place in the wood before the turning is carried out, but even so both bowl and lid should be partly turned, almost - but not quite - to completion, and

Plate 12. A nicely turned pedestal bowl with lid, produced from yew.

allowed a few more days indoors before they are taken back to the lathe and finished.

If this procedure is not carried out it is quite likely that, shortly after the bowl has been completed, the lid will either be jammed in place so that it is virtually immovable, or if it has been left off the bowl it will not be possible to fit it. Timber does shrink along the length of the grain, but only by a very small amount. Shrinkage across the grain, however, could be considerable, and if the lid of a bowl has been placed with its grain running at right angles to that of the bowl, shrinkage will result in the two becoming locked together.

If the lid of a bowl is to have a knob or handle this is best turned as a separate item, using a small woodscrew chuck. If the knob is turned as a separate item the turning of the lid of the bowl becomes somewhat easier, since a single screw can be used in a large woodscrew chuck, and the hole left in the bowl lid will accept a brass screw fitted from the underside which will hold the knob in place. In some cases the knob is turned as an integral part of the lid, but this is rather wasteful of timber and creates certain problems in the turning.

If the disc of wood is thick enough to permit the knob to be turned as part of the lid, it can be fitted to a faceplate and the outside of the lid, including the knob, can be turned using a deep-fluted gouge and one or two scrapers if necessary for the more detailed parts of the knob. When the turning has been completed, the job can be thoroughly sanded, given a coat of sealer, resanded, and in fact completely finished off.

The inside, or underside, of a bowl lid is normally shaped with a gouge into a concave form, and in order to do this it will be necessary to make up a home-made chuck which will hold the lid without the necessity for using screws. A disc of softwood $1\frac{1}{2}$ to 2 inches thick is fixed to the faceplate, and a hole is drilled at the centre large enough to give clearance for the knob. A recess is now formed in this disc with a sharp parting tool, working very carefully so that the recess ends up exactly the right size to accept the lid as a tight push fit. If the outside of the lid has a marked degree of curvature, it may be helpful to give a convex shape to the bottom of the recess in the scrap disc. As usual in these cases, if the hollowing out of the recess has been overdone and the lid is a slack fit, the situation can be remedied by placing a sheet of stout brown paper across the recess as the lid is pushed into position.

With the lid held securely the shaping of its underside can be carried out, and a recess can be cut around its outside edge to permit it to be neatly fitted to the bowl. The usual sanding, sealing and finishing processes follow.

Another approach to the mounting of bowls for hollowing, which finds favour in some quarters, is what is known as the 'glue and paper sandwich system'. For this the bowl blank is attached to a faceplate with screws, in the normal way, and the outside of the bowl is turned and finished. The surface of the base of the bowl is left absolutely flat. When this has been done, the bowl is taken from the faceplate and a disc of scrap wood is screwed on. This scrap disc is recessed very slightly with a sharp parting tool, not with the object of holding the bowl blank but in order to make certain that when the blank is fitted to the disc it will be centred accurately. The inside of the recess is now coated with adhesive, a sheet of thick blotting paper or heavy brown paper is placed across the recess, the bottom of the bowl is coated with glue, and the bowl is forced into the recess.

This assembly must be given sufficient time to dry and harden at room temperature. The hollowing of the bowl can now be carried out in the normal way, and when the job is finished a sharp thump with the fist should split the paper between the bowl and disc so

that the two can quite easily be separated. The bottom of the bowl will now, of course, be left covered in glue and brown paper, but this can be roughly cleaned up and the bowl base covered with self-adhesive green baize.

The 'glue and paper sandwich' system is quite effective, though many inexperienced turners are rather wary of it, being convinced that bowl and disc will part company halfway through the job. I have never known this to happen, and the only objection I have to the system is that in some operations green baize is not used to cover the base, and it is necessary to remove the glue and paper which adheres to the bottom of the finished job. This can be a difficult and tiresome process.

Once 'the glue and paper sandwich', and the home-made wooden chuck, have been used in the making of one or two articles, many other uses should suggest themselves to the ingenious woodturner. A typical situation where the two can very satisfactorily be combined is in the making of wooden plates, which have become extremely popular. If these are turned in really beautiful timber such as yew, they will not only be attractive on the dinner table but also make an excellent talking point.

Plates

During a discussion with a group of students on one of my courses the conversation got around to the vast number of questions I am asked each year through letters, telephone calls and personal contact. One student wanted to know what I consider to be the most common question. I had no hesitation in answering this, since it is without doubt 'What is the best wood for turning?' This question is asked several times every week, but there is no simple answer.

One has to know, in order to answer satisfactorily, exactly what information is required. It may be which timber is easiest to turn, or which timber looks best when turned properly, or which timber is most stable and least likely to give trouble through shrinkage after turning, or any one of a number of other things. In my opinion the best wood for a beginner to use is tree wood; in other words, any piece of timber available should be tried, provided always that it is sound and in no way dangerous.

I do not believe there is a 'best wood for turning', all timbers being grist to the wood-turners' mill. One thing, however, is quite certain. If a group of woodturners is asked to give opinions as to the woods which they most enjoy turning, quite a range of timbers will be mentioned. My own favourite timber, among all those I have turned over the years, which is quite a number, is, without a shadow of a doubt, yew. This is a colourful timber of high density and close grain, a joy to turn and a delight to look at if the turning has been done properly. Unfortunately, it is becoming extremely difficult to obtain in reasonable quantities, and it is also a timber which is very prone to cracks and shakes, many of which are not apparent until the turning is well under way. However, a set of side plates made from yew, if the job has been done properly, will enhance the table of prince or pauper, so let us consider the making of a wooden plate from a disc of yew, taking the design from an ordinary breakfast plate.

Whenever I mention plates to my students, one will always come up with the obvious question, 'How can you hold a plate on a lathe, when it is certainly not possible to use screws?' This is a good question, but fortunately there is a good answer.

The first stage in the turning of a plate is the shaping of its upper surface, in other words, the surface upon which the food will rest, and this is done with the disc of wood attached to a disc of scrap wood by means of a 'glue and paper sandwich'. The disc of scrap wood is

Plate 13. Wooden plates and platters are popular but can be uneconomical for the professional wood-turner in view of the problems involved in mounting the blank on the lathe.

fixed to the faceplate with screws. This is a straightforward piece of faceplate turning, most of it done with a deep-fluted gouge, but it will be necessary to use a square-ended scraper very lightly to make certain that the central area of the plate is absolutely flat and true.

When all this has been done, a thorough sanding, followed by an application of sealer and further sanding, can be carried out. Do bear in mind of course, that with any 'glue and paper sandwich' assembly, sufficient time must be given at room temperature for the adhesive to set or harden properly.

When the turning of the upper surface of the plate has been satisfactorily completed, the plate blank can be split away from the scrap disc by placing an old chisel at the joint between the two and striking it smartly with a mallet.

The disc of wood attached to the faceplate is now recessed with a sharp parting tool so that it will accept the plate blank as a tight fit. It is not necessary to make the recess deep, but just sufficiently to provide an adequate grip on the blank. With the blank mounted in this manner, the shaping of the underside of the plate becomes a reasonably simple matter, though it is doubtful whether the making of wooden plates is a good project for a beginner. Timber used for this sort of purpose must be as thoroughly seasoned as possible and must definitely be kept indoors for a reasonable period of time before it is used, otherwise the finished plate will warp and twist.

Using Green Timber

One further aspect of the turning of bowls which must be dealt with before we leave the subject is the use of bowl blanks which are wet, or 'green'.

Elm is very much the favourite for this sort of work, and it is extremely sad but nevertheless true that there are ample supplies of wet elm at this time due to the ravages of Dutch elm disease. Trees which have been afflicted, unless they have been allowed to stand too long, will yield timber which is perfectly usable in every respect.

Timbers other than elm can also be used for green turning, and the woodturner should experiment in order to establish some kind of reference. Assuming that a turner has purchased a number of freshly sawn elm planks, these should be converted into squares suitable for the production of discs for bowl-turning, and great care must be taken to see that these green squares of timber do not, in fact, dry out. If they do, very serious splitting will occur on the end grain. The best way to prevent this sort of thing from happening is to place the squares in some suitable receptacle such as a tea chest with a layer of damp shavings at the bottom. A layer of squares is placed upon the wet shavings, further shavings are put in to cover them, another layer of squares is put in, followed by more wet shavings, and so on until the container is full.

The squares should not be bandsawn into discs until they are required for turning, when they should be taken one at a time to the bandsaw and thence to the lathe. The turning of a bowl from green timber follows the same procedure outlined for normal bowl-turning, except that it is a great deal more messy. As the disc rotates on the lathe centrifugal force will drive the sap to the surface, where it will be flung in all directions. It will run in a river down the flute of the gouge, soak the turner, and drip from the walls of the workshop. On the credit side, green timber turns very easily indeed with a sharp gouge, and the inside of a bowl will end up on the floor as a series of very long shavings.

No attempt should be made to finish a bowl in one session from green timber, unless there is a particular requirement for a grotesque fruit or salad bowl. If the turning is taken to completion the bowl is unlikely to split, provided no heartwood is present in the disc, but it will certainly distort very badly indeed as it dries out. Some rather attractive bowls have resulted from this sort of situation, usually by accident.

The correct procedure is to shape the outside of the bowl and then take out about a third of the waste from the inside, leaving the 'wall' of the bowl about $1\frac{1}{2}$ to 2 inches in thickness. A number of blanks can be treated in this way and then placed under a bench well out of direct sunlight with free circulation of air. They should be left in this position for three or four weeks. At the end of this time they can be taken back to the lathe, the bases having first been planed so they are absolutely flat, since considerable distortion is likely to have occurred. They will be fixed one by one to the faceplate and the turning taken a stage further, now leaving the 'wall' of the bowl $\frac{3}{4}$ to 1 inch thick. When this has been done, they can be hung up across a garage or in the workshop, out of direct sunlight, in a piece of old fruit netting. They should remain suspended in this way, so that the air can circulate freely around them, for several more weeks.

The experienced turner will be able to

determine by the weight of the blank when it is ready for its final turning, but this is difficult for an inexperienced worker, who must adopt a trial-and-error method. When the final turning is done, bringing the bowl to completion, sealer should be used generously, as many as five or six coats. When I make bowls by this method I finish them off with at least two coats of Rustins plastic coating, which I find gives them an excellent and extremely durable finish and inhibits any further drying which might cause distortion. Beautiful bowls can be made in this way from timber which is extremely inexpensive, since one does not have to pay for the expensive process of seasoning.

LAMPS AND CANDLEHOLDERS

Among amateur woodturners table lamps undoubtedly rank next to bowls in popularity. Standard lamps are also well liked, but they require rather large quantities of timber, which is nowadays an expensive item. The turning of a table lamp is a straightforward piece of spindle-turning, and in cases where the base of the lamp is made as a separate article they make a very good combination of spindle and faceplate work.

In making either table or standard lamps the turner should not lose sight of the functional aspects of the object being constructed. I refer to the large number of lamps which I have seen in my lifetime whose design has been so poor that they would fall over at the slightest provocation. It is, of course, quite possible to make a table lamp complete with base from one piece of wood, but since the base must have a width which will give stability to the lamp, it is normally necessary to make the base as a separate item to conserve timber.

Lamps designed for bedside use or as reading lamps are often no more than 5 or 6 inches

Plate 14. Two pairs of candlesticks. Accuracy in copy turning is absolutely essential in such jobs.

high, and if they are 3 or 4 inches in diameter they will have sufficient stability without a separate base. Table lamps as such are generally between 9 and 12 inches in height and therefore will need a base which will render them stable.

Any worker who is no longer greatly concerned about the application of the tools to the wood and the grinding of them, or who has achieved a reasonable degree of competence as a spindle turner, will have very little trouble with the turning of lamps. There are, however, various points relating to the making of table or standard lamps which should be mentioned, and a few words on the subject of wall light fittings will not be out of place.

It is surprising how frequently amateur designs for lamps overlook the vital aspect of stability. There is no specific formula which can be used to relate the size of a table lamp base to a stem of given dimensions, but this is largely a matter of common sense, and the turner will in a very short time be able to recognize an overall lamp shape which is both pleasing to the eye and functional.

Stems for table lamps are turned between centres with the top of the project at the tailstock end. This is usual, but the process can be reversed if required. When a lamp is drilled for the flex after it has been turned it is important that the turning should be done as described, since the boring is done from the tailstock end and the hole should be central. If any error is present in the drilling it will be evident at the base of the stem where it joins the lamp base itself, and it will be hidden in the finished job.

Drilling of this kind is discussed in chapter 7, so there is no need to deal with the details of it here. It should be noted, however, that most table lamp or standard lamp work is best approached by preparing a reasonable number of blanks and drilling these through while they are still in their square form, rather than adopting the procedure of turning a lamp and drilling it afterwards. The reasons for this are fairly obvious to anyone accustomed to wood-turning, but they are often overlooked by beginners.

Firstly, it must be expected that, whilst the drilling process is very simple and straight-forward and almost invariably presents no problems, there will still be occasions from time to time when things go wrong. This being so, if the drilling of a square piece of wood has not been successful it can be dis-carded without undue waste of time, and in most cases such a piece of timber can be utilized for some other purpose at a later date. Secondly, once the project has been com-pleted and brought to a high standard of finish, it is patently unwise for it to be sub-jected to a further process such as drilling in which it may be damaged.

The finish of such an item will certainly not be improved by the general handling and rigours of the drilling procedure, and if the workpiece is dropped it is almost certain to strike some sharp part of the machine, thus forming a dent in the surface which may be impossible to eradicate without returning it to the lathe and cutting the surface again.

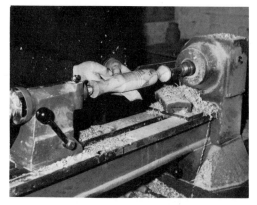

Plate 15. Stem of a yew table lamp being sanded with fine paper. Note how the abrasive material is held, and that the toolrest holder has been swung clear.

In the construction of lamps which have separate bases, the round tenon system is almost invariably employed. This simply means that a short pin is formed at the bottom of the stem and a recess made at the centre of the base to accept the pin as a close fit. This system, coupled with the tremendously strong adhesives which are now available, gives great strength to the finished project. The bottom of the lamp stem itself, which fits down onto the central area of the base, should be made slightly concave by cutting across the end grain with the point of a sharp skew chisel. This will ensure that there is contact between stem and base around the outside edge. If this point is overlooked there is a possibility of a slight gap, and little points like this can take the edge off otherwise good work.

Any lamp, large or small, must obviously be fitted with a bulb holder. In the past these were made of brass, and in fact this type is still available. It must be noted, however, that if a metal bulb holder is used it is necessary for the cable to be of the three-cored variety, which includes an earth lead. This earth lead must be securely connected to the bulb holder and to the earth pin of the plug. The plastic bulb holder, usually incorporating a switch, is now far more commonly used, and there is no necessity for this to be earthed since it is manufactured from a material which is an insulator.

It is a great pity for the results of long effort to be spoilt by lack of attention to details, and some thought should be given to the type of connector used to join the bulb holder to the stem. Three types of connector exist, and by far the best of these is a short brass cylinder. Part of its length carries a coarse thread which is screwed into the wooden stem, and the remainder is of a slightly larger diameter and is threaded at 26 TPI to accept the bulb holder. Once this type of connector has been correctly fitted to a lamp it is virtually impossible for it to be torn from the wood, even if the lamp should suffer a severe fall.

Beginners in woodturning are often advised to drill through their table lamp stems with a $\frac{5}{16}$-inch diameter auger and then to force the brass connector to cut its own thread in the wood by twisting it in with the tang of a file, using a rotary motion. This system does work, but I have always preferred to run a $\frac{3}{8}$-inch Whitworth tap into the hole in the wood, which provides the correct thread internally and enables the brass connector to be screwed in neatly by hand without risk of damage.

The other two types of connector are not, in my opinion, as useful to the woodturner. One of these consists of a brass tube about $\frac{3}{4}$ inch long which is threaded all along its length at 26 TPI. A thread as fine as this is not suitable for connecting the metal to the wood; therefore it is necessary to drill a short hole to accept the connector and to fix it in place with a strong adhesive. This type of connector is mainly used on lamps manufactured from ceramic materials.

There is perhaps a case for the use of the third type of brass connector, which if properly fitted can look very attractive. This type is best described as a flat brass disc about the size of a two-pence piece, on one side of which is centrally mounted a short length of tubular brass which carries a thread to fit the bulb holder. Three holes are provided in the brass plate for fixing screws, which should, of course, also be brass. These holes are very small, and the screws which are used to fit the disc to the lamp stem do not provide a very firm grip in the end grain of the wood. In addition, a connector of this type which is simply screwed to the surface of the top of the lamp does not look attractive.

In order to make a first class job of the fitting, it is necessary to recess the top of the lamp carefully so that the brass disc will fit exactly into the recess and be flush with the surface of the wood. In view of the inadequate support provided by the tiny brass screws, it is as well to smear the inside of the recess with a strong two-part adhesive such as Araldite. In deciding between the use of the connector first described and the flat disc type, one has to consider whether to make a feature of the brass connector or to hide it altogether. The disc type when properly fitted is very attractive, and I invariably use this on expensive lamps. The cylindrical version first discussed is invisible when in position with the bulb holder connected to it.

There is little more to be said about lamp stems as such. They are straightforward pieces of spindle-turning, and if the shape is not too complex projects of this kind should be well within the capabilities of any reasonably competent turner.

Lamp Bases

Since the turning of a base for a table lamp is a quick and simple process, it is quite possible that insufficient thought may be given to the matter. A base must be made with a diameter and thickness in proportion to the stem. Those unaccustomed to designing shapes for jobs like this should always bear in mind that, to the user, a table lamp consists of a base, a stem, a bulb holder, bulb and shade. Woodturners frequently overlook the fact that the lamp is not complete without its shade. They should try to picture the finished article with a shade in place. It is a matter of proportion, and fortunately it will cease to be a problem after a few lamps have been made.

The prime prerequisite in a lamp base, having accepted that its proportions should fit the overall design, is that it must provide adequate stability. In the case of a table lamp this is largely a matter of giving the base sufficient diameter, but with a standard lamp it is also necessary for the base to be heavy. This requirement is frequently dealt with by inserting lead weights into the bottom of the base after turning.

The making of a lamp base is, of course, disc turning in a very simple form, and the deep-fluted gouge used in bowl-turning is the tool for the job. Small lamp bases can be turned quite satisfactorily on a 1½-inch woodscrew chuck, to which they are attached by means of the one central screw. This screw is, however, going into face grain, as distinct from the end grain situation which pertains to the turning of an egg cup, and if the gauge of screw used is over 14 there should be no trouble.

In the case of larger bases, of course, the 2½-inch chuck will be used, giving greater support by means of its increased diameter and the use of extra screws. When the disc has been fitted to the chuck and mounted in the lathe, it is reduced to the required diameter by means of a gouge, the handle of which must be kept as low as possible to avoid the chance of a dig in. The shaping of the base can, in most cases, be done with the same tool, which must of course be sharp, but if the base has

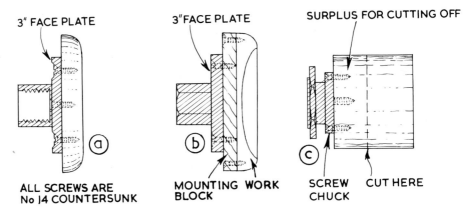

Figure 84. (a) In the turning of discs for lamp bases and similar items, direct screwing to a woodscrew chuck or small faceplate is acceptable, provided that screw penetration is not sufficient to impede the free movement of the tool. (b) Mounting by the method shown here enables screws to pass through the waste piece of wood into the thicker areas, thus leaving the thinner parts free from screws. (c) Many small jobs can be turned with a waste section next to the chuck, the finished item being separated from this by means of a parting-tool cut.

complicated detail the turner may be forced to use scraping techniques in places. This must be avoided if possible in view of the inferior surface which will inevitably result.

A flat area must, of course, be left at the centre of the base, regardless of the details of the design in other respects, in order to accept the bottom of the lamp stem. If this point is overlooked and the upper surface of the base is given some curvature, there will inevitably be a gap around the bottom of the lamp stem after it is fitted.

Some people advise cutting a pin of specific size on the lamp stem so that a drill may be used to form the recess in the base. This system, however, involves operations which could quite easily be avoided, and I have always found it preferable to cut a pin on the stem without bothering too much about its exact size.

The fit of such a pin into the base is best effected by means of the Columbus pattern vernier caliper. The version of this tool used by woodturners is similar in shape to that used by engineers, but whereas the woodworkers' vernier caliper is relatively inexpensive the engineering pattern may cost ten times as much. This type of caliper has parallel jaws which can be opened and closed by the movement of a small wheel. There are parallel jaws on both sides of the tool, and if the pin is measured with the jaws designed for outside measurement the other pair of jaws can be used to mark on the disc of the base the exact areas to be recessed.

When the turning of the base has reached this stage, the toolrest is placed in position across the face of the work, fractionally below centre, and the jaws of the tool are applied to the wood. It is essential that the toolrest be close up to the disc, to avoid any danger of the tool being tipped forward and jammed between the rest and the work, and that the vernier caliper be firmly in contact with the toolrest throughout the operation. With a little practice it is possible to get the marking process right almost every time, but it will be appreciated that if the jaws do not contact the work at points equidistant from the centre the result will be two concentric rings on the wood instead of one. If this occurs, it is only necessary to repeat the marking process, this time ensuring that the points of the jaws touch the wood midway between the two previously marked lines.

The cutting of the recess can most easily be accomplished by means of a sharp parting tool held in a roughly horizontal position. There is no alternative to holding the tool in this manner even though the result is a scrape rather than a cut, but with a recess of this nature, where another piece of wood is to be glued in place, the rough finish is preferable to a smooth one.

It is necessary to exercise caution in cutting a recess of this kind, and the presence of the holding screw or screws must be borne very much in mind. If it is necessary to make a recess, the depth of which will involve the exposure of the screw point, a small pin of wood about $\frac{3}{8}$ inch in diameter is left uncut at the centre, and is broken off when the job has been completed and removed from the lathe.

Beginners are frequently worried by the possibility of tools contacting holding screws, visualizing a situation where the tool is wrenched from their hands. This, in fact, is extremely unlikely. In the case of a workpiece held by a single screw, which is rotating very slowly relative to the speed of the edge of the disc itself, the only results of contact between the screw and the tool will be a blunting of the tool edge and damage to the thread of the screw. The edge of the tool can quickly be reinstated by application to the grindstone, and the centre screw of a properly made wood-screw chuck can easily be removed and replaced. If contact occurs between the tool edge and a number of screw points which are set at a distance from the centre of the chuck, a rattling sound will be heard, and the edge of the tool will be found to have suffered minor damage. The idea is, or course, to avoid this sort of occurrence, but from time to time such instances are bound to arise.

A further point in relation to the turning of bases for lamps is that provision must be made for the electric flex. This normally passes through a hole drilled horizontally in the base connecting with a hole at the centre which has been drilled vertically. An alternative sometimes adopted is the cutting of a groove running radially on the underside of the base, the flex passing through this groove and being held in position by a strip of wood which has been cut to fit the groove exactly, glued into position, and sanded flush.

The drilling of a radial hole from the edge of the base through to its centre is a simple process if tackled the right way. Those with considerable experience find it quite simple to mount a Jacobs chuck in the headstock of the lathe, fitting a drill of suitable size to the chuck, and to push the disc onto the rotating drill, achieving the successful drilling of the hole entirely by eye. This, however, is by no means as easy as it sounds, and fortunately there is a procedure which guarantees complete success.

Many lathes have available as an optional extra a flat table which can be attached to the saddle or the toolrest holder. If such a table is not available, an average woodturner can manufacture one from a piece of fairly thick plywood or blockboard and a length of steel pipe, which can be attached to the table itself by means of a pipe flange connector.

The idea is to set up the Jacobs chuck in the headstock complete with drill bit and to position the table so that it passes under the drill bit at a height which will give the correct location for the hole in the base. With the lathe

running, the base can be placed flat on the table and pushed slowly forward until the point of the drill bit reaches the centre. This process is safe and extremely simple, but like most other operations in woodturning and, indeed, in general woodwork it is as well to prepare a batch of bases, set up the lathe table and drill the whole batch at one setting. It is best to drill holes of this kind across the grain of the wood rather than into the end grain. If the drilling is done in this way the cutter operates more efficiently and the base is not unduly weakened.

Standard Lamps

The turning of a standard lamp is, or course, basically very similar to that of a table lamp, but certain problems exist which are peculiar to the standard lamp and must be taken into consideration.

Most lathes available to the home woodturner are designed to accept about 30 inches between centres, though this can sometimes be increased by the manufacturer at little extra cost if so desired. Considerations of space in the workshop, coupled with the fact that long workpieces are difficult for anyone but a very competent turner, means that very few lathes with extra-length beds are sold.

The overall height of an average standard lamp is approximately 5 feet including its base, and the normal approach is to manufacture the stem of the lamp in two sections, each of which will fit a standard lathe bed. The two sections are subsequently connected by the round tenon system. A pin about $1\frac{1}{2}$ inches in length is turned on the end of one section to fit into a hole of suitable dimensions drilled in the end of the other section prior to turning. If such a joint is assembled with a epoxy adhesive such as Aerolite, the finished lamp will be quite as strong as if it had been made from one length of timber. It is, of course, necessary to position the joint where there is a change in the design, so that, if the grain in the two pieces of wood is carefully matched, the joint itself becomes extremely difficult to detect.

The turning of long workpieces like this will be greatly facilitated by the provision of a toolrest which runs the full length of the work. Where long slow curves have to be produced, for example, the repositioning of the toolrest partway through the cut makes the production of a smooth continuous curve very difficult.

A query which arises very frequently among my students and other turners who contact me for advice is how to deal with the problem of turning thin workpieces. Before any comment can be made on this, it is necessary to realize that the word 'thin' is strictly relative. In other words, a workpiece which is 4 inches long and 2 inches in diameter can be classified as thick, whereas a workpiece 2 feet long and 2 inches in diameter is thin as far as the turner is concerned.

Thickness is thus relative to length, and the same problems which might be experienced on a workpiece $\frac{3}{4}$ inch in diameter and 7 inches long are likely to be found in the turning of a section of a standard lamp 30 inches in length and perhaps averaging 2 inches in diameter. The major problem is that of 'ribbing', which is caused by the work bending slightly under the pressure of the tool. This produces spiral markings on the timber which are not easy to remove once they have been allowed to form.

To most people, the obvious answer to this lies in the use of some form of lathe steady, a device manufactured either by the maker of the lathe or by the turner, which can be fitted to the bed of the lathe to give support to a long workpiece. The idea sounds very good, but the perfect lathe steady has yet to be invented, and in general such devices are not entirely satisfactory since most of them create un-

wanted marks on the wood, and all of them, once fitted, are very much in the way.

With a certain amount of practice, which should be undertaken on scrap timber rather than on actual projects, it is possible to develop the necessary skill to support the timber by keeping one hand around the back of the work whilst manipulating the gouge or chisel with the other. It is only necessary to counter the pressure of the tool by means of pressure from the hand, and provided that the pressure of the tool against the work is light, this can be done without danger of any kind and is extremely effective. The great advantage of this system is that the hand supporting the timber will move along it at the same rate as the tool, so that the point of support remains close to the point at which the tool is operating throughout the cut. This is not the

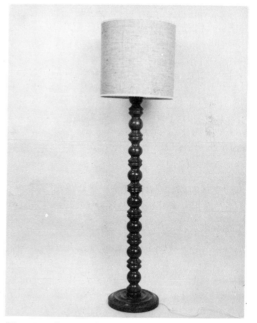

Plate 16. An attractive standard lamp. It is an easy matter to mask the join on a job like this, if the job is done in two halves.

case if a lathe steady is used, as this gives maximum support only in the areas immediately adjacent to it.

Bases for standard lamps are frequently quite large and heavy. This is desirable in view of the requirement for stability, and provided the lathe can be run at a reasonable speed relative to the size of the workpiece no real difficulties should be experienced. In most respects the turning of a large base is very similar to that of a small one, except that for reasons of economy or availability of suitable timber large bases may need to be built up from several pieces of wood. If two or three planks of wood are edge-jointed to form a square from which a disc can be cut for the turning of a base, a straightforward edge-to-edge glue joint can be used, but this does not in my view represent the best method, as strength is important in the finished job.

If a little more trouble is taken, a very strong structure can be produced by splining the joints with strips of plywood. This involves cutting slots, say, $\frac{1}{2}$ inch deep in the edges to be joined, which stop short of the ends of the timber by 1 inch or so and must not run right through to the ends, because this would render the plywood strips visible in the finished project. Strips of plywood can be cut to fit in these grooves, and if the assembly is done in this manner it will be very strong indeed.

The design of a base for a standard lamp should allow for a reasonably large diameter and as much thickness as is compatible with the shape and diameter of the stem. This in itself will give reasonable weight, keeping the centre of gravity of the finished lamp low. If there is any doubt as to whether the base is in fact heavy enough to be functional, a groove can be turned in the bottom of the base, of suitable dimensions to accept a length of lead pipe, which can be held in place by means of small nails or tacks. The presence of this pip-

ing will be concealed, of course, by the green baize or other material covering the bottom of the job.

In making a standard lamp of a specific height some difficulty may be experienced because the length required for the sections of the stem exceeds the available distance between centres. This problem is quite easily resolved by turning up three or four small feet which are screwed to the bottom of the lamp base, raising it clear of the floor by an inch or two.

The necessity for drilling holes of the length required in such workpieces is daunting to a beginner, but the process is relatively simple and is covered in chapter 7. Those who do not have the necessary facilities for drilling holes of this length do have an alternative, which will serve until they acquire the necessary equipment. Assuming no long-hole boring kit is available, provision can be made for the passage of the flex in the following manner. Two square lengths of timber from which the sections of the lamp stem are to be turned are cut exactly in half along their length by means of a circular saw. Grooves about $\frac{1}{4}$ inch wide by $\frac{1}{8}$ inch deep are then cut in the faces of the timber which have been exposed, and the two pieces are glued and clamped together. If the grooves are taken through the full length of the timber it will be necessary to plug the holes in the ends of the glued-up squares in order to facilitate centring in the lathe. An alternative is to start and finish the grooves an inch or so short of the ends of the wood, and to drill in from each end after the turning is complete. The unfortunate aspect of this system is that, even if the greatest possible care is taken, the joint will be fairly obvious in the finished lamp.

Wall Light Fittings

In dealing with the making of matched pairs of wall light fittings we come to the system

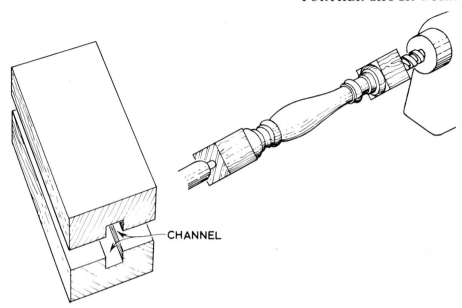

CHANNEL

Figure 85. If no suitable tool is available for drilling through table or standard lamps to take the electric cable, square blanks can be constructed by grooving two rectangular pieces of timber as shown. This method is not strongly recommended as the join is almost invariably obvious.

known as split turning, which is also useful in various other projects. A pair of objects made by the split turning method will be identical in every respect, regardless of the skill of the turner. If it is necessary to make two pairs, then considerable skill is needed to ensure that both pairs are exactly alike. The making of a pair of wall light fittings, perhaps to fit either side of a fireplace, is by no means difficult and represents a very interesting project.

Split turning is simple enough in itself, but there are two approaches which should be explained. In situations where the back of the finished project is of no great importance, the two pieces of material which make up a blank can be glued together with a piece of blotting paper or thick brown paper interposed. The removal of the resulting glue and paper mess is always something of a problem, but since

the back of the fitting is to be fixed against the wall it can in this case be ignored. In other projects, where the back of the finished turning does have significance, it is necessary either to clean off all the glue and paper or to approach the turning by a different method.

The basic idean of split turning is to form a square blank for turning between centres from two rectangular pieces of wood, so that when the turning is completed these two pieces can be separated. If the workpiece is not too long the rectangular stock can be an inch or two longer than the overall length of the finished project, so providing about an inch of waste material at each end through which screws can be driven to hold the job securely while it is turned.

This means that the rectangular stock must be accurately planed before it is assembled into a square, so producing very smooth surfaces. The turning is carried out in the normal manner, taking the job down to a diameter of about $\frac{1}{4}$ inch at the ends, and after removal from the lathe the waste pieces can be carefully cut away. This system is not advisable for use on long projects, since the two sections of the blank will tend to separate at the centre when the lathe is in motion due to centrifugal force.

It might seem that a simpler method would be to do the turning from a solid blank and to cut this in half along the centre line afterwards. However, this is by no means as effective as it sounds, since if a circular saw is used for the purpose, there is difficulty, and some danger, in holding the workpiece satisfactorily while it is sawn. If a bandsaw is employed, the blade will tend to follow the grain of the wood to some extent, giving uneven surfaces. One must also remember that if the process of sawing the job into two exactly equal parts does not go smoothly the job may well be ruined, and the time spent in turning it will have been wasted.

The making of a pair of wall light fittings is described below. The first part of the operation is the manufacture of the two main parts, which fit against the wall. Often a shape which suits a table lamp will work well for wall light fittings. The blank from which these two main parts are to be turned should be assembled with care from exactly rectangular stock, so that the blank itself forms a perfect square. Two lengths can be cut from this to provide a pair of blanks. These will be turned by normal spindle-turning methods and finished in exactly the same way as other forms of spindle-turning.

When the turning has been completed the workpiece is taken from the lathe, the waste sections if any are removed, and the two halves of the project are separated. If the glue-and-paper method of assembly has been used, the two pieces can be split apart by means of an old chisel placed exactly along the line of the joint and given a sharp tap with a mallet.

Wall light fittings normally have two arms projecting from them which carry small cups into which the bulb holders will be fitted. These arms project from the backing piece at a set angle, and obviously the angle of the two

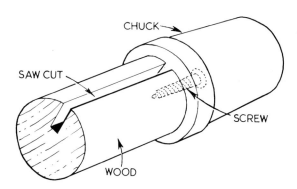

Figure 86. Bobbin sander. A cylinder of wood is turned to a suitable diameter and a saw cut is made laterally along it. Abrasive paper can be wrapped around the cylinder, its ends tucked into the saw cut and secured by driving in a strip of scrap timber.

arms must be the same. In order to fit the arms to the backing piece, it will be necessary to drill two holes, and the greatest possible accuracy is required in the process. It is not necessary for the angle chosen to be precise, but it is essential that it be the same for both arms. The method normally adopted by woodturners not in possession of a drilling machine is to make a cradle from scrap timber to which the workpiece can be secured, so that it is presented at the correct angle to a drill which rotates in the headstock. The auxiliary table of the lathe is used to support the cradle, and with the wood in position the table is advanced to the rotating cutter. In order to ensure that the two holes are drilled to exactly the same depth, some form of stop can be fitted to the lathe bed, so that the forward movement of the table is arrested at the same point for each hole.

The turning of the arms and the cups, if these are to be turned, is quite straightforward and will be done by methods already described. In many cases, however, the arms and cups are not turned but formed from square stock, in which case the arms may have to be let into the main sections by taking out square mortises with a chisel.

An 'antique' effect is often given to arms of this kind, and this is best produced with a small sander. The type of sander used for such an operation can be made in the workshop by the woodturner himself, and it is commonly known as a bobbin sander. This is made by turning up a short cylinder of wood on a small woodscrew chuck, its length not exceeding 3 inches and its diameter being such as to suit the job for which it is intended. When the cylinder has been turned a saw cut is made along its length or a groove can be taken out with a carving tool.

A piece of abrasive paper can now be wrapped around the cylinder and its ends tucked into the slot. If a small strip of soft-wood is cut to fit and tapped firmly into the slot, it will secure the abrasive paper, tightening it around the sander at the same time, and this system is preferable to that of gluing the paper to the cylinder. It is a simple matter to remove a worn piece of abrasive paper and replace it with a fresh one. With a little practice on scrap wood, the turner will find that it is very easy to produce the effect desired by applying the square arms for the wall light fittings to the rotating bobbin sander.

Sanders of this kind should not be discarded after use but kept in a box so that a collection in various diameters is built up. These will be found extremely useful in the course of a great many woodworking operations. A typical example is the fitting of legs to the centre pillar of a tripod table. The legs themselves will have square faces, which have to be fitted against the cylindrical pillar. If the bobbin sander is the same diameter as the pillar and the ends of the legs are applied to this exactly on the centre line, a curvature which matches that of the pillar will be produced and the legs will fit neatly.

The arms of a wall light fitting can be drilled through to take the flex, but a more common method is to run a groove along the upper surface of each arm, and since the unit itself is normally secured to the wall above eye level the flex will not be visible.

Candle Holders

Not a great deal needs to be said about the actual turning of candle holders and candlesticks, since the turning techniques involved have already been discussed in the earlier chapters. A general discussion on the subject may, however, be valuable.

The accepted difference between a candlestick and a candle holder lies in the fact that a candlestick is usually fairly thin and has a base turned from a disc. It is in some respects a very similar proposition to the turning of a table lamp. Candlesticks as such were at one time extremely popular, but they seem to some degree to have lost favour.

A candle holder, on the other hand is usually shorter and of greater diameter, and in most instances it does not have a separate base. The candle holder is nowadays used mainly for large-diameter decorative candles, which have gained popularity in recent years and which can quite easily be made at home. Kits for this purpose are available from craft suppliers.

Since the procedure for the turning of candlesticks which have a base turned from a separate blank follows so closely the procedure used for the turning of a lamp, there is little to be said on the subject other than to point out that it is essential to drill the hole which is to take the candle before the turning is undertaken. When this hole has been drilled a small wooden block is placed in it to facilitate centring the job in the lathe, and from that point on the project can be treated as a piece of normal spindle-turning.

In the making of candle holders, the wood-turner can indulge creative fantasy to the limit, there being no right or wrong apart from the production of a satisfactory finish on the wood. Candle holders can be turned from discs, so that they are in effect small trays with a recess at the centre to accept the candle, but they are more commonly produced from short lengths of wood in which the grain runs parallel to the bed of the lathe. This type of work is usually carried out on the larger of the woodscrew chucks, using as many screws to support the workpiece as is possible. This depends on the number of holes provided in the chuck by the manufacturer.

If a boring bit of suitable size is available, this can be used in the tailstock to produce the hole for the candle by the method described in chapter 7. Home-made candles, however, tend to come in a very wide range of sizes, and it

may well be preferable to use the vernier caliper in the manner described for the fitting of a lamp stem to its base, measuring the candle diameter and transferring this dimension to the end of the rotating blank prior to the excavation of the recess.

The recess is best cut with a parting tool, initially making a cut just inside the marked line to roughly the required depth and working towards the centre with successive cuts. The recess can be brought to exact size by trimming carefully with the parting tool, and it should receive a thorough sanding, since the action of the parting tool in a cut of this nature is a scraping one and the surface produced will be fairly rough.

When the recess has been brought to a satisfactory size and condition, the remainder of the turning can be carried out. If the projection of the material from the face of the chuck is likely to cause any problems during this stage of the turning, a wooden plug can be inserted in the candle recess and the tailstock can be brought up to give light support.

The blank is brought to a cylinder with a sharp roughing gouge, and the shaping of the design is carried out by means of gouges and chisels in the normal manner. Since the turning of candle holders is so frequently allied to the home manufacture of candles, and there is considerable scope for imagination in the design of both, this aspect of woodturning is very popular among beginners, who find the end product acceptable as a gift and easy to sell. The beauty of this is that a candle holder can be turned to suit a candle of specific size, shape and colour using timber which seems to lend itself to the project. This is more satisfactory than buying suitable candle holders in a shop.

COPY TURNING

While some people start their woodturning

careers by making a table or a chair, which involves the production of four identical legs and perhaps a number of stretchers or rails which are to the same pattern, the recommended approach is rather different. Jumping in at the deep end by making something which requires copy turning is perhaps not a good idea. The majority of beginners start their woodturning careers by learning as much as possible about the lathe and its ancillary equipment and studying the methods by which the tools are sharpened and manipulated in order to produce good surfaces and high-quality work. This in itself can take quite a considerable time, and it is probably fair to say that anyone who cannot produce a specific shape in a reasonable time, complete with a good surface finish, is not yet ready to undertake copy turning.

The turner whose intentions are in any way commercial will find that it is quite essential to understand copy turning and to be able to produce within a reasonable period of time articles which are, to all intents and purposes, identical. Those who set up as commercial woodturners often find that much of the work which comes to them is what others do not want because it is too difficult or involves the turning of workpieces too large or awkward for the average home turner.

An analysis of woodturners would undoubtedly reveal that a very small percentage were capable of good copy turning, a larger percentage were capable of some sort of copy turning, and an even larger percentage would have nothing to do with this work if they could possibly avoid it. This is a pity in many ways, but it is nevertheless encouraging

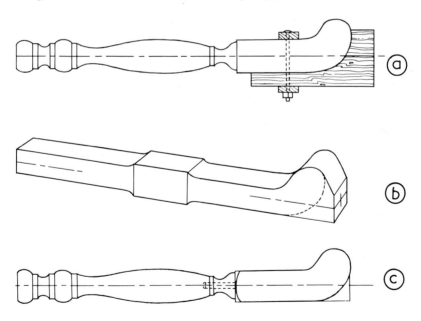

Figure 87. Methods of mounting chair legs for turning. (a) The leg has been bandsawn and mounted in a wooden clamp. (b) Leg partially bandsawn with some waste left in position to facilitate centring. (c) Leg made in two parts, these being joined by means of a wooden pin glued into a hole.

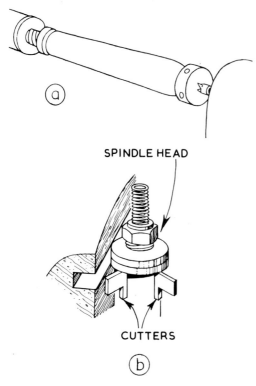

SPINDLE HEAD

CUTTERS

Figure 88. (a) Four identical table legs can be turned at once by glueing together four small square lengths of timber to form one large blank, with paper interposed between the glued joints. (b) Mortises for legs of this type can be cut after turning using a spindle moulder with a ring fence which runs along the material to prevent over-cutting.

from the point of view of the person starting out to make money with a lathe. Anyone prepared to work hard and master the finer points of this sort of work, can make a very good living. Antique dealers, in particular, are always on the lookout for woodturners who will take on the reproduction of parts of furniture from a pattern or even from a drawing.

The road to excellence in copy turning is a long and hard one, consisting mainly of practice, followed by more practice, followed by even more practice. Assuming a reasonable control of the tools and a thorough understanding of the machine and the material, however, there are certain points which can assist the would-be copy turner, and the most important of these is a logical approach.

Let us examine the fairly simple case of a pair of electric lamps, to be positioned in alcoves on either side of a fireplace. There is perhaps no requirement for a specific shape for these lamps, but they do need to be identical, or at least as nearly so as possible. The making of the first lamp is therefore a straightforward piece of spindle-turning, and the shape is a product of the imagination of the turner, who should have no difficulty in producing an attractive unit.

Having sailed confidently through the making of a lamp, in half an hour or so, one fact has to be faced. This is that the making of the second item may take three or four times as long. If great care is not exercised throughout the whole operation the workpiece may have to be rejected and the whole process started again from the beginning. It is easy enough to cut wood away from the workpiece, but it is quite impossible to replace it once it has been removed, so any attempt to hurry the job is likely to lead to disaster.

Basic equipment required for copy turning consists of calipers, dividers, a clearly marked ruler of some kind, and preferably a device which will allow the item being copied to be held in clear view of the turner at the rear of the lathe, so that comparisons can be made while the turning is in progress.

Many of the very old procedures which have been in use in the craft of woodturning for centuries are still extremely useful, and among these is the hinged-board system for comparison between patterns and work in progress. The idea is extremely simple, and like many simple ideas it works very well indeed. The equipment needed to make up a hinged-pattern board will be found lying around in most workshops, and little time is needed to prepare it.

This copy turning device consists of a hinged board which normally lies flat on the bench at the rear of the lathe, but which can be raised to a vertical or near-vertical position by pulling a string. The pattern or drawing is attached to the board, and when the string is pulled it is possible for the turner to sight across the workpiece against the outline of the drawing or pattern and immediately see where more timber needs to be removed – or where too much has been cut away.

The idea is simplicity itself; it consists of screwing to the bench a strip of softwood about the same length as the lathe itself. The board can be plywood or hardboard and should be equipped with clips or some system of rubber bands so that the pattern can be attached firmly. A string taken from the centre of the upper edge of the board through a hook

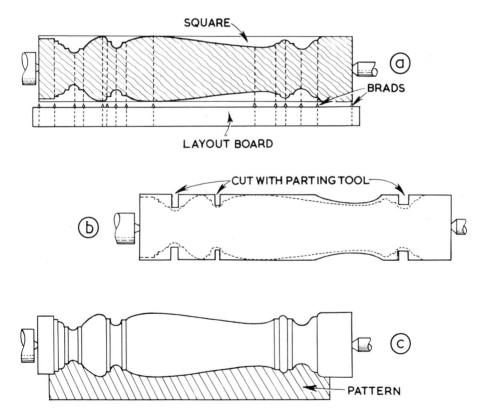

Figure 89. (a) Production system for furniture legs. Layout board with sharp-pointed brads is placed firmly on toolrest and applied to rotating workpieces. (b) Waste is removed by parting-tool and gouge cuts. (c) Finished job is checked against pattern which is made from plywood or hardboard.

in the ceiling completes this unsophisticated piece of equipment.

Many beginners buy a needle-type copying device, which they seem to imagine will remove all the problems connected with their copy turning. I have tried these several times but find them of very little assistance. They consist of a bar about an inch or so in width, through which are passed, at right angles, a large number of thin steel rods. These rods are held by friction and move under pressure. If the ends of these rods are placed against a piece of turning and pressure is applied, the rods move and the outline of the turning is produced on the edge of the copying device. Some workers like these devices, and if they are found helpful then there is no reason whatsoever why they should not be used. It should be noted, however, that quite considerable pressure is required to force the rods to take up the pattern of the turning, and if they are placed against the finished item they may damage its surface.

Assuming one lamp has been made, the production of the second can commence. A blank of timber of the same size as that used in the making of the first lamp is mounted in the lathe and reduced to a cylinder with a sharp roughing gouge. The diameter of this cylinder should be about $\frac{1}{16}$ inch greater than the maximum diameter required in the finished lamp.

Good copy turning consists in part of marking out with great accuracy the salient changes of design along the length of a workpiece and exercising care during the turning itself to make sure that the shaping of each section ends exactly where it should. The second ingredient of good copy turning is the maintenance of the exact diameter at any given point along the work.

The first point can be achieved with the aid of a good pair of dividers set from the pattern and used to transfer the measurement to the work. Calipers will take care of the second

point if the lathe is stopped frequently in order to check the diameters. It is advantageous for the turner to possess a number of pairs of calipers, for if a strong interest in copy turning develops, as many as ten or twelve pairs may be needed in order to produce work at an economic speed.

While a production run is in progress a separate pair of calipers is set to each of the diameters to which the turner is working. These should be laid out in a row so that once set there is no need for them to be moved. If only one pair of calipers is employed, a great deal of time will be wasted in resetting them for each diameter.

When the blank is reduced to a cylinder of the required size the marking out can be undertaken. In the case of a table lamp there is likely to be a pin at the left-hand end of the blank which has to be cut to fit into the base. This is marked out first either by measuring and marking with a pencil or by measuring with the dividers and then placing them firmly on the toolrest and applying them to the work, so that a line is drawn with the divider point. The lamp shape may consist of a foot, a stem, a curved centre portion, a neck and an upper section. If this is the case the sections should be marked out in that order.

The procedure for setting in the diameters along a piece of copy turning worries some beginners, who consider that it looks dangerous. Many things in life are dangerous to some degree, but I have used the method outlined here for more than thirty years without difficulty. It is not really the sort of operation for anyone who has not gained confidence in the handling of the tools, since it involves the use of a parting tool held in one hand while a pair of calipers, held in the other, is applied to the work from the rear of the job.

The danger most beginners imagine is that the wood may snatch at the calipers and fling them into the face of the operator. It should be remembered that it is not necessary to stand directly in line with the calipers. Those who still feel slightly nervous can wear one of the high-impact lightweight visors currently on the market, which may bolster their confidence.

The parting tool should be pushed forward onto the work, cutting until the calipers will slip over the workpiece. It is not necessary for the calipers to contact the workpiece at all until the end of the cut is near. Some people place them against the work at the commencement of the cut and keep them there until they slip over, but at least two-thirds of the cut can be completed before the calipers are placed against the wood. They should rest against it lightly, and care should be taken to see that the pressure against the rotating wood does not cause the calipers to open, thus rendering the work inaccurate. For this reason the type of caliper controlled by a transverse threaded bar and a knurled nut is preferable to that which is simply opened and closed by pushing and pulling. If the latter type is used, then the nut or rivet which holds the two sections of the caliper together must be kept very tight.

Most parting tools have a $\frac{1}{4}$-inch-wide blade while some are $\frac{3}{8}$ inch wide. In some forms of copy turning even the $\frac{1}{4}$-inch version may produce a cut which is too wide, and if this is the case the diamond-section type of parting tool should be employed. This is a thin-bladed tool, the section of which takes the form of a diamond in order to reduce friction while the tool is in the cut. It is not suitable for some parting tool work because in many cuts, being thin, it will flex and bend away from the wood. The type of cut described here is known as a sizing cut and should not be taken to the full depth. In other words, the diameter left when the cut is finished should be slightly greater than that required in the finished turning. This allows final gouge or chisel cuts to be used to clean up the finished surface.

When all the sizing cuts have been put in on a spindle-turning of this nature, certain areas will need to have bulk waste removed. In this particular instance these areas are between the parting tool cuts which mark out the length of the stem and the left-hand end of the turning and the length of the neck at the right-hand end. A common method of removing such bulk waste is to divide its length up with further parting tool cuts, leaving short blocks of waste about $\frac{3}{4}$ inch in length which can be dealt with by means of a $\frac{3}{4}$-inch square-ended chisel.

This is the only situation in woodturning in which I use a square-ended chisel. Use this chisel as a parting tool – in other words, place it completely flat on the toolrest with its edge square to the work in a position where it will be cutting as high up on the work as possible or at the point where, if it is pushed forward any further, there will be no cut. The cut is executed by pushing the tool forward, raising the handle very slightly at the same time, and the whole block of waste should be removed in the form of a shaving $\frac{3}{4}$ inch wide. This cut is extremely simple and requires little skill. The prime prerequisite is that the tool should be kept firmly in contact with the toolrest across its width throughout the cut.

This does seem to be a spectacular cut, and some writers even give detailed descriptions of the lengths of the shavings produced in such a cut and the time taken to produce them allied to the rpm of the machine. Such information is of purely academic interest to anyone who is trying to become a good woodturner, and fortunately most people grow out of such childish enthusiasms. Many people seem to fear that the chisel may suddenly kick violently during the cut, but there is no logical reason for supposing that this is likely, and in fact this type of cut can be executed by anyone capable of using a parting tool.

There is no valid reason why the waste

should not be removed simply by making a series of parting tool cuts, but in production work this takes up a lot more time. The reason for using a square-ended chisel, as distinct from a skew chisel, is simply that if the cut is deep the skew chisel, which has to be held at an angle to the work, will be able to proceed for only a relatively short distance before it fouls the wood.

When these operations have been completed the blank which is to form the second of the pair of table lamps will have a pin cut to fit the base and an obvious section which is to form the foot. Another two will form the short stem and the neck, a main portion will form the curved centre part of the lamp, and finally a section at the right-hand end will form the upper part of the job. With the major portions of waste removed it will now be possible to shape the foot of the lamp, the centre section, and then the top part using a $\frac{1}{2}$-inch spindle gouge, following this if possible with a smoothing cut from a very sharp skew chisel. This leaves the stem and the neck to be dealt with, and again a $\frac{1}{2}$-inch spindle gouge, working partly on its side so that it is cutting with the section of its edge which lies between the centre and the corner, should be used. This is the stage at which the turner should take the greatest possible care to ensure that too much wood is not cut away. The lathe should be stopped frequently in order to check diameters by means of the calipers.

In connection with copy turning one frequently comes across references to professional turners in days gone by, who would produce a leg for a Windsor chair, for example, in two and a half minutes. It should be remembered, however, that those who were employed day in and day out to make the same article, as was frequently the case, developed tremendous speed in the turning of that particular item. Had they been called upon suddenly to produce some alternative artefact, for example a chair leg of an entirely different pattern, the high speed they had developed would undoubtedly have dropped drastically.

In the same way the home woodturner who begins to enter the commercial market will find that the making of the second of a pair of table lamps is a fairly lengthy process, whereas in the turning of a hundred or so identical articles, such as balusters for a staircase or even skittles, after the first couple of dozen a speed will develop which may be amazing. If a regular habit is made of turning batches of a hundred or so items to a given pattern, it will not be long before the stage is reached where they can be produced without the aid of calipers, the turner's judgement having reached a point where they are superfluous.

My students always seem very interested in this question of copy turning and usually want to know if there is some magical system which will render the process easy. The answer to this is that there is not, although there are certain types of lathe still in existence which were designed for copying. I am not referring here to the automatic 'lathe', which is a very expensive machine designed to produce large numbers of articles such as ladder rungs, handles for pickaxes or tapered legs for furniture. The type to which I do refer is no longer made but was once marketed as a copying lathe. It worked on the principle of a lathe in the sense that the wood was mounted between centres and rotated under some form of power. Manual turning methods were not used, however, and the shaping of the workpiece was done by a series of specially shaped scraping cutters which were attached to a bar. By pulling on a lever the operator could cause these cutters to contact the work, and careful pressure on the bar would gradually cut the work to shape.

The process was one of scraping, and therefore the finished surface produced by a lathe of this nature was never particularly good. Considerable abrasive work was required to bring the object to a reasonable condition.

Furthermore, it was difficult or impossible to carry out work on a lathe of this type which had any degree of crispness to it, or sharp fine edges of any kind. Such edges would be

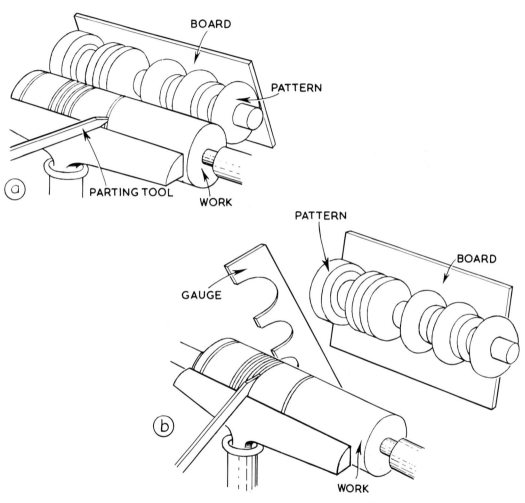

Figure 90. Aids to copy turning. (a) A pattern or drawing, attached to a board hinged to the bench top, will facilitate marking out for copying. The parting tool can be used initially to mark off salient changes in design. (b) A gauge board made from plywood or hardboard can be used for repeated checking of diameters as they are cut with the parting tool. As the shaping proceeds the turner can sight across the work at the pattern to check progress.

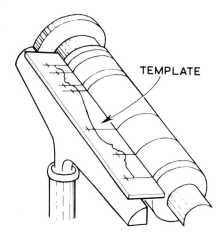

Figure 91. The use of the template in copy turning. The salient features of the design are marked off on to a cylinder which has been turned to a diameter fractionally greater than that required for the finished job.

damaged by the action of the scraping cutters, as is the case in spindle-turning if a hand-held scraper is used. On timbers of a very dense nature where the fibres of the wood are tightly packed, it is possible to produce a fairly wide range of items on a lathe of this kind, provided sufficient speed is available.

The making of the first of a pair of lamps is a relatively straightforward procedure, but it must be remembered that although no copying is in progress in the making of the first one, the curves and the straight sections must be either curved exactly as they should be or be perfectly straight. This means that some time must elapse before a beginner is capable of producing a really first-class example of a table lamp. At this stage the turning of the second of the pair may be quite beyond the capabilities of a novice since it requires not only the ability to turn a high-class table lamp but also the ability to remove exactly the right amount of wood while manipulating the tool in exactly the required way in order to produce the shape desired, with no bumps or hollows. The only answer to all this is continual practice, and anyone who has managed to learn to use gouges and chisel correctly need have no fear. If copy turning is practised as frequently as possible, skill will develop rapidly.

Some people find the system of sighting across the workpiece, against a pattern or drawing held on a hinged board, difficult and in some cases impossible. The vast majority of turners like the method, however, and once they have become used to it they may use it to the exclusion of all others. Those who do not find it suitable usually prefer to make up patterns or templates in hardboard or plywood. This is a time-consuming process, but it does suit large numbers of woodturners. The idea is to use the template to check the progress of the turning, and ideally when the job is finished the template will fit snugly against the workpiece, so that if a strong light is placed behind it no light will be visible at any point between it and the workpiece.

It should be obvious that the accuracy of the turning produced in such a manner will be entirely dependent on the accuracy with which the template was made in the first place, so no attempt should be made to hurry the making of templates, and they must be checked against pattern or drawing with a very critical eye before they are used.

A point worth noting is that items which are to be sold in sets, as for example egg cups, skittles or goblets, are best made in reasonable quantities before being finally selected to form sets. It is relatively easy to pick out six or eight items from several dozen which are sufficiently alike to defy detection of differences by the average eye, but it is much more difficult to make only six or eight objects to form a set which are equally accurate. The method I like to use is to have a reserve bank of several dozen or so articles, from which I select my sets, and to have frequent turning sessions during which I add to this reserve bank.

In the making of a pair of table lamps as discussed earlier the system of marking out the blank by means of a pencil or with a pair of dividers is quite adequate. Where large numbers of any given object are required, however, a great deal of time will be saved if a marking board is made up. This consists of a straight piece of wood with a number of small nails or panel pins driven into its edge. These are positioned to coincide with the points which are to be marked on the workpiece. The heads of the nails are cut off and the nails are then filed to sharp points. The use of such a marking board is a very simple matter. The toolrest is placed as close as possible to the work, so that there is no danger of the board being tipped forward and jammed between workpiece and toolrest. The board is then placed firmly on the toolrest and advanced to the work, so that each nail will scribe a line around the wood. Such marking boards should have their purpose clearly inscribed on them with pencil or ballpoint pen and can be kept for future use.

A marking board does away with one problem which besets some turners simply because they have not grasped a certain concept. It is not uncommon for inexperienced operators who are faced with the necessity to make, say, forty or fifty items, to proceed with great care and industry but to do the marking out of workpieces from any one of the previously completed turnings which happens to be conveniently to hand. The use of workpieces picked at random from a pile for marking out further blanks is not a very sensible system, since it leads to inaccuracy. The easiest method is to keep one workpiece on the lathe bench as a master pattern from which the marking out of all subsequent blanks will be done. This prevents cumulative error.

BUILT-UP TURNING

Built-up turning is a highly fascinating aspect of the woodturner's craft. Many woodturners, myself included, are not particularly enamoured of turnings formed from varieties of timbers. These can look extremely attractive, however, and many people seem to like them. The trick is to make things the customer will like, and for some reason people who have no knowledge of woodturning tend to regard a completed piece of built-up work as an example of tremendous skill.

The skill called for in projects of this nature, however, is not really a matter of woodturning know-how. Once a blank has been satisfactorily built up it may be regarded to all intents and purposes as a solid blank, and the woodturning method used is the same as for normal turnings. What is required is not so much a high degree of skill as a high degree of accuracy in the preparation and assembly of the materials which form built-up blanks. There is no room whatsoever for errors of any kind, which may well be extremely dangerous and will certainly result in a poor-quality piece of work, since the glue lines will be thick and in some cases there may be gaps which have to be filled with some form of stopper.

Unfortunately, even in this manual, which is larger than the average book on the subject of woodturning, there is not sufficient space to cover the entire subject of built-up turning as I would have liked. A complete book could be written on this subject – and in fact I am preparing one at the moment. However, the main points and features which relate to the most common forms of built-up work are covered here.

References are made in this section to built-up turning, laminated blanks, wedge-sectioned constructions, post-blocked turnings and so on. This aspect of the craft is wide open to the ingenious woodturner, who would

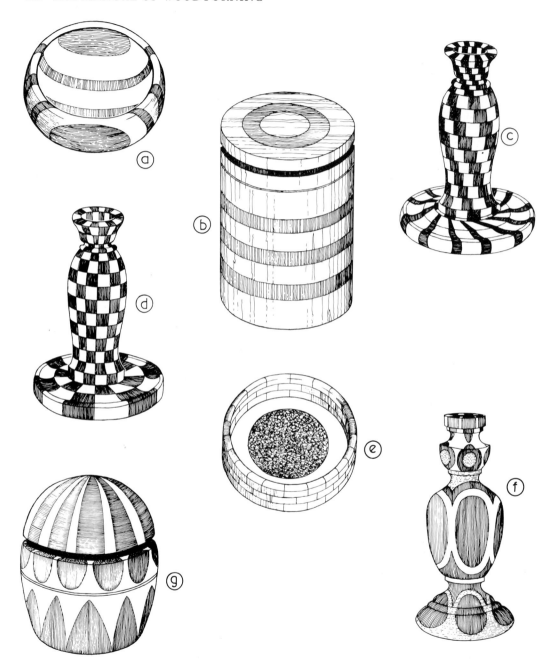

be well advised not to follow slavishly along the lines already laid down. Whole lifetimes have been devoted to various forms of built-up and laminated turnings, often by people who were not particularly good woodturners but who were fascinated by the various forms of build-up and by the varying results which can be achieved according to the shaping of the blank when it is mounted in the lathe. I would strongly recommend anyone to try out the various types of basic build-up which are outlined here, but to follow on from this by building up blanks and ideas of their own. Some of these will be successful and some will inevitably have to be classified as failures, but overall the enjoyment which can be derived from this branch of the craft is tremendous.

When built-up turning is mentioned it is frequently assumed that the reference is to the gluing together, in the form of blanks for turning, of timbers which are of contrasting colours. Certainly this forms a very large part of built-up turning, but, as we saw earlier, certain methods of building up are used for tankards and deep boxes, and in some cases bowls, in which only one type of timber is used throughout.

When my wife and I moved from Tewkesbury to Bath we were fortunate enough to buy a small chapel in a little hamlet a mile or two beyond the edge of the city. This chapel contained the pulpit, still there today, and the pews, which were painted blue. In removing these pews I discovered that they were made of Columbian pine, and they had in fact been in position for over a hundred years. Columbian pine has a very strong grain and is extremely pleasing to the eye, and it seems a pity to me that it was ever considered necessary to paint them at all.

I experienced a certain amount of difficulty in dismantling these pews, since anything which has held together for a hundred years in regular use without disintegrating does not come apart easily. The timber is now stacked in a corner of the chapel and will be reclaimed, most of it for furniture work. There will be many pieces which are too short to be of any practical value, and these will be built into blanks for turning. I have made one or two experimental blanks and turned them, and the results are very striking, since this form of pine is very dense and turns extremely well. The grain itself is very strongly marked, and since the built-up pieces have their grain direction alternated in the build-up for purposes of stability, the result can be extremely interesting.

I have mentioned this purely to point out that it is not always necessary to use different timbers in a build-up; some excellent results can be obtained by using one variety of timber only or one variety of timber with thin spacers of a different colour.

It will perhaps be as well to look at some of the simple forms of build-up first. Two of

Figure 92. The possibilities in built-up turning are almost infinite. (a) Some attractive bowls can be made by laminating strips of light and dark timber side by side. Very accurate centring is required, or the two opposing oval sections will be of different sizes. (b) A useful technique for boxes, such as biscuit barrels or tobacco jars. Rings of timber are prepared by means of bandsaw and jigsaw, then glued together in a vertical formation, the grain direction in each piece being altered by 90° to give stability. (c) and (d) Table lamps or candle holders made by cross-cutting segmented cylinders are assembled to give chequered or spiral marking. (e) Bowl built up from a large number of small 'bricks'. The base of such bowls is normally made from stout plywood to obviate the risk of shrinkage which might break the bowl. (f) Attractive results for such items as table lamps and candle sticks can be obtained by post-blocking. (g) Trinket bowl with segmented lid.

these are the bread-and-butter and the side stack, which are American terms for which there do not appear to be equivalents in Britain. A bread-and-butter build-up is one in which flat pieces of timber are glued one on top of another. The pieces are usually in the form of discs for convenience, and this type of build-up is extremely useful for making containers for biscuits or tobacco, vases or pots, and even such items as tankards.

In all forms of built-up or laminated work it is essential that the timber be prepared with extreme accuracy. I appreciate that numerous people are capable of achieving such accuracy with smoothing planes and other forms of hand tool. I regret, however, that I am not among their number, being by inclination a woodturner and woodcarver and only an average cabinet-maker. I therefore use machinery wherever I can, since it gives me a combination of speed and accuracy which is quite impossible to surpass. The machine which will best serve those who wish to go in seriously for built-up turning is the planer/thicknesser. Cheap examples of any form of woodworking machine should be avoided if possible, since although they may render some form of assistance for occasional work, they generally lack accuracy and are in some cases not entirely safe. A good-quality planer/thicknesser will be of tremendous value to the woodturner, and is probably the next in order of priority after a bandsaw has been purchased.

All timber which is to be used in built-up turning should be passed through a planer/thicknesser, and it is very important, as I mentioned earlier, that this timber should be kept strictly in the batches in which it was machined.

For certain forms of build-up this is not quite so important, and the bread-and-butter system is an example. Minor variations in the thicknesses of the pieces in the stack will have no adverse effect on the turning. In the making of a bowl which is composed of numerous bricks built up in rings, however, any variation in the thickness of the segments which make up any given ring will result in gaps and heavy glue lines in the finished job. Timber which has been thicknessed for the purpose of building up blanks for turning should be used immediately, or as soon as possible, since if it is kept around the workshop for a long period before being used it may well warp or twist.

The adhesives used in built-up turning will vary from one country to another as far as brand names go, but in Britain the adhesives I find most satisfactory for operations of this nature are Cascamite and Aerolite 306. The poly-vinyl acetate type of adhesive, or pva as it is commonly known, while possessing tremendous strength, is not entirely suitable for built-up turning. A blank built up with this type of adhesive will not fly apart on the lathe if the job has been done properly, but when the turning has been completed and the finish applied the adhesive has a habit of 'creeping' from the joints very slightly over a period of time. This results in a rather rough feel to the job. Cascamite or Aerolite 306 do not have this characteristic. Poly-vinyl acetate glues are not waterproof, and this point should be borne in mind for certain operations.

A bread-and-butter construction, like most other blanks which have been built up, will look extremely rough, and it is difficult for anyone who is not familiar with this sort of work to see how anything worthwhile can come from it. But if the quality of the woodturning is good and the edges of the tools are sharp, the results will be excellent.

The usual system with blanks of this kind is to mount them on a faceplate, centring them as accurately as possible, and then to drill a large hole at the centre of the blank to a depth just short of that required in the finished article. The procedures for such drilling are

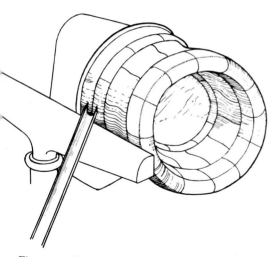

Figure 93. Final shaping of a built-up blank using a deep-fluted square-ended gouge. The handle must be kept very low to avoid digging in.

outlined in chapter 7. I invariably use saw-tooth pattern bits for this kind of job, and in fact I keep a $2\frac{1}{2}$-inch-diameter bit for opening up blanks of this type.

A $1\frac{1}{2}$-inch-diameter bit would do the job, since the purpose of the drilled hole is to provide access for the tool which will enlarge the hole and complete the bulk of the hollowing. The Gordon Stokes deep-hollowing tool, which we now send all over the world in large numbers, is the ideal tool for the removal of the bulk waste in a project of this nature. Being extremely heavy, it can be projected over the edge of the toolrest for some consider-able distance without any danger whatsoever of the blade flexing and causing either damage to the surface of the wood or a dig in.

The side stack is a method of building up a striped plank of wood from various timbers, from two timbers of contrasting colours which are alternated, or from timber of one variety only with fine veneer spacers between the pieces. The first operation is the ripping up of a number of rectangular staves of a size to suit the relevant purpose. Normally they will be 2 inches by 1 inch, 3 inches by 1 inch or there-abouts. These staves should be passed over the planer on two adjacent sides, care being taken to make certain that the fence of the planer is at exactly 90 degrees to the table. When all the staves have been treated in this manner they are passed through the thick-nesser to machine the two remaining surfaces. If this method is adopted, the staves will be exactly rectangular and completely uniform.

In building these staves into a laminated plank (I usually work on a length of about 3 feet) it is only necessary to apply glue to one side of each stave. If too much adhesive is used, much of it will be squeezed out when pressure is applied with clamps, resulting in an extremely messy-looking blank. By the same token, only sufficient pressure should be used with clamps to hold the staves reasonably firmly together while the adhesive sets. If too much clamp pressure is used, most of the adhesive will be forced out from between the staves, which is not desirable.

Slight movement of some of the staves is quite likely to occur while the assembly is cramped, resulting in a faintly uneven surface to the built-up board. This can quite easily be corrected by passing both sides of the lamin-ated board over the planer.

These striped boards, which have been so carefully laminated, should be kept at room temperature for a minimum period of two days – as indeed should all built-up blanks. No attempt should be made to turn them before this period of time has elapsed. Adhesives of the contact or impact varieties should not be used for built-up work.

In most cases there is little point in building up one blank at a time, since when the machinery has been set up and the cramps and adhesives are to hand a great deal of time can be saved by making up a reasonable batch to be kept for future use. Side-stack boards, as described here, are mainly used in the turning of bowls, dishes, bases for standard lamps, lids and so on. Blanks for such purposes need to be in the form of discs, therefore at some stage a larger pair of dividers will be used to mark out circles on the boards, which are then taken to the bandsaw for the production of the disc. If the discs are cut from the boards with the intention of storing them against the day when they will be turned, the edges should be protected by the application of a fairly thick layer of paint or some molten wax. There is end grain present around the periphery of such a disc, and if not protected this may crack.

Much of the more complicated built-up turning which one sees is simply the result of combining various basic forms of build-up into one blank. A typical example of this, which is well within the capabilities of even a relatively inexperienced woodturner, is the combination of bread-and-butter build-ups with side stacks in the construction of bowls, pots or deep boxes. This, if done well, can give striking results.

In all forms of build-up a careful watch

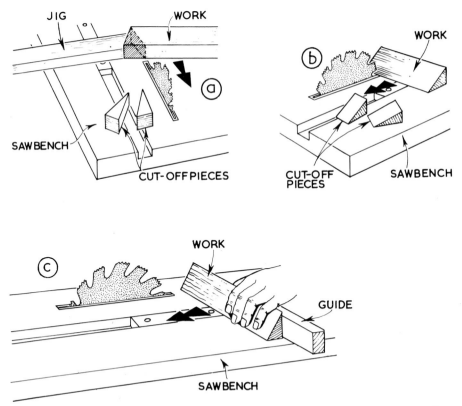

Figure 94. Sawing operations for built-up work. (a) Wedges cross-cut from a plank. (b) Cross-cutting wedges from a bevel-ripped strip. (c) Alternative cutting method. Saw guard not shown, but should be used.

should be kept to ensure that the grain in one piece of wood wherever possible runs the opposite way to that in the next piece. If the end grain of a board is examined curvature will be found in the grain. If the grain of the bottom board curves upwards away from the bench, then the second board should have the grain curving downward towards the bench. Examination of the end grain of short pieces

of board will soon make this point quite clear.

Another very basic form of build-up, commonly known as the 'pie-wedge', is by no means difficult but does present certain problems not present in the types mentioned above. The term 'pie-wedge' is self-explanatory, in that a blank made by this method resembles a circular pie cut into equal sections prior to serving. The difficulty is the accurate

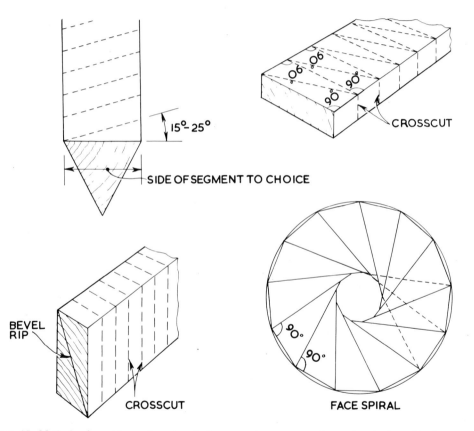

Figure 95. Methods of marking and cutting timber to produce segments for various built-up blanks. (Above left) Cross-cut or bevel-ripped strip. Saw blade or saw table will be tilted in order to produce segments for spiral blanks. (Above right) Method of cutting a rectangular board to produce 90° triangles. (Below right) Assembly of right-angled triangles to form blanks. (Below left) Alternative method of producing right-angled triangle sections by bevel-ripping without cross-cutting.

cutting of the angles in the wedges. Unless a very high degree of accuracy is maintained, the resulting blank will be of no use whatsoever.

A saw bench can be used for this operation, though I always prefer to use a radial arm saw, which I consider vastly superior for the cutting of any form of angle. Whether a bench or radial saw is used, however, a template should be made and checked for accuracy, and this should be used to set the angle between the blade of the saw and the mitre fence or the fence of the radial saw, as the case may be. Such templates must be one hundred per cent accurate and should be carefully guarded and marked for future use. The type of blade used on the saw is also of some significance, since if too coarse a blade is used it will be necessary to take the wedges on to a process of sanding, and this may result in an alteration in the angle. If a tungsten carbide-tipped sawblade with a minimum of forty-two teeth is used, the results should be smooth enough for assembly without further treatment. If the wood is not too thick I prefer to use what is known as a thin rim plywood blade. This is a blade made from high-speed steel, which has about 1 to $1\frac{1}{2}$ inches of its outer diameter ground thinner than the centre part. There is no set on the teeth, which are of the cross-cut pattern and very small indeed. Such blades should not be sharpened by amateurs but returned to a saw doctor when necessary. They must be kept very sharp and will produce a beautiful finish even on end grain. I use a blade of this kind for small picture frames and find it extremely satisfactory.

It is unlikely that any attempt to use a bandsaw, no matter how good the machine may be, will give satisfactory results. It is not impossible to make reasonable blanks this way, but a bandsaw is a shape cutter, and because its blade is so extremely thin, there is inevitably some movement during the cut. The blade of a circular saw is a great deal thicker and works in a totally different manner; therefore it is to be preferred for work of this nature.

If a circle is divided up into any given number of sections by means of straight lines, the angles subtended at the centre must of course add up to 360 degrees. It is therefore not a difficult matter to ascertain the angles for the cutting of a specific number of wedges to form a pie-wedge blank.

In this type of build-up timbers of contrasting colours can be used or timber of one variety can be employed, with thin strips of veneer or strips of oil-tempered hardboard used as spacers. It should be borne in mind that when spacers are used on a build-up of this kind there is no effect on the angle required for cutting up the wedges, but a hole will be produced at the centre of the blank, the diameter of which is dependent upon the thickness of the strips used as spacers. Hardboard is often employed in a variety of ways in built-up work, but there are cheap types of hardboard on the market which are totally

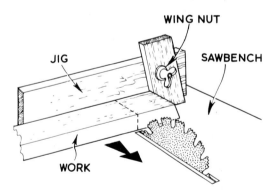

Figure 96. Jig for cross-cutting segments of precise length in built-up work. Jig is attached to mitre guide of saw and a stop block attached by means of a wing nut. The stop block should not touch the surface of the table, a gap being left to allow sawdust, etc., to escape. Saw blade is tilted as required.

unsuitable since they can split when the work is on the lathe. The only kind of board which can safely be used is the oil-tempered variety such as Masonite.

The pie-wedge, like the side stack, produces a flat blank which is normally cut to a circle prior to turning. Such a blank can be made sufficiently thick to permit the turning of a bowl or dish, or it may be made thinner so that a number of such blanks can be glued together to give varying patterns. If this is done the discs can be glued directly to one another or, if desired, a thin sheet of contrasting veneer can be interposed between them which will produce interesting effects in the final turning.

The time taken in building up a blank for bowl turning can often be compensated for by building up the blank as a hollow structure so that very little work has to be done on the shaping of the inside. The pie-wedge assembly as such is normally used for the bases of table or standard lamps, trays, shallow dishes and similar items. If a large quantity of such built-up discs is available and it is desired to turn a bowl, the centres of the discs can be cut out with a jigsaw and the outer rings built up one above another on a solid base to form a bowl blank. The inner sections which have been cut away can be retained for use in other projects.

This is often done, but if the intention is to make a bowl it may be better to build up the blanks as rings rather than as solid discs. In order to understand the principles involved in this it is only necessary to draw out the project accurately on a piece of paper. Taking a twelve-sided figure as an example, a large circle should first be drawn, its circumference then being divided into twelve equal parts. Lines are then drawn from the centre of the circle to each point.

Assuming that the project is a 10-inch-diameter bowl, the circle can be drawn slightly larger than this in order to allow for the final cutting out of a 10-inch disc. When the radial lines have been drawn in, the points which divide the circumference of the circle can be joined together by means of a sharp pencil and a ruler, working as accurately as possible. The drawing now shows a typical pie-wedge assembly, and it will be obvious that since it is divided into twelve equal parts the angles at the centre will each be 30 degrees, making up a total of 360. Since the angles of the triangles formed add up to 180 degrees, it follows that 150 degrees are contained in the two angles at the base of each triangle, each of which is 75 degrees. The cutting angle for the segments of a twelve-sided figure is thus 15 degrees, the result of subtracting 75 from 90. In other words, if a circular saw is used the mitre guide will not be at 90 degrees to the saw-blade, as it would be for normal cross-cut work, but it is swung through 15 degrees to produce the required 75-degree angle.

Many people seem bewildered when cutting up timber for assembly into blanks of this nature, initially finding difficulty in working out the lengths and widths of the segments. Those unused to this sort of work will find that the easiest solution is to complete the drawing. For example, if the diameter of the circle is $10\frac{1}{2}$ inches on the paper, a point can be marked at $7\frac{1}{2}$ inches from the centre on each radial line, these points then being joined by means of the ruler and pencil as before. Since the drawing is full size, the worker can see at once exactly how the blank will look when it is finished, and if necessary adjust the width of the staves to be used. Many people like to put rather wider strips in the bottom ring, which is attached directly to the solid base, making it slightly easier to curve the interior of the bowl neatly into the base when the turning is done.

Note that timber used to make bases for bowls which are constructed from built-up rings or discs must be thoroughly seasoned. Even if it is considered to be ready, it should be kept at normal room temperature for a week or two before it is used, since if there is any shrinkage or movement in it after the turning is completed it will almost certainly break the bowl. For this reason many workers prefer to use plywood.

Another very popular approach to the making up of blanks for bowl-turning is extremely simple and very effective indeed, particularly when the work is carried out in good-quality pine. The turning of pine calls for rather more skill on the part of the turner than is the case when working with hardwoods, but if such skill can be acquired through diligent practice and effort is is certainly well worth the trouble. This system calls for the preparation of a considerable quantity of timber, which needs to be exactly square. The length of the pieces should be slightly greater than the intended diameter of the bowl, so that if the intention is to turn 12-inch bowls, the timber should be cut to $12\frac{1}{2}$ or 13 inches, and it might well be $1\frac{1}{2}$ inches square.

Successful results are unlikely if timber is purchased from the local handyman's store already planed to this size, since it will undoubtedly have warped and twisted after planing. It is better to rip up timber to, say, $1\frac{3}{4}$ inches square and to do the planing immediately prior to building up the blanks. The lengths of timber should be planed on two adjacent sides over a machine planer, with the fence of the machine set precisely to 90 degrees. When all the timber has been treated in this way the remaining two faces are dealt with by passing them through the thicknesser. This will produce timber which is exactly square and true and will greatly facilitate the assembly of these pieces into blanks.

When the preparation of the timber has been completed, the pieces are assembled with a good quality glue, side by side, to form squares. This work should be carried out on a surface which is absolutely flat, and care must be taken to see that the pieces do not move when cramps are applied.

When the squares have been formed in this way and sufficient time has been allowed for the adhesive to set, they are cleaned up and assembled by glueing them one above another. The grain in each layer should be at 90 degrees to the layer above and below. These build-ups are again cramped and kept at room temperature until the adhesive is completely hard, and when they are ready a circle of the required size can be drawn with a pair of dividers on one face of the blank, which is then sawn to a circle on the bandsaw ready for mounting on the lathe.

Bowls made in this way are extremely attractive, particularly if the pine used is of a high quality and has a strong and striking grain. It is necessary to use tools which are razor sharp and to cut with care and precision. Plenty of good-quality sealer will be required in order to obtain the first-class finish which is desirable.

Interesting results can be obtained with blanks of this nature, as is the case with many other types, if very thin sheets of contrasting veneer are interposed between the vertical and the horizontal joints. A great many things are possible in the field of built-up woodturning, but it is undoubtedly true to say that many of the more striking examples of this art are to some extent the result of fortuitous error.

Another system which was once widely used, though its popularity seems to have waned in recent years, is the building up of bowl blanks from small 'bricks'. In principle this is very similar to the methods described earlier for building up bowls from rings of segments, except that in this case there are a greater number of segments in each ring, usually from thirty-six to forty-eight. The building up of bowl blanks from bricks calls for the highest possible degree of accuracy, since any error will occur twice in each brick. In a blank composed of forty-eight bricks to the ring there will be ninety-six errors, so even if the error is as small as 0.1 degree, the resulting build-up will not be suitable for turning. It may be this fact which discourages so many people. The use of a really accurate template will help to remove any problems.

The construction of a bowl by the brick method calls for the use of some kind of thin steel band cramp, and the Flexicramp is the most widely used. This is a circular steel band which can be tightened up on the work by twisting a handle. In the most common procedure a large quantity of bricks is prepared for which the material has first been thicknessed. They are cut with the utmost accuracy, and the bowl blank is assembled by building up the bricks in layers inside the Flexicramp, working on a completely flat surface. Here, as in the making of other hollow built-up blanks for bowl-turning, it is customary to make the bottom ring of bricks wider than those above it to facilitate blending the internal shape of the bowl into the base. It would at first appear necessary to leave the resulting build-up inside the Flexicramp until the adhesive was thoroughly hard, which would mean that the Flexicramp could not be used again for a day or two. In practice this is not necessary, since there is a simple and extremely effective method of securing the blank so that the Flexicramp can be removed.

Prepare a number of discs of blockboard or plywood cut to a size to suit the diameter of bowl being constructed. The diameter of the discs should permit them to fit neatly inside the Flexicramp. Once the bowl has been assembled in the cramp one of these cramping discs is placed on either side of the build-up, a steel bolt is passed through holes which have been drilled at the centre of the disc, and the discs are drawn together under high pressure

by means of a large butterfly nut or wing nut. When the blank has been secured in this way the Flexicramp can be removed, and the construction of the next blank can commence.

A point worth noting is that in segmented blanks of this nature the grain of the wood runs round the bowl, and there is no end grain to be dealt with. This means that quite satisfactory results can be achieved even using a scraper, but there is no real reason why anyone capable of using a gouge should use this sort of approach. It is sometimes suggested that scrapers should be used on all forms of built-up turning, since the possibility of a dig in is thereby removed. It should be pointed out that some people do manage to dig in in a quite spectacular manner even with the scraper. It would be more accurate to say that a correctly used scraper is preferable to a gouge in the hands of anyone who has not yet arrived at the stage where dig ins can be avoided.

Bowls constructed from bricks can be turned so that the walls are quite thin, provided that the bricks have been cut with complete accuracy. Should there be any doubt on this point, however, it is advisable to leave a reasonable thickness in the bowl wall to give it strength.

There is another simple approach to the built-up bowl which appeals strongly to beginners because it requires just a modicum of care in the preparation of the blank. The process is described below in logical sequence for the benefit of those who may wish to try it:

1. Prepare and thickness a piece of material from which a disc of the desired size can be cut. The use of a thicknesser will ensure that both faces of this material are parallel.

2. Mark out a circle on this material using a heavy pair of dividers, ensuring that the centre remains clearly marked. Then cut out the disc on a bandsaw, cutting fractionally outside the marked line.

3. Step out the radius of the circle around its circumference, which will accurately divide it into six parts.

4. Carefully connect the points so marked by means of a sharp hard pencil and a steel ruler.

5. Having ensured that there is a good blade in the bandaw which can be relied upon to cut accurately, cut carefully and exactly along the lines which have just been marked, so producing a hexagonal blank.

6. Set the planer to take a fine shaving and pass each flat face of the hexagon over it. The job can be done by hand if preferred.

7. Small blocks of wood which are contrasting in colour are now glued onto the flat surface of the hexagon. These must be cut to a size which will exactly fit the flat surfaces, and no gaps should be apparent between the ends of the blocks after assembly. Cramp up and allow the adhesive time to harden.

8. When the adhesive has thoroughly hardened, take the dividers and, without altering the setting, scribe another circle which will this time pass through the blocks which have been added. When this has been done cut the blank once again to a disc, taking care to cut exactly on the line.

9. Mount the prepared blank on a faceplate, taking the greatest possible care to ensure that it is centred with complete accuracy. Any inaccuracy in centring the blank will result in a lopsided pattern. This type of build-up will turn very nicely, since once again the end grain problems have been largely removed, and the result will be a beatutifully scalloped effect around the bowl.

I have also made bowls, with varying degrees of success, from blanks which have been built up from square pieces with the

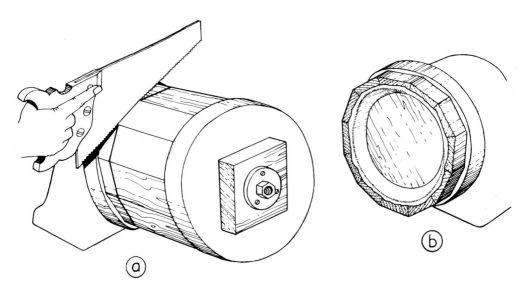

Figure 97. (a) If the assembled blank is marked out with precision, and a good quality hand saw, which is sharp and correctly set, is employed, a box can be cut accurately to sections. This operation is performed manually, with the lathe switched off. (b) Careful sawing will leave a perfectly smooth surface to each ring of segments. These can then be glued up and re-assembled.

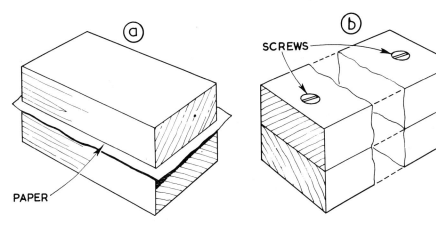

Figure 98. Split turning. (a) Rectangular lengths of wood, accurately prepared, can be glued together with paper between the glued surfaces. The two parts can easily be split after turning. (b) Alternative method of uniting rectangular lengths to form squares for split turning involves provision of waste section at each end to take wood screws. This method is not suitable for long workpieces which will 'flap' under the effect of centrifugal force.

grain running vertically, as distinct from those in which the grain runs around the bowl. In this type of build-up very interesting results can also be obtained by incorporating a thin veneer of contrasting·colour between all the joints.

The blank is constructed from short square lengths of timber, the lengths of which are equal to the desired thickness of the bowl. In other words, they will be glued together standing on end, and when the bowl is turned the hollowing will be done into end grain. Workers who are not completely at home with the deep-fluted gouges may prefer to use heavy sectioned scrapers with very sharp edges for the actual hollowing.

Naturally the material from which the blank is to be built up must be prepared so that it is exactly square. After the blank has been assembled and the adhesive has thoroughly hardened, great care should be taken in drawing a circle with the dividers so that the pattern enclosed by this circle is completely regular. The job is then cut to a disc on a good bandsaw, and once again the greatest possible care must be taken in centring it to the faceplate.

Woodturners who have access to metal lathes, or who have friends who could do the job for them, might like to make or have made a centring device to be used with the faceplate of their own lathe. The process is perfectly simple. A piece of steel rod which exactly fits the hole at the centre of the faceplate is turned down for $\frac{3}{8}$ of an inch or so at one end to give a pin about $\frac{1}{8}$ inch in diameter. This pin is then brought to a sharp point, but it must be noted that the pointing of the pin has to be done on the lathe, so that the point itself is central to the device.

By placing the faceplate on the prepared blank, with the side marked for cutting the disc facing upwards and the mark made by the leg of the dividers visible through the hole in the faceplate, it will be quite a simple matter to place the centring device into position and move the faceplate around slightly until it is felt to drop into the hole. It can now be given a sharp tap with a hammer, after which the faceplate can be screwed to the blank. When this has been done the centring device can be removed and the blank, together with the faceplate, mounted on the lathe.

Many other ideas for built-up blanks for bowl-turning will suggest themselves to enthusiastic turners, and all of these can be tried, always with the proviso that the cutting of joints and the preparation of segments or squares which are to be built up is carried out with the greatest possible care. A blank which

has been built up should always be checked thoroughly to see that there are no gaps. If any gaps are present there may be a danger in attempting to turn the blank, since it could possibly disintegrate at some stage during the turning. No matter how much time has been spent in the preparation, the thing shoud be consigned to the waste bin. The last method suggested above for bowl blanks, where short square pieces are laminated together with the grain running vertically, could be used for the preparation of blanks for spindle-turning or for the making of egg cups, pots, candle holders and the like. The length of the pieces

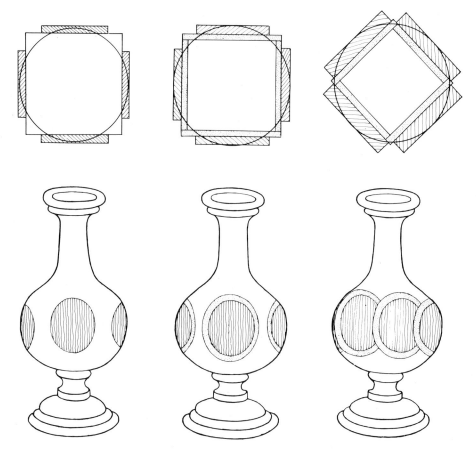

which are to be glued together for this sort of work will be much greater, but the size of the section of each piece will be a good deal smaller. In this way as many as sixty-four tiny squares can be glued up to form a blank, say, 2 feet long. This blank can be cut into sections of varying lengths for use in different projects. Some of the sketches provided in this section may themselves provide further ideas for the interested reader. I have room only to outline the processes involved and to sow some seed which I hope will produce in many people a desire to pursue the matter further.

Blanks which are laminated or built up for

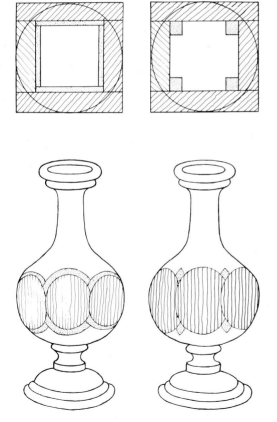

spindle-turning are normally done on the post-blocking system, which is clearly shown in the accompanying illustrations. In this process a central, square length of wood has further small blocks built up around it – in other words, the post, or central square, is blocked. The most important aspect of this is the preparation of the central square itself, which must be absolutely accurate. It is impossible to build anything accurate on a base which is not, so the greatest care should be taken over this.

The second point, which is vital to successful work, is that the central square must be centred with complete accuracy in the lathe. Any inaccuracy will produce imbalance in the pattern and will make the job look dreadful. Once the squares have been centred they can be removed from the lathe so that the process of building up the blocks around them can be undertaken. It is not a good idea to prepare a central square and then build up the blank with the idea of centring the whole thing in the lathe. Sometimes the centring process goes wrong, and if it does valuable time will have been wasted in assembling the parts.

Lengths of wood being prepared for use as central squares in post-blocked blanks should always be cut with their ends absolutely at 90 degrees to the sides, and a fine-toothed saw should be used so that the end grain has a very smooth surface upon which fine marks are easily visible. The procedure for centring such squares in the lathe is set out below:

1. Carefully mark the diagonals at each end of the square workpiece with the aid of a sharp knife and a steel rule. No errors can be permitted at this or any other stage.

Figure 99. A wide variety of effects can be produced by post-blocking, as indicated by these drawings. There is ample room for experiment and the sectional sketches show what is removed from the timber in roughing down.

2. Make a small depression at the intersection of the diagonals using a sharp bradawl.
3. Place the workpiece in position in the lathe, where it is held lightly between centres.
4. Place the toolrest in position along the work, parallel to it and about $\frac{1}{8}$ inch away from it at centre height. If point three has been correctly attended to, it should now be possible to rotate the work without its fouling the toolrest.
5. Check the centring of the workpiece with a bradawl or the point of a skew chisel. Place the tool on the toolrest at one end of the work and move forward until it will just touch a corner of the wood. By slowly rotating the

wood by hand it is quite a simple matter to check whether or not the tool will touch all four corners. If it will not, the position of the wood relative to the centre must be altered. This process should be carried out at both ends of the wood until everything seems satisfactory.
6. Using a parting tool, take a cut no more than $\frac{1}{16}$ inch wide at the extreme end of the work, pushing the tool forward until it has cut past the corners and leaves a disc shape on the end of the wood. It will be necessary to stop the lathe once or twice to check the progress of the cut. Once the cut is continuous check the position of the disc which is left for accuracy with the square workpiece. Repeat this process at the other end of the job.
7. Tighten up the tailstock fully. Give the job a final check to make certain that this tightening has not put the workpiece off centre.

If at this stage any inaccuracy is present, something must be done about it. If the inaccuracy is not great it may be possible to plane a little from one side of the square in

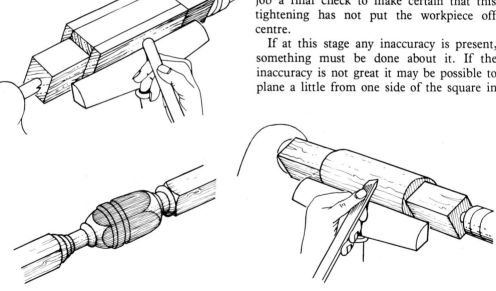

Figure 100. In the production of furniture legs it is often necessary for the turned section to have diameters greater than those of the square parts which have to be left. These drawings show how this can be achieved by building up timber around the section which is to be turned. The wood used for this may be of the same type, or of a contrasting colour. The type of gouge used in the turning is not important but it is usual to reduce the job by means of the roughing gouge and continue the shaping with a spindle gouge, finishing off with a smoothing cut from a skew chisel where possible.

order to correct the situation. If this appears unlikely to give a satisfactory result because the error is too great, the workpiece should be abandoned.

One of the simplest forms of post blocking is that which was once in very common use for the preparation of certain furniture legs which had turned parts that were greater in diameter than the overall width of the square sections which carried the rails and stretchers. Whilst

it was possible to cope with a situation of this nature by means of a bandsaw, reducing the sections at the ends of the job to a small square and leaving a larger one to be turned in the centre, this was extremely wasteful of timber. It was much more usual to employ a central square of timber the correct size for the pummels which carried the mortises for the frame, and to build up the job with blocks at the point or points where the turning was to

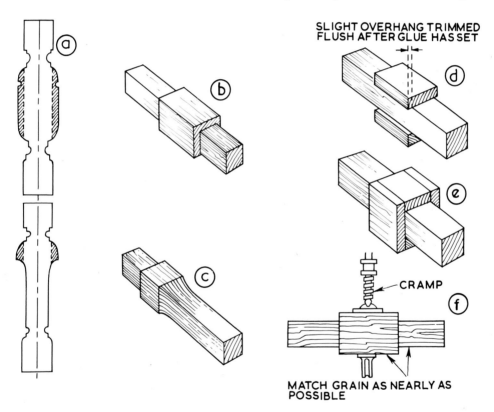

Figure 101. (a) Design for chair leg, where maximum diameter for turned parts is larger than for square sections. Note that this design is made up from two pieces joined together after turning. (b) Large square length of timber reduced on the bandsaw to form a blank for turning an item such as is shown at (a). (c) Alternative bandsaw operation which is slightly quicker and easier. (d) Built-up blank showing how first two sections are glued but with slight overhang. (e) Second part is glued to sections in position after initial overhang has been trimmed. (f) Work is held under pressure in a clamp while glue sets.

be larger than the square sections. This simple method can be used effectively in the production of a wide variety of articles on the lathe.

Timber to be used for blocks in post-blocked work should always be planed using a planer which has very sharp knives and is set to take a fine cut. It should also be thicknessed to avoid any possible inaccuracies. The whole length of the central square can be covered by successive layers of blocks, but it is much more common to find that certain sections are built up while others are left untouched.

For a simple build-up all that is necessary is to build round the square at the desired points with lengths of prepared timber of equal thickness. In order to achieve accuracy it is necessary first to build up on two opposite sides of the central square, using strips of wood which overhang the square very slightly. When these have been cramped and the adhesive allowed to harden, they are trimmed back either with a hand plane or on a spindle moulder so that their edges are completely square and flush with the central part of the build-up.

Blocks are now attached to the remaining sides. These blocks should be wide enough to cover both central square and the pieces of wood which have already been attached to it. The assembly is now cramped, and again the adhesive is allowed to set. In view of the time spent waiting for adhesive to set, it is advantageous to have a session of building up blanks of this nature so that they can all be taken through the various stages without any waste of time. If so desired, a build-up which has reached this stage can be replaced in the lathe and turned, and quite pleasant patterns can be achieved with just one layer of blocks. Full post-blocking, however, as shown in the illustrations, is a more complex business.

Some workers like to continue layer by layer, working as described, until they have completed their post-blocked blank. I have always found it more satisfactory, however, to laminate the remaining pieces and then apply the lamination in one piece. This makes life easier because it is possible to work with strips of wood of varying thicknesses and widths up to about 2 feet long.

These are laminated one on top of another, with the widest at the bottom and the width of each successive layer decreasing. They can then be cramped up and set aside for the hardening of the adhesive and are subsequently cut up into lengths suitable for the projects in hand. Many workers keep boxes or plastic bags full of sections of laminated material to draw upon at any time.

Blanks for spindle-turning and for use on chucks in the making of such things as vases or candle holders can also be prepared by laminating rectangular-sectioned pieces of

Plate 17. Roughly post-blocked blank for a lamp, awaiting final cleaning up.

timber in contrasting colours to form squares. The grain of these squares runs lengthwise. Again, timber of the same type can be used throughout, with sheets of thin veneer placed between to give a contrast. The rectangular strips used in this kind of work are in effect small planks, and they should be laminated so that the curvature of the end grain is alternated. The effects produced in the turning of items in this way are greatly enhanced if striped strips are placed in the build-up at certain points. These strips are built up as separate items, and again a session can be devoted to this work so that they are always available.

The method of building-up such striped pieces of material is not at all difficult, though once again it calls for precision. The process can be modified to suit whatever the turner

has in mind, but basically it is as set out below.

The size of the stock selected for an operation of this nature depends on the width of the strips required. In this case, we will assume that 3-inch-wide strips are called for, so the stock with which the job commences will be two lengths of 3-inch by 3-inch timber which has been planed true and square.

This is now carefully ripped into strips about $\frac{1}{8}$ inch thick, preferably using a saw blade with tungsten teeth which will give a really smooth finish. When the stock has been ripped into strips it is rebuilt into squares, using strips of alternate colours. These are then glued together and cramped. These blocks can be passed over a planer to smooth the laminated surfaces before being ripped again with a sharp circular sawblade into $\frac{1}{8}$-

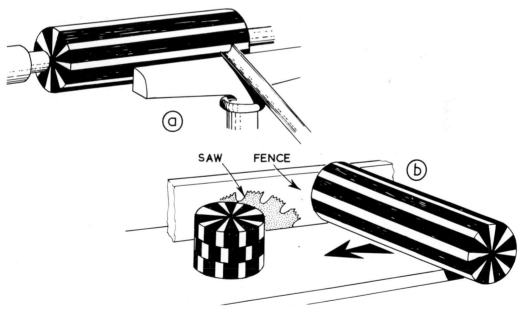

SAW FENCE

Figure 102. Built-up work. (a) Blank is centred accurately and turned to a true cylinder by means of the roughing gouge. (b) Blank is cross-cut into sections on the circular saw, holding the blank firmly against the mitre guide while cutting.

inch strips, which will be formed from $\frac{1}{8}$-inch square pieces of wood in alternating colours. Care must be taken to ensure that the timber is kept firmly against the fence of the circular saw throughout the ripping cut, or inaccuracies may develop.

Striped strips of this nature can be used as they are, but they are very effective if a sheet of veneer is glued to each side. There are many ways of building pieces of this striped material into various types of blank, and experiments can be carried out to discover just what sort of results can be achieved by turning different shapes. This is an extremely fascinating aspect of the craft of built-up turning.

It is necessary also to consider the cylindrical type of blank built up from strips of timber which has been bevel-ripped. Here the grain of the wood runs along the cylinder rather than around it, as is the case in the pie-wedge discussed earlier. Cylinders of this type are usually turned about 30 inches long, since this is the maximum capacity of the average lathe, and they are then cut into lengths suitable for intended projects. The most common approach is to build them up in strips of alternate-coloured timbers, or to use one timber with thin veneer strips of a contrasting colour between each piece.

One of the most spectacular and attractive forms of built-up turning is a derivative of this form of build-up, and it is worthy of mention. The number of sides in a blank for this purpose is usually about sixteen, and there should be as much contrast as possible in the timbers used.

The timber is ripped on a saw bench with the saw table or the blade tilted by the required amount and, as in any other form of built-up work, extreme accuracy is essential. When the cylinders have been assembled with the strips alternating in colour around them they are glued and cramped using the normal methods. Once the adhesive has completely hardened, the next stage can be undertaken, which is the cross-cutting of each cylinder into discs, the thickness of which will equate to the width of the strips used in the build-up. This cross-cutting must be done with great accuracy or the results will not be pleasing.

The cylinders can be dealt with one at a time by reassembling the resulting pile of discs into a cylinder, either staggering the discs in the build-up so that the cylinder becomes chequered or offsetting each disc by one section so that a spiral is formed. The spiral is perhaps the most impressive version. No matter what shape is given to the project the spiral will remain constant when the cylinders are turned, and in a tall item, a half standard lamp for example, the appearance of the finished job will be very striking indeed.

There is a lot of work in projects of this nature, and they cannot be hurried in view of the high degree of accuracy required. The greatest possible care should be taken in the turning and finishing of these jobs.

Another approach to the turning of built-up bowls or very large boxes is shown in the illustrations. This is to build up a deep box from segments assembled on a base by slicing the whole thing into rings which are then reassembled, after staggering them in a manner like that described above.

In the absence of a very large power saw of a type not normally available to home woodworkers, this calls for the very careful use of a handsaw. The system will not give good results except in the hands of an expert woodworker. The illustrations should suggest various ideas, which can be modified and adapted by the ingenious woodturner.

7 Drilling and Boring

The cutting of holes in timber by means of drill bits and cutters is a very important aspect of the woodturner's craft. It is often necessary to produce holes for a number of purposes in a very wide range of sizes. The smaller ones are produced with what are known as twist bits, as used by the home handyman in an electric drill. Such bits come not only in a wide range of sizes but also in a surprisingly wide range of qualities.

As with almost everything purchased for use in the workshop, it is rarely an advantage to buy cheap items. The cheap twist bit, like a cheap chisel or gouge, will not hold an edge for any length of time and may either snap or bend in use, depending upon the degree of error in the tempering of the steel. Good-quality drill bits are readily available, and although they are initially more expensive they will last many times longer than cheaper versions, so if they are looked after their purchase represents an economy.

It is sometimes said that it is not necessary to worry about keeping sharp edges on drill bits which are used in woodwork, in view of the relative softness of the material. This is quite untrue, since unless the drill bit is correctly ground so that it does have sharp edges and the point of it is central, it will not produce accurate holes. It will be found that for a great deal of work undertaken with this type of bit the wood can be hand-held and simply pushed onto the rotating drill. This is a quick and easy operation which permits the worker to use both hands to control the movement of the material.

Holes from about $\frac{1}{2}$ inch diameter upwards need to be produced with cutters of a different type. Many kinds of boring bits are available, but without any doubt the most effective for most work is the saw-toothed pattern variety. It is not necessary to buy a full set of these cutters unless money is no object, in which case they are certainly well worth having even if not essential. Most woodturners, in fact, buy one or two saw-tooth bits in sizes which they feel are likely to be useful to them, subsequently adding two or three more for specific operations.

There is considerable difference between a saw-tooth bit and a Forstner bit. The latter is often recommended for use in woodturning, but it is more expensive than a saw tooth and less efficient. The advantage of a Forstner bit is that is produces a hole with a completely flat bottom with only a small mark at its centre. The same effect, however, can be produced by using a saw-tooth bit, which will give a flat-bottomed hole like the Forstner but has a longer point at its centre, and so leaves a deeper mark at the centre of the drilled area. If the hole is taken in slightly short of the required depth, the bottom can be cleaned up with a narrow square-ended scraper, bringing the hole to the required depth and removing the mark made by the cutter point.

The saw-tooth pattern bit cuts more freely than does the Forstner, and it is less likely to become overheated by friction in use. These bits are also very much easier to sharpen for workers who are not skilled in this aspect of woodwork. They have a number of coarse teeth around their edge and a cutter which runs across the centre to remove the waste. These teeth can be sharpened quite easily with a small triangular file, and even the inexperienced can make a reasonably good job of this. Frequent sharpening is not necessary unless the timbers being worked are unusually hard or abrasive.

Some workers use Jennings pattern auger bits, of the type supplied for use in a carpenter's hand brace. These when purchased have a square section on the end of the shank, designed to be gripped by the chuck of the hand brace. It is necessary to cut this piece off with a hacksaw and to remove the thread of the lead screw. This is a small point at the centre of the business end of the bit which has a thread on it to assist its penetration into the wood. The point itself must be retained, but the thread must be removed by careful work with a small file. These cutters if kept sharp work very well indeed, but in fact there are machine versions produced with a $\frac{1}{2}$-inch-diameter parallel shank with a machine point which does not have a thread on it. It is also possible to buy a wide variety of machine bits for use in the wood lathe which have a shank tapered to suit one of the three commonly used forms of Morse taper. If bits of this kind are used there is no necessity for a chuck of any kind, since they can be inserted directly into the headstock or tailstock, according to the type of work in progress. They are, however, very expensive and are therefore not in common use.

Another popular form of drill bit or cutter is the spade bit, often referred to as a 'flat bit'. This performs very well in electric drills, but since it is a high-speed cutter it does not work at all well at low speeds. Unlike most other bits it does not cut in the accepted sense of the word but has a scraping action. It is sharpened by means of a file or on a grinder if the worker has sufficient skill, and the resulting burr or

wire edge does the cutting, in a similar manner to the edge of a woodturning scraper.

As is the case with the twist bit, cheap versions of the spade bit are available from various sources, but these should be avoided for use on powerful machines. They are generally too soft and are quite likely to bend if sufficiently provoked, and in some cases they have been tempered to a point where they are in fact too hard, which could result in a fracture of the metal during a cut. Good-quality spade bits such as those manufactured by Messrs. William Ridgway are not cheap, but they are entirely satisfactory. They should be run at as high a speed as the lathe will permit, and if kept in good condition they will cut very rapidly, producing clouds of fluff rather than shavings and giving clean and accurate holes. The spade bit has a pronounced point with a cutting edge on either side at right angles to the shank. These cutting edges are ground or filed at an angle of approximately 45 degrees, though this is not critical.

The type of chuck in general use for boring and drilling on the woodturning lathe is the Jacobs pattern which is described on page 88. Two points of vital importance from a safety angle must be noted and remembered. Firstly, the majority of Jacobs chucks are attached to the lathe by means of a Morse tapered shank. When fitted into the machine this taper should be 'set' by giving the nose of the chuck a smart tap with a piece of wood. There is little danger of a chuck working loose and flying from the lathe when it is used for boring, since it will be under pressure most of the time, and in fact the grip of the taper is such that it is far more likely to be difficult to remove. When used for other purposes such as the mounting of a drum sander, the tailstock must always be brought along the lathe bed so that its point lightly touches the sanding drum, thus effectively preventing any forward movement.

Secondly, it is necessary to point out that some very nasty accidents have occurred with chucks of this type. Its jaws are operated by means of a small key, the end of which carries the equivalent of a small bevelled gear wheel with a pin protruding from the centre. In adjusting the chuck, this pin is engaged in one of the several holes which are drilled around the chuck casing, and the teeth of the small gear wheel engage with teeth in the outer casing of the chuck. By turning the key, the jaws can be opened or closed. Most woodworkers will be familiar with this system, since it is used on nearly all electric drills. The danger lies in leaving the key in the chuck after adjustment has been carried out. If the lathe is started with the key in position, it may be flung violently across the room by centrifugal force. If it should strike the operator or an onlooker, serious injury could result.

Two basic systems are available to the woodturner who wishes to use the lathe for drilling or boring. A chuck can be fitted either to the headstock or to the tailstock. Both positions are in fact used, and the choice will depend upon the nature of the work. It is sometimes more convenient to have the drill chuck secured to the headstock, in which case a workpiece being drilled or bored out is held firmly with the left hand while it is pushed forward onto the rotating cutter by means of the tailstock hand wheel. This results in a hole which follows the longitudinal axis of the workpiece, since it is held accurately in a position parallel to the lathe bed. This system is often used in drilling out the ends of candlesticks or in drilling through short table lamps.

Most people seeing this done for the first time are convinced that there is grave danger in the operation. It appears, to an inexperienced observer, that the wood may suddenly be snatched by the cutter and rotated rapidly, so injuring the hand of the operator. Cutters used in this type of work are kept extremely sharp, as indeed all cutters should be. Having used this system for more than thirty years, however, I have no hesitation in recommending it to anyone.

The alternative system, in which the drill chuck is positioned in the tailstock, has a wide number of applications. A typical one is the opening out of a blank which is to be used in the construction of a vase, small pot or a goblet. The workpiece is attached securely to the chuck, and the tailstock, complete with chuck and boring bit, is brought up to touch it lightly.

At this stage the blank from which the vase is to be made may still be in its square form. The tailstock securing lever is firmly clamped. The lathe is switched on at low speed if a sawtooth bit is being used or at high speed in the case of a spade bit, and the cutter is fed into the rotating work. If it is not possible to achieve the desired depth because the travel of the cutter is limited by the tailstock movement, it will be necessary to wind the tailstock back, release the securing lever, move the tailstock forward until the cutter reaches the bottom of the hole, re-tighten the securing lever, and repeat the process. This is a typical case where the provision of a lever feed facility for the tailstock is desirable, especially if large numbers of blanks have to be drilled.

LONG-HOLE BORING

Of all the procedures likely to be undertaken by an average woodturner, the boring of long holes, usually to accept the flex in a table lamp, is undoubtedly the most difficult to describe. I have found it necessary to explain the system over the telephone on innumerable occasions and have described it in print on a good many more, yet although the process itself is really very simple it is an incredibly difficult thing to describe to someone who has never seen it done. It always sounds a great deal more awkward and complicated than it is in reality. If it were not for the necessity to drill holes through the centres of lamps the whole process might by now have died a natural death, since it is used for virtually nothing else in woodturning today.

Many years ago the production of wooden rollers for the printing industry was a job which fell to professional woodturners along with a great deal of other work which required the drilling of holes of considerable length. Modern machinery does not call for such rollers, at least not wooden ones, so the only augers available in shops now are almost invariably $\frac{5}{16}$ inch in diameter, though a few of $\frac{3}{8}$ inch may be found here and there. The reason for the predominance of the $\frac{5}{16}$-inch auger is that this is the tapping size for a $\frac{3}{8}$-inch thread, and the type of connector used in the making of table lamps almost invariably carries a $\frac{3}{8}$-inch Whitworth thread.

The auger used in long-hole boring is the shell auger, which has a flute 4 or 5 inches long and a small lip on its extreme end, which does the cutting. The overall length of such augers is normally about 18 inches to 2 feet. It is usual to purchase what is described in manufacturers' catalogues as a long-hole boring kit. This consists of the shell auger, a centre finder, a counterbore tool and a drilling jig which fits into the toolrest holder of the lathe.

It is probably true to say that the best advice that can be given to a beginner regarding the sharpening of shell augers is, don't. Whilst this may seem a negative approach, it must be borne in mind that the cutting lip of the auger is very small indeed, and frequent sharpening will soon destroy it. Once this has happened the auger must be discarded. Unlike the gouge it cannot be sharpened until it is quite short, since the tiny lip is essential to its correct

operation. Furthermore, if a shell auger is sharpened other than by an expert it is highly probable that the angle formed on it during its manufacture will be altered, and should this happen the tool will no longer run true.

It has to be accepted that these augers do become quite hot in use, and it is difficult to avoid discolouration of the steel which is an immediate indication of an alteration in the temper of the metal. One can only describe a shell auger of this type as a crude tool, and in fact it will continue to produce perfectly satisfactory holes when both blunt and discoloured.

It is undoubtedly better to drill through the blanks to be used in the making of lamps prior to turning them, for reasons which have already been described. I still prefer, however, to make a lamp and to drill the hole after it is finished.

The system used in the boring of long holes is perhaps best explained by indicating a logical sequence of operations, as enumerated below:

1. Remove the tailstock centre and replace it with the centre finder.
2. Set up the drilling jig in the toolrest holder and bring up the tailstock so that the centre finder passes through the body of the drilling jig and so through the ring centre. The latter has a threaded shank which allows it to be attached to the drilling jig and enables it to be adjusted.
3. The drilling jig will now be in position at centre height, with the horizontal hole which passes through it exactly parallel to the lathe bed. The clamp which holds it in the toolrest holder can now be tightened.
4. Place the work against a normal driving centre and move the tailstock and the saddle, which is carrying the drilling jig, towards the headstock until the point of the centre finder engages with the wood. At this point the

turner may wish for several more arms, since the process is awkward, but the knack will soon be acquired.

5. Tighten the tailstock clamping lever securely and apply pressure to the workpiece by tightening the tailstock. Move the saddle forward so that the ring centre of the drilling jig is contacting the wood. Tighten the clamp of the saddle securely.

6. Apply a few drops of oil or wax polish to the ring centre to reduce the friction and prevent burning and partially unscrew the ring centre itself from the drilling jig by means of a tommy bar or a pair of grips. This is done with a reciprocal action until the ring centre can be seen to have bitten into the wood.

7. Tighten the thumbscrew on top of the drilling jig to prevent the ring centre from moving while the wood is rotating. This should be done with a pair of pliers, making sure that the thumbscrew is really secure. The direction of rotation of the material enables it to rotate a ring centre which has not been properly secured, driving it back into the drilling jig, and this can result in the timber flying from the lathe.

8. Slide back the tailstock, complete with centre finder, along the lathe bed, leaving the work firmly supported between the driving centre and the drilling jig. Remove the tailstock from the lathe or swing it underneath the bed, according to the type of lathe used.

9. Start the machine at about 800 to 1000 rpm. Pass the auger through the drilling jig and push it firmly into the work.

The auger can only be fed into the wood in any one movement to the depth of its flute, and if this depth is exceeded the tool will become extremely hot and may jam in the wood. Once the depth of the flute has been reached, the tool should be withdrawn from the material so that the waste can be emptied from the flute.

In the case of fairly short workpieces, say up to 10 to 12 inches in length, the drilling can be done at one setting, taking the hole through to a point just short of the end of the work. With

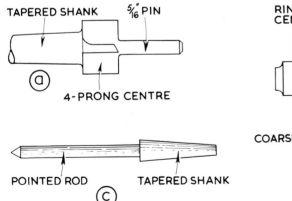

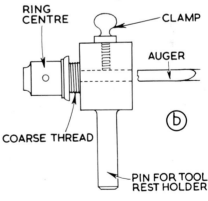

Figure 103. Equipment for long-hole boring. (a) Counterbore tool with tapered shank to fit headstock, and with projecting pin $\frac{5}{16}$ inch in diameter. The counterbore tool acts as a driving centre, the projecting pin, when fitted into a previously drilled hole, ensures that the blank is mounted centrally. (b) Drilling jig. (c) Centre-finder fits into tailstock to support end of workpiece and so facilitates setting up of drilling jig.

experience the turner will be able to detect the point at which the drilling operation should be stopped because the wood around the driving centre has been compressed, and a slightly bumpy sensation will be experienced. This is difficult to describe, but the phenomenon will soon become evident after a few holes have been drilled. Should the auger be taken too far through the wood so that it contacts the driving centre, there is no danger as such, but the auger itself may be damaged.

Having drilled as far as possible through a workpiece of this length, the turner can take the wood from the lathe, reinsert the auger, and complete the drilling by rotating the auger by hand in the wood under firm pressure. Alternatively, an electric drill can be used to drill in through the end grain to connect with the previously drilled hole.

An experienced worker can complete an operation of this nature in a fairly short time, but in the early stages of learning to perform it the ring centre may require further lubrication before the job is completed. This will be made evident by a high-pitched squealing noise and by the smell of burning which will arise due to friction. I have found that the most satisfactory method of renewing the lubricant is simply to touch the ring centre briefly with a piece of beeswax. The ring centre will be hot enough to melt the beeswax, which will run down into the wood.

For tall lamps, or for sections of standard lamps, it is necessary to complete the drilling in two stages. The first stage will be identical to the procedure described above, but for the drilling of the second stage the work has to be reversed in the lathe so that the end which has been drilled goes against the headstock. If an ordinary driving centre is used for this purpose it will be very difficult to centre the work accurately. The driving centre should be removed from the lathe and replaced by the counterboring tool.

This is, in effect, a four-pronged driving centre with a $\frac{5}{16}$-inch pin protruding for a distance of about $1\frac{1}{2}$ inches from its centre. This pin will fit the hole which has been drilled in the wood, thus centring it exactly to the counterboring tool, the fangs of which will drive it in the usual way.

The drilling jig is set up as before, and the drilling process is repeated until the auger meets up with the original hole. The shell auger works with reasonable accuracy, but there will be occasions when for some reason it does not run absolutely true. If this occurs on a long workpiece, the error will only be evident where the two holes meet, but this is not a serious matter, though it may cause some problem when the flex is fitted.

It is appreciated that this description of the system of drilling long holes may not be immediately clear to some readers. The description should be studied again in the workshop with a long-hole boring kit set out on the lathe.

8 Finishing Procedures

It is necessary to be careful about the exact definition of the word 'finishing' in the context of woodturning. For the purpose of this manual, I refer in this section to the application of various finishing materials to surfaces which have already been brought up to the highest possible standard of quality by means of the turning tools.

Unfortunately, in many forms of woodwork, the expression 'finishing' means to many people a process in which damage done to the wood by inexpert handling of the tools is repaired. A woodturner should achieve a good finish in two stages. The first is the process of cutting the wood with sharp cutting tools, paring away clean shavings, and leaving the fibres of the timber as undisturbed as possible. Only when this has been correctly done is there any real point in proceeding to the second stage, which is the use of abrasive material (if necessary) coupled with the application of some kind of sealer, and followed by waxing, oiling or varnishing of the surface as required.

I have a sneaking suspicion that many people who telephone me to enquire about the best method of achieving a really beautiful finish are, in fact, hoping to be told of some magic potion in a tin or bottle which, when poured upon the tortured remnants of a woodturning blank, will change it miraculously into a thing of beauty. I have as yet been unable to trace any such mysterious substance. The old saying about sows' ears and silk purses is true, and there is little point in trying to impart a gleaming lustre to a surface which

resembles a doormat.

Let it not be thought that I am in any way patronizing those whose tool work is not yet expert. There is not the slightest doubt in my mind that in my early days of woodturning, which are too far distant to be recalled with clarity, the sow's ear was the order of the day. Everyone has to start somewhere. If a start is made along the right lines, success is virtually certain given sufficient effort and determination. Those who begin their woodturning without the benefit of sound advice on the basic principles, however, will encounter far more difficulties, and it will be much less easy for these difficulties to be overcome.

Having said that the expression 'finishing' as regards woodturning refers to the two stages of completing the turning itself to the highest possible standard, and to the logical sequence of operations which follows this and includes the application of the finishing medium, the reader will appreciate that the first of these two stages has already been fully covered. This section of the manual, therefore, refers to the second stage only, and presupposes a workpiece which is ready for final treatment. Certain statements have already been made in various parts of this book which refer directly or indirectly to the second stage of finishing, but it is necessary to repeat these now in more detail and to consider the second stage of the finishing process as a whole.

The second stage of finishing in woodturning can itself be divided into two parts. These are the preparatory work which brings the wood to a stage where it is ready for the application of polish, varnish, or some other finishing medium, and the application of the medium itself.

ABRASIVE WORK

The most commonly used abrasive medium among woodturners is now undoubtedly garnet paper. Sandpaper as such is still extant, but it is not sufficiently durable for satisfactory use in machine woodwork. Garnet paper, on the other hand, although more expensive, has a far greater life expectancy and is very satisfactory from a woodturning point of view.

The abrasive grains which coat this paper are orange in colour. Two types of garnet paper are marketed; the first is open coat and the second closed coat. In woodturning open-coat paper is used almost exclusively, since it does not clog with wood dust and resin deposits as rapidly as does closed-coat paper. Given the same grade of abrasive, the size of the abrasive grains is the same with both types, but open-coat paper has less grains per square inch and thus has wider spaces between the grains, so it can shed dust in much the same manner as a coarse-toothed saw blade.

Newcomers to the craft may well be confused when attempting to purchase abrasive paper by the fact that manufacturers have not as yet standardized their system of describing the coarseness of their products. Various systems are in operation, but the one which appears likely to take over completely in due course is that where the abrasive material is described by the number of apertures per square inch in the sieve through which the grains have been passed. In other words, if the abrasive particles have been put through a sieve which has 100 apertures per square inch, the grade of paper is 100, and there will be no

grains present on the paper which could not pass through this sieve.

The grades of paper of most interest to a woodturner, based on the system mentioned above, are perhaps 100, 150, 240 and 320. These can, of course, be varied slightly without detriment, but a beginner who has these grades of open-coat garnet paper at hand need not be concerned with others for some considerable time.

It would perhaps appear that the use of abrasive paper requires little discussion, since one has merely to hold it against the wood to achieve the desired result. This is not the case, though, and there are a number of points which must be carefully noted if satisfactory results are to be achieved.

Abrasive paper must always be bone dry when it is applied to the work. If it does not crackle when moved around between the hands it is not dry enough for use, and unless it is dry before it contacts the wood it will rapidly become clogged. If it is held to a fire for a few seconds the small quantity of moisture present will soon be driven out.

Many workers like to tear a sheet of abrasive paper in two and then rub the two sheets together on a flat surface for a few moments before using them. This slightly dulls the cutting points and may seem to be a negative approach, but it can help to prevent some nasty scratches appearing in the wood if one or two stray grains which are larger than they should be happen to be present.

In sanding work which is rotating in a lathe, considerable friction is obviously present, and since friction produces heat it is advisable to fold the paper once or twice into a pad. If it is used in a single thickness the heat may be sufficient to burn the fingers of the operator.

Under no circumstances should abrasive paper be applied to a workpiece in a manner which necessitates the worker's fingers pointing against the direction of rotation. In the vast majority of cases this will mean that the paper is held underneath the work with the fingers trailing against the surface, so that there is no danger of them being suddenly bent backwards. If the lathe is fitted with a reversing switch, the paper will need to be held on the upper surface of the job when the lathe is running in reverse. The fingers must trail over the surface at all times, and a little more thought needs to be given to the matter when operating inside a bowl.

The use of abrasive paper and other abrasive materials inside deep-box structures, such as biscuit barrels, vases, tobacco jars and the like, calls for the exercise of common sense, since the aperture is not particularly wide in most cases and it is very dangerous to allow the hand or any part of it to enter the workpiece. In such circumstances the abrasive material should be wrapped around a cylindrical piece of scrap timber.

In spindle-turning, assuming the correct methods have been used in conjunction with really sharp tools, little or no abrasive work should be required. The turner who finds that spindle work cries out for abrasive paper should return to a serious study of basic principles. In sanding a workpiece between centres, the abrasive particles must cross the grain of the wood at right angles. Unless care is exercised in the choice of the correct grade of paper, therefore, there is a serious danger of the work becoming deeply scored.

Scratches produced around a piece of spindle turning by the use of too coarse a grade of paper can be very difficult to remove, and the obvious solution to this problem lies in preventing it from occurring in the first place. What this means is that, if abrasive paper is to be used on spindle work, nothing coarser than 240 should be employed, and even then care must be exercised. In view of this, unless the turning itself is of a high standard a great deal of time will be wasted in the entirely uninteresting process of sanding.

Work which has been sanded with a medium grade paper such as 240 should also be given thorough treatment with 320, after which a few moments' work with steel wool will finish the job.

Steel wool, or wire wool as it is sometimes called, must not be of a coarser grade than 000. This grade is not easy to obtain in hardware stores, and woodturners normally purchase such items from specialist suppliers. The steel wool on general sale for rust removal or the cleaning of domestic cooking utensils is quite unsuitable for woodturning applications, since it is likely to contain odd strands which are very coarse indeed, and this will defeat the entire object. It is as well to avoid the use of steel wool on timbers which may react unfavourably to it. Oak is the most common example. Tiny fragments of steel wool, although invisible to the naked eye, will remain embedded in the timber, and these can react with the acid in the wood to cause discolouration.

Great care should be exercised in the use of steel wool, which must be held so that it can be plucked from the fingers of the operator if it should become entangled with either the workpiece or one of the lathe centres. If it is held in such a way there is no risk of injury, but it must *never* be twisted around the fingers in order to provide a firmer grip, since this practice can result in serious injury.

Although the point has little to do with abrasive paper, it may be as well to mention the practice of using a woodworker's smoothing plane in woodturning. This is sometimes advocated by people who have never mastered the skew chisel, and if there is any merit in it, it is unlikely to be discovered other than by turners who have the same problem. I will not describe the manner in which the plane is used, since its use merely represents an avenue of escape for those who do not wish to make the necessary effort to master their chisels. A sharp skew chisel, properly handled, will produce a better effect with considerably less risk.

SEALER

The importance of a good sealer in woodturning is often not appreciated. It has been my custom for many years to employ sealer in preparing almost all workpieces for their final finishing.

In cases where the intention is to give the material some kind of oil finish, it might appear that the use of a sealer would be undesirable since it would prevent the entry of the oil into the grain of the wood. In fact it will be found advisable to give such material a liberal coat of sealer and to sand the job thoroughly when the sealer has dried to a point where the sealing medium has virtually been removed. If the functions of a sealer are examined, the reason for this will become obvious.

The first function of a sealer is to swell the grain of the wood and raise it up above the surface of the work. In many forms of woodwork a damp cloth is passed over the surface which is then allowed to dry, so that the grain will be raised and subsequent sanding will produce a marked improvement. The sealer, which is liquid, raises the grain, but in drying to a hard skin it locks this roughened grain so that it cannot bend away from the abrasive particles when the job is sanded. The first application of sealer, therefore, is liberal, and the sanding is as thorough as circumstances require.

Secondly the sealer will, after a number of coats have been applied, effectively prevent the finishing medium itself from being forced into the wood. This is very important, and ignorance or neglect of this point is frequently the cause of frustration when it becomes impossible to produce a really attractive polished or varnished surface.

Almost any liquid which can be applied to the wood and will dry rapidly will be beneficial in the early stages of finishing, but considerable research over a long period of time has gone into the production of certain proprietary brands of sealer, and, although the woodturner can experiment for amusement, it is unlikely that any superior substance will be discovered.

The first application of sealer to any job should be generous, and it is vital that this application is given sufficient time to harden before any further work is undertaken. In view of the thickness of the first coat, some fifteen or twenty minutes in a warm room will be required. Subsequent coats, however, will be very much thinner, since the first coat will prevent them from being soaked up by the wood, and they will not require more than a few minutes for drying. If the first coat is sanded with 240-grade paper, subsequent coats can be treated with 320 or with very fine steel wool.

By working in this manner it is possible to produce a really beautiful lustrous finish with sealer alone, applying several coats and buffing the last coat with a soft dry cloth. A workpiece which has been finished in this manner will not require any further treatment unless a very high gloss is desired, but a little household furniture cream can be used at the discretion of the woodturner, which, if it does nothing else, will certainly give the finished article a pleasant odour. It seems that one of the first actions of anyone who is handed a piece of finished woodturning is to sniff it.

The use of a sealer requires little skill, but it does call for an understanding of basic principles. One other virtue of a sealer, which does not actually relate to this section of the manual, is its ability to help the woodturner over certain problems which may arise with timbers which have difficult working qualities.

When certain areas of grain cannot satisfactorily be conquered by normal techniques because the fibres of the wood are soft and easily distorted, an excellent solution is to apply a good coat of sealer and to allow it to dry thoroughly, overnight if possible. If when this sealer has dried completely one or two further cuts are taken with freshly sharpened tools, the results can be quite startling. The sealer, having soaked into the wood, will have locked the fibres which were causing trouble, enabling the cutting edge to pass through them cleanly.

An alternative to sealers which have a shellac base is the use of clear cellulose lacquer which has a quantity of French chalk mixed with it. A sealer of this nature must be thoroughly shaken up before use, and it is not effective on dark timbers, since the French chalk tends to give them a greyish appearance. One of my students, to whom I had explained the manufacture of this type of sealer, subsequently telephoned me to say that he had been visited by his local police. Apparently he had found difficulty in obtaining the necessary ingredients and some alert chemist had reported his requirements to the police, who were disturbed by the fact that only one other substance is necessary for the production of an eminently satisfactory bomb. He did escape incarceration, but there must be a moral in it somewhere.

WAXES

There may be a little of the mad scientist in all of us; those who find the idea attractive can experiment with various mixtures of basic waxes to provide substances which they can apply to their carefully turned workpieces. It has, however, always been my view that the highly paid research chemists who are employed by the manufacturers of household and other waxes are considerably more likely to achieve success on a full-time basis in their lavishly equipped laboratories than is the untrained woodturner in a garden shed. Apart from one simple wax mixture which can be prepared at home if the turner can find the time, there would seem to be little virtue in such activity other than the passing of a few hours on a wet afternoon.

The waxes in common use in woodturning are refined beeswax, carnauba wax and paraffin wax. The latter is used almost entirely for the protection of the end grain of timber as it dries out. Refined beeswax should always be used in preference to the cheaper forms, which are darker in colour and in some cases quite unsatisfactory. Beeswax used by itself can be considered a form of finish, though its function is really that of a filler and it will not impart a high gloss.

The process of applying beeswax to a finished piece of woodturning is very simple, consisting of spreading the wax evenly over the rotating work and subsequently melting this wax by means of a folded pad of soft cloth applied with heavy pressure and moved slowly along the workpiece. This will create considerable heat, melting the wax and driving it into the surface of the wood. The position of the rag should be changed occasionally so that the excess wax is removed from the job.

Some woodworkers apply beeswax in the manner described above and follow this with an application of carnauba wax, which is not subjected to heavy pressure from a cloth, but to relatively light pressure; this will, if circumstances are right, bring up a brilliant gloss. The application of carnauba wax in this manner, however, is very difficult, and even expert woodturners sometimes fail to achieve their objectives. Unless the carnauba wax is applied in a perfectly even film and the pressure applied with the cloth is exactly right, which is unlikely, the result will be streaky in appearance. This is caused by the wax failing to cover the whole job evenly. Should such a situation arise it can be remedied by heavy pressure with a folded rag, which will melt the rings of carnauba wax and blend them with the beeswax, thus enabling the operator to repeat the carnauba wax application, hopefully with a greater degree of success.

Carnauba wax, unlike beeswax, is extremely hard, and if a freshly broken piece is applied to a rotating workpiece its sharp edges can scratch the surface very badly. Some workers like to pulverize carnauba wax by wrapping it inside a folded cloth and beating it with a hammer. The pad containing the powdered wax is then applied to the work so that the frictional heat draws the melting wax through the cloth and deposits it on the wood. This does work, but it will not be long before the friction breaks the fibres of the cloth, allowing the powder to fall through.

The most effective approach to the use of these waxes, and the one which is most commonly employed, is the mixing of the two together with a little turpentine or white spirit. This operation should be carried out with care in view of the possibility of fire. The waxes are mixed in proportions of two parts beeswax to one of carnauba by volume, and the amount of turpentine added will govern the consistency of the resulting paste. Since carnauba wax is not particularly easy to melt in lump form, we purchase it for sale in our showroom in large sacks of what is known as 'flake'. These are sold in 1-pound bags, and the small fragments melt down very easily.

The melting should be done in an empty tin placed in boiling water, and for convenience the molten wax can be poured out into suitable receptacles such as discarded yogurt or ice-cream containers. This mixture can be spread evenly over a workpiece, and, when buffed with a pad of soft dry cloth, it will give a very satisfactory finish indeed.

Just as there will always be the woodturners who like to grind the ends of old files in order to impress acquaintances with the fact that they make their own tools, so there will always be individuals who manufacture strange mixtures of wax, the 'secrets' of which cannot be extracted from them by anything short of torture. The good woodturner, however, will be too busy to wander around in useless fields of endeavour. For a final film of wax which will enhance the work there is nothing to beat a really good-quality proprietary product.

After considerable research over many years I discovered a polish which fulfills my requirements in every way. It is not available from normal stores, but we now purchase it in large quantities and can supply it on request. This material is marketed under the trade name 'Melshine' and is available in two forms, one an almost clear mixture and the other a rich dark brown. Whilst a pack of this is not particularly cheap, only a very small quantity is required in the finish of a given article, and it is therefore extremely economical in use.

When using 'Melshine' I find it best to apply a coating of beeswax to the timber after the abrasive work has been completed and to melt this into the wood as described above. The beeswax fills the grain and provides an excellent surface for the Melshine itself. Experiments can be carried out with other forms of household furniture wax or cream, and indeed with the various wax polishes sold for use an automobile bodies. I have achieved less successful results with silicon-based products than with straightforward wax mixtures, but individual preferences vary considerably regarding finishing materials, and the experience gained in trying out various types can only be valuable.

FRICTION POLISH

The form of friction polish most likely to be encountered in woodturning is marketed under the name of 'Speedaneez'. This is popular with many woodturners, particularly for small articles, and provided the turning has been properly executed and the sealing procedure followed, a beautiful shine can be produced by repeated applications of Speedaneez. On articles of small diameter it is extremely effective, although rather more skill is required to achieve good results on bowls and other items of relatively large size.

In considering the finishing medium to be used for a specific turned article, it is necessary to consider the use to which the object will be put. Woodturning projects which are mainly ornamental and unlikely to be handled except infrequently can be finished quite satisfactorily with wax or friction polish. Other items, such as sugar bowls or pepper mills, which will be handled several times a day, do not lend themselves to this type of finishing, since the durability of wax or friction polish is not great. Wax can develop a grubby appearance due to dust and dirt becoming ingrained in the surface. If Speedaneez is used this is less likely to occur, but an article finished in this way should be kept away from water, which will cause discolouration.

A large number of woodturners become very actively engaged in the production of tableware, which has quite a hard life and requires a finishing medium which will stand up to everyday use. A popular item which is easily saleable, not too difficult to make, and therefore popular with a great many beginners, is the salad bowl. Various kinds of finish can be employed on these projects, but the traditional one is oil. Some workers finish their salad bowls with salad oil, which they apply as thinly as possible in a series of coats, each of which is given a thorough buffing with

a dry cloth prior to the application of the next. A better medium for finishing salad bowls is Danish oil. This is a very thin oil which has a pleasant odour and is far easier to apply than teak oil, which is much thicker and unless applied with some care, does not harden properly, leaving the bowl with a faintly 'tacky' feel.

Polyurethane is used by a great many people, but it is necessary to use a really good quality product such as that produced by Rustins. This is available in either high gloss or matt, but most workers purchase only the gloss variety, which they can rub down with fine steel wool when a matt finish is required.

Finishing media such as polyurethane are best applied with a soft brush while the work is stationary, though it can be rotated slowly by hand in the lathe to facilitate the process. It is also possible to apply the first one or two coats by means of a soft rag. If two or three coats are to be used, the final one should be diluted with thinners by about fifty per cent. When carrying out operations of this nature some newspaper or old cloth should be placed over the lathe bed to protect it, since some types of finishing material contain acids which can attack the metal, and the free movement of the lathe saddles may be impaired.

A product which has become very popular in the past few years is Rustins plastic coating. This is a two-part catalyst resin which is mixed prior to application in a glass or ceramic container. Under no circumstances should the container be metal, since the acid will immediately react with it. The resin is mixed according to the instructions provided, usually on a basis of one part hardener to four of resin.

The instructions given by the manufacturers should be followed as closely as possible if satisfactory results are to be achieved. This type of finish, like polyurethane, can be applied either with a rag or with a brush. It is self-levelling, which means that there is no need to do anything about brush marks, since these will disappear. This type of resin finish is the most durable of those which are freely available to the woodturner. It is capable of withstanding boiling water, mild acids, and reasonable impact. For these reasons such finishes are eminently suitable for various forms of tableware, particularly drinking vessels, and if two or three coats are applied the object can be washed in lukewarm water.

It is possible to apply a medium of this nature while the lathe is rotating, but a very low speed will be required, like 50 to 100 rpm. Very few lathes provide such a speed, and it is doubtful whether the expense involved in producing a countershaft or gear system which will do so is justifiable.

Successive coats of plastic coating can be cut down to a beautifully smooth surface by means of burnishing paste, which is also available from the manufacturers. This is applied to the rotating work by means of a soft cloth, and the workpiece is burnished with a dry cloth before the next coat is applied. The final coat, once it has hardened completely, can be polished to a very brilliant gloss by means of the wadding sold for cleaning silver, or it can be cut back with steel wool to give a Scandinavian effect.

FUMING

This process is used in connection with work turned in oak, and if correctly carried out it can darken timber in a most pleasing manner. It calls for exposure of the finished workpiece to the fumes of full-strength ammonia in a confined space over a period of some hours, and the exact period of exposure will depend upon the amount of darkening desired.

No skill is required, the workpiece being suspended by a nylon thread inside a large box such as a tea chest at the bottom of which has been placed a dish of ammonia. Household ammonia is useless for this purpose – only the full strength variety will do the job.

In order to check the progress of the fuming operation without the necessity for the removal of the lid of the box, which will fill the workshop with unpleasant fumes, a hole can be drilled in the side of the box and a tapered peg of oak inserted. Progress can be checked quite easily by removing this peg. Once the fuming has been completed the workpiece can be subject to any of the finishing processes describe earlier.

In the matter of finishing, personal preference is to some extent the deciding factor, and groups of woodturners argue among themselves on the subject if given the opportunity. Certain processes appeal to certain people, and unless a specific finish has been requested these tend to be the ones in general use in any workshop. Beginners, however, should experiment with all the finishes I have mentioned here, and with any others which may occur to them, to test their efficacy and value with regard to specific varieties of timber.

9 Woodturning Projects

NAPKIN RINGS AND CHESSMEN

A set of napkin rings represents a simple and straightforward project for a turner who has reached the intermediate stage. These are always in demand, make excellent gifts and will sell readily to gift shops and the like. They have, as do chessmen, the added merit of requiring very little raw material. A point worth noting is that whilst it is not normally advisable to use green or unseasoned timber for woodturning projects, napkin rings can be made from branch wood taken from fruit trees which is by no means fully seasoned.

Since the centre of the stock is removed in the process of making the napkin ring, the wood dries out evenly without splitting, and shrinkage is minimal. Branches from yew trees are frequently used in this way with entirely satisfactory results, and the turning of yew which is not fully seasoned is a very pleasant experience. Two basic methods should be described, both of which are in general use, and individual turners should experiment with both in order to establish which suits them best.

NAPKIN RINGS

Method 1

A napkin ring can be produced by mounting on a small woodscrew chuck a suitable piece of timber the length of the napkin ring plus a little more for the screw which projects from the chuck. Care must be taken to see that the

end of such a blank which fits against the chuck is absolutely flat. The blank is reduced to a cylinder a little larger than the required finished diameter of the project, and the parting tool is taken across the end to make certain that it is square.

The length of the napkin ring is now marked on the material measuring from the unsupported end, and the shaping of the outside of the project is carried out, avoiding the use of scrapers if possible. At this stage the job can be given a thorough sanding, after which the toolrest is positioned across the face of the work and the napkin ring is hollowed by means of a sharp parting tool, taking the depth of the hollow to a point just beyond the length of the workpiece. While it would appear simpler to fit a saw-tooth pattern bit into a chuck in the tailstock and feed this into the rotating workpiece this is not a practical proposition since the grip provided by a single screw in the end grain is not sufficient to withstand the torque which would result. The difficulty experienced by most people in hollowing out such a job with a parting tool is that of keeping the inside face of the job parallel to the lathe bed. Unless this is done with care the finished ring may well be thinner at one end than the other.

It is usually suggested that when this stage has been reached and the inside of the job has been thoroughly sanded, the ring should be separated from the waste section by cutting through with a parting tool. Whilst this sounds quite reasonable, it does not work well in practice, since the action of the parting tool will cause spelching, which is a breaking away of the fibres of the wood on the inside of the ring. It will be found far more satisfactory to cut the ring away from the waste part of the job with a sharp fine-toothed saw.

It is best to prepare a number of rings to this stage before setting up for final finishing work which, if the procedure outlined above has been followed correctly, should consist merely of sanding off the sawn end of the job. This can be done by rubbing the ring carefully on a sheet of paper placed on a flat surface. If the turning has not gone completely according to plan, however, it may be better to adopt the procedure for final finishing outlined in the second method, which follows.

Method 2

Whilst the procedure described above may be quite satisfactory, it does have some drawbacks, and I have always preferred to adopt the method described here. The first stage of this is the production of a sufficient number of blanks, this time cut to the exact length required for the finished ring. These are usually square, but there is no reason why sections of branch wood should not be used. As is the case with any other aspect of woodturning, great care must be taken to ensure that the material selected is sound and free from cracks.

The centres of these blanks now have to be removed, and the most convenient method is to drill them out with a large saw-tooth pattern bit. Those whose lathes provide a device for the cutting of mortises will find the drilling of such blanks a simple process. The mortising attachment will hold the blank securely, and it can be fed to the rotating cutter by means of the forward feed lever. A piece of scrap wood must be attached to the mortiser so that neither it nor the cutter are damaged. In the absence of such an attachment, the operation can be quite satisfactorily performed on a pillar drill. As is the case with so many operations of this nature, there is considerable advantage in the preparation of a fairly large number of blanks, so that, having set up machinery for the drilling, no time is wasted.

The problem facing the woodturner at this point is that of holding the small blank in a satisfactory manner in the lathe, and this can be solved by the use of a tapered wooden mandrel. A piece of wood 7 or 8 inches in length is set up in the lathe between centres and reduced to a cylinder with a diameter slightly greater than that of the hole in the blank. This cylindrical length of wood is now given a slow taper for which it may be found beneficial to use a scraper, since the rough surface produced by such a tool will provide an excellent grip for the blank. The taper produced on mandrels for this kind of work should not be of too rapid a nature, or the grip is likely to be inadequate.

The wooden mandrel is removed from the lathe, and a napkin ring blank is pushed along it as far as it will go then tapped securely into position with the edge of a skew chisel. Care should be taken to see that it is parallel to the mandrel when fully tightened. The mandrel and blank are now placed between centres, and the outside of the napkin ring can be turned using a roughing gouge to bring the job to a cylinder. The shaping is completed by means of spindle gouges and skew chisels. At this point a thorough sanding is carried out and, if desired, some form of finish can be applied. The remainder of the blanks will now be treated in the same manner.

In order to deal with the internal surfaces of the blanks it will be necessary to mount a 2- or 3-inch-thick disc of wood on a large woodscrew chuck and to take out a recess at the centre of this disc of a size which will accept the rings. The fit should be a firm one if possible and if there is any doubt at this point some paper can be used as packing. There is no necessity for the recess to be deep enough to accept the full length of the ring as long as the grip is sufficient for the sanding process. If the rings are mounted in this home-made chuck their ends can be thoroughly sanded and the inside surface brought to a smooth finish. While the processes described may sound complicated to anyone who has not tried them out, they are in fact very simple.

CHESS PIECES

Being strongly addicted to the game, I have over the years made numerous sets of chess pieces in both traditional and modern styles. This is a project which attracts many wood-turners whether or not they play chess, and apart from the repetitive and rather boring process of producing the pawns, it is quite interesting.

There are now shops in various parts of the country which sell chess sets almost exclusively and which carry vast ranges of designs and styles. For the purpose of this section of the manual, however, I have restricted myself to the traditional Staunton pattern, the type used in championships because its design provides the best possible recognition of the pieces when viewed from any angle. Most of the remarks made concerning the production of such a set apply equally to other designs.

The timber selected for the production of chess pieces should ideally be close-grained and dense. Commonly used varieties are ebony, box, beech and yew. The timber must be hard because some of the finer detail of the pieces is quite vulnerable to damage by accidental knocks. The normal procedure is to select two contrasting coloured woods. Box and ebony are good if the ebony is obtainable. As an alternative, the plastic coating referred to elsewhere in this manual is available not only in clear form but also in black or white. A perfectly satisfactory set of chessmen can therefore be produced from almost any timber, and the black pieces can be ebonized with black plastic coating and the white pieces treated with white. This is unlikely to appeal to anyone who is a true lover of wood, however, since most of us avoid at almost any cost obscuring the natural grain of the timber.

The greatest possible care should be exercised in the selection of the wood to be used in a project of this kind to ensure that no cracks or other faults are present, since a great deal of work goes into the making of one small piece, and it is a pity to discover a fault when the lathe is stopped.

My own preference in making a set of chess pieces is always to deal with the sixteen pawns first, on the basis that since this is the least interesting aspect of the operation it is best dealt with while enthusiasm is at its height. In the production of chess pawns there is a case for the home manufacture of what are known as 'form tools', scrapers carefully ground to the outline shape of the pawn. Some workers may prefer to make up two form tools rather than one. One of these can deal with the lower half of the pawn, and the other can be ground to the shape of the upper section.

It is not advisable simply to turn the material down to suitable diameter and then produce the complete pawn by means of a form tool, though this is possible. It is far better, in my experience, to turn the pawn roughly to shape and size by means of small gouges and chisels, and to use the form tool or tools to trim this shape. Bearing in mind that this is a small piece of material with fine detail, the form tools must be kept extremely sharp and must be used with light pressure only.

Some books suggest the turning of items of this nature between centres, making four or five pawns in a 'stick'. If this system suits the individual turner there is no reason why it should not be adopted, but it will give rise to certain problems which can only be dealt with effectively by an experienced worker. The foremost of these is the movement of the timber during the cutting operations, brought about because the wood is so slender. Whilst a little more time may be required, the system of making chess pieces individually from short lengths of material mounted on a small wood-screw chuck has always seemed to me to be the better one. By working in this way projection of the timber from the screw chuck can be kept to a minimum, and the job will remain quite rigid throughout.

A chess piece which has been turned in this way can be parted off from the waste section of the blank in which the screw of the chuck is concealed by means of a sharp parting tool. The tool is fed into the wood with the right hand, and the workpiece is caught in the left hand as it drops clear. This system is quite satisfactory if the bases of the chess pieces are to be covered with baize or some other material. If it is not intended to cover the bases in this way, the use of the parting tool to separate the project from the waste timber may cause a bundle of fibres to be ripped bodily from the centre of the base of the job, leaving a small hole. In such cases it is better to part through with the parting tool, leaving $\frac{1}{8}$ inch or so of material connecting the workpiece and waste, and to complete the separation by means of an old hacksaw blade.

Once the pawns have been dealt with and checked carefully to ensure that they do represent sixteen identical shapes, the more interesting parts of the job can be undertaken. An ideal size chess set for a beginner to tackle would be one which has a 4-inch king with the other pieces in proportion. The king, the most significant piece in the game, can be given priority, followed by the queen and their entourage in rough order of seniority. The turning of the king and queen is quite straightforward, and since the pieces themselves are in pairs rather than sets of eight (as the pawns), the problems of achieving exact similarity in the pairs are quite minor.

While the pawns themselves can be completed in their entirety by means of woodturning tools, the main chess pieces will require a certain amount of hand tool work, which can be tackled by any normal woodworking techniques which appeal to the individual concerned. The king and queen require some attention to their crowns, which can be successfully carried out with a short length of broken hacksaw blade. Working with great care the turner can utilize the indexing head of the lathe to ensure that the castellations are equally spaced around the piece.

The bishops are a perfectly straightforward piece of woodturning, but they are easily spoiled by sloppy workmanship in the cutting of the slits in their upper sections. The rooks, or castles if you prefer, are easy enough, but the piece which most worries those making their first chess sets is undoubtedly the knight. The production of a knight is not, however, as difficult as it may first appear. The piece consists of a carved representation of a horse mounted on a small wooden plinth. It is therefore made in two parts, and it is the problem of holding the work while carving the horse section that seems to worry the majority of people. This task will be greatly facilitated if a piece of wood of suitable thickness and 4 or 5 inches in length has the outline of the horse drawn on it. The waste can then be cut away by means of a fret saw and the piece of timber gripped firmly in a vice. When the horse has been carved it can be cut free and mounted on the turned plinth by means of a strong adhesive.

While difficult to describe, the carving of a knight is not really difficult, even for those with no knowledge of woodcarving as such, and the best advice one can offer to anyone who is concerned about this is to study the knight from a Staunton pattern set for a few minutes. This will show that the operation is merely one of whittling and does not represent a complicated piece of woodcarving.

The various methods by which chess boards and chess tables, with boards let into their centres and drawers on either side to contain the pieces, can be made is not in any way connected with woodturning, and I must regretfully exclude them from this manual. The making of a chess board from two contrasting colours of timber calls for extreme accuracy and a certain amount of common sense, but it should not pose much of a problem to any reasonably competent woodworker. As regards 'modern' style chess sets, I leave these to the imagination of the individual, and imagination is the right word.

Index

Page numbers in *italic* refer to the illustrations